Learning Phalcon PHP

Learn Phalcon interactively and build high-performance web applications

Calin Rada

BIRMINGHAM - MUMBAI

Learning Phalcon PHP

First published: August 2015

Production reference: 1210815

Published by Packt Publishing Ltd.
Livery Place
35 Livery Street
Birmingham B3 2PB, UK.

ISBN 978-1-78355-509-3

www.packtpub.com

Credits

Author
Calin Rada

Reviewers
Altaf Hussain
Stephan A. Miller
Dilanka Somarathne

Commissioning Editor
Kunal Parikh

Acquisition Editors
Harsha Bharwani
Rebecca Youe

Content Development Editor
Amey Varangaonkar

Technical Editor
Menza Mathew

Copy Editor
Vikrant Phadkay

Project Coordinator
Bijal Patel

Proofreader
Safis Editing

Indexer
Tejal Daruwale Soni

Production Coordinator
Aparna Bhagat

Cover Work
Aparna Bhagat

About the Author

Calin Rada is a full-stack developer with over 10 years of experience in web development; system architecture; database modeling; the setup, configuration, and administration of servers and hosting systems; and understanding customer and business needs. He is always interested in learning new things and working with new technologies.

I'd like to thank my family and all the people involved in writing this book.

"Touch the untouchable star and don't forget about the people who believed in you."

– *Octavian Paler*

About the Reviewers

Altaf Hussain is an electrical engineer on paper and a software engineer at heart. He is an e-commerce and mobile applications enthusiast. He acquired his BE degree in electrical engineering (with specialization in computers and communication) from Pakistan. He then worked for numerous organizations as a backend developer and moved to Saudi Arabia to work as a software engineer.

Currently, Altaf is working in the fashion industry at Shy7lo.com. He manages dedicated servers, different VPSes, Staging Servers, and GitLab instances for fast deployment. As a senior team member, he is responsible for creating cross-platform mobile applications and APIs. He also works on different caching systems, such as Varnish and Full Page Cache. In his free time, Altaf writes posts for `http://www.programmingtunes.com`.

Stephan A. Miller is a software engineer from Kansas City, Missouri, USA. He is currently working for Kinetic Supply Company. He has worked with open source software technologies for over a decade. Some of the languages that he uses are PHP, JavaScript, and Python. He also uses various frameworks in these languages, including Phalcon, Zend, Laravel, jQuery, AngularJS, and Flask. Stephan has written *Piwik Web Analytics Essentials* and *Getting Started with Phalcon* for Packt Publishing.

Dilanka Somarathne has worked with the LAMP stack for 2 years. He always tries to learn something new. He performs experiments in PHP to find out the best PHP framework for programming. He also conducted a tech talk session in benchmarking several PHP frameworks at his previous organization, thinkCube Systems, for which he received good feedback from the audience and appreciation from other technical leads and architects. Dilanka has experience of working on Laravel, Zend Framework 2, CodeIgniter, and Phalcon. He has worked on Node.js and Angular projects too.

Phalcon is a new and very fast PHP framework. He started following and learning Phalcon after he attended a Phalcon meetup. As his first step, he created a small application with Phalcon. Because of his amazing experience with the application, he was able to get a clear idea about it.

I feel fortunate to get a chance to join the reviewing panel of Packt Publishing. Leena Purkait gave me this awesome chance. I would like to take this opportunity to thank her. Then, Bijal Patel joined the team. From the first day, she has been very helpful and has always replied to my e-mails patiently. Thank you very much, Bijal.

Working as a Phalcon reviewer for Packt Publishing was a really good experience for me. Thank you very much guys for giving me this huge opportunity.

www.PacktPub.com

Support files, eBooks, discount offers, and more

For support files and downloads related to your book, please visit www.PacktPub.com.

Did you know that Packt offers eBook versions of every book published, with PDF and ePub files available? You can upgrade to the eBook version at www.PacktPub.com and as a print book customer, you are entitled to a discount on the eBook copy. Get in touch with us at service@packtpub.com for more details.

At www.PacktPub.com, you can also read a collection of free technical articles, sign up for a range of free newsletters and receive exclusive discounts and offers on Packt books and eBooks.

https://www2.packtpub.com/books/subscription/packtlib

Do you need instant solutions to your IT questions? PacktLib is Packt's online digital book library. Here, you can search, access, and read Packt's entire library of books.

Why subscribe?

- Fully searchable across every book published by Packt
- Copy and paste, print, and bookmark content
- On demand and accessible via a web browser

Free access for Packt account holders

If you have an account with Packt at www.PacktPub.com, you can use this to access PacktLib today and view 9 entirely free books. Simply use your login credentials for immediate access.

Table of Contents

Preface

Phalcon is the fastest PHP framework out there, and it is delivered as a C extension. More than that, you will find it very easy to learn. This book will present in detail the most common and useful parts of Phalcon PHP, as well as guide you to lean towards making the right decision when developing a Phalcon-driven application.

Learning Phalcon PHP is an interesting journey that starts with guides for installing the required software and preparing the working environment and project structure, and continues with a step-by-step approach development of each module.

By the end of this book, you will have developed a simple but fully functional news website and gained advanced knowledge on how Phalcon works.

What this book covers

Chapter 1, Getting Started with Phalcon, introduces the Phalcon Framework. In this chapter, you learn how to install and configure Phalcon.

Chapter 2, Setting Up the MVC Structure and the Environment for Our Project, helps you get to grips with the basics of MVC (Model-View-Controller) and setting up the work environment.

Chapter 3, Learning Phalcon's ORM and ODM, is about Phalcon's ORM (Object-relational Mapping) and ODM (Object-Document Mapper). You learn how to connect to a database and create models and relations between them.

Chapter 4, Database Architecture, Models, and CLI Applications, teaches you how to create the database architecture and the models needed for our project. You also learn about Phalcon CLI and develop a simple CLI application.

Chapter 5, The API Module, helps you start the development of a RESTful API module.

Chapter 6, *Assets, Authentication, and ACL*, explains assets management (JavaScript files, style sheets, and images), and you create a simple authentication system based on an ACL (access control list).

Chapter 7, *The Backoffice Module (Part 1)*, shows you how to develop CRUD operations. This first part is about CRUD for categories and hashtags.

Chapter 8, *The Backoffice Module (Part 2)*, is a continuation of the previous chapter. Here, you develop CRUD operations for users and articles.

Chapter 9, *The Frontend Module*, helps you develop the frontend template. You learn how to implement Elasticsearch and Mongo to improve the speed of your application.

Chapter 10, *Going Further*, teaches you common operations, such as file uploads and annotations.

What you need for this book

The most important thing that you need is some knowledge of PHP 5.3 or later and Linux environments (this book is written based on Ubuntu/Debian). If you are not using a Linux distribution, or you are using a distribution other than Ubuntu/Debian, you will need to look up their official documentation to install the required software.

Who this book is for

If you are an intermediate PHP developer with some basic knowledge of installing and configuring your environment, then this book is for you. Familiarity with PHP frameworks will make your life easier.

Conventions

In this book, you will find a number of styles of text that distinguish between different kinds of information. Here are some examples of these styles, and an explanation of their meaning.

Code words in text are shown as follows: "Deleting data is easier, since we don't need to do more than calling the built-in `delete()` method."

A block of code is set as follows:

```php
<?php
$di['session'] = function () {
  $session = new Phalcon\Session\Adapter\Files();
  $session->start();
  return $session;
};
```

When we wish to draw your attention to a particular part of a code block, the relevant lines or items are set in bold:

```php
public function registerServices(\Phalcon\DiInterface $di) {
  $config = include __DIR__ . "/Config/config.php";
  $di['config'] = $config;
  include __DIR__ . "/Config/services.php";
}
```

Any command-line input or output is written as follows:

```
$ cd modules/Frontend/Views/Default
$ mkdir index
$ cd index
$ touch index.volt
```

New terms and **important words** are shown in bold. Words that you see on the screen, in menus or dialog boxes for example, appear in the text like this: "Going back to the article list, you will see the new title, and the **Updated** column will have a new value."

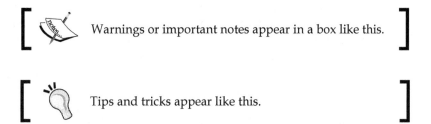

Warnings or important notes appear in a box like this.

Tips and tricks appear like this.

Reader feedback

Feedback from our readers is always welcome. Let us know what you think about this book—what you liked or may have disliked. Reader feedback is important for us to develop titles that you really get the most out of.

To send us general feedback, simply send an e-mail to feedback@packtpub.com, and mention the book title via the subject of your message.

If there is a topic that you have expertise in and you are interested in either writing or contributing to a book, see our author guide on www.packtpub.com/authors.

Customer support

Now that you are the proud owner of a Packt book, we have a number of things to help you to get the most from your purchase.

Downloading the example code

You can download the example code files for all Packt books you have purchased from your account at http://www.packtpub.com. If you purchased this book elsewhere, you can visit http://www.packtpub.com/support and register to have the files e-mailed directly to you.

Errata

Although we have taken every care to ensure the accuracy of our content, mistakes do happen. If you find a mistake in one of our books—maybe a mistake in the text or the code—we would be grateful if you would report this to us. By doing so, you can save other readers from frustration and help us improve subsequent versions of this book. If you find any errata, please report them by visiting http://www.packtpub.com/submit-errata, selecting your book, clicking on the **errata submission form** link, and entering the details of your errata. Once your errata are verified, your submission will be accepted and the errata will be uploaded on our website, or added to any list of existing errata, under the Errata section of that title. Any existing errata can be viewed by selecting your title from http://www.packtpub.com/support.

Piracy

Piracy of copyright material on the Internet is an ongoing problem across all media. At Packt, we take the protection of our copyright and licenses very seriously. If you come across any illegal copies of our works, in any form, on the Internet, please provide us with the location address or website name immediately so that we can pursue a remedy.

Please contact us at `copyright@packtpub.com` with a link to the suspected pirated material.

We appreciate your help in protecting our authors, and our ability to bring you valuable content.

Questions

You can contact us at `questions@packtpub.com` if you are having a problem with any aspect of the book, and we will do our best to address it.

1
Getting Started with Phalcon

What is Phalcon? Let's start by quoting from the documentation of the official website (`http://phalconphp.com/`):

> *"Phalcon is an open source, full stack framework for PHP written as a C-extension, optimized for high performance."*

Version 2.0 of Phalcon was released in April, and it was developed with a new language called Zephir (`http://zephir-lang.com/`). Zephir was designed especially for developing PHP extensions, and it is quite user friendly for both (PHP and C) developers.

There are many frameworks out there. The main reasons why we choose Phalcon were for its steep learning curve, speed, and because it is decoupled. (We can use any of its components independently.) If you have some knowledge of the **Model-View-Controller** (**MVC**) and some experience with any **Object-Relational Mapping** (**ORM**), you will find working with it pretty straightforward.

We will start our journey with this first chapter where we will:

- Configure our web server
- Install Phalcon
- Discuss a bit about how Phalcon works

Before starting, we assume that you are using a *nix environment. Personally, I feel comfortable with Debian distributions, especially Ubuntu, which I am using on a daily basis; so, the installations steps that we will talk about are for Ubuntu. The OS is a matter of personal choice, but I highly recommend any *nix distribution for development. (Even Microsoft decided to open source their ASP.NET for Linux early this year)

For other types of OS, you will have to search their official documentation, in terms of "how to". This book is intended to be about Phalcon and tutorials on installing different software on different kinds of OS are out of the scope of this book.

Here is the list of URLs that contain installation instructions for different operating systems:

- `http://docs.phalconphp.com/en/latest/reference/install.html#windows`
- `http://docs.phalconphp.com/en/latest/reference/install.html#mac-os-x`
- `http://docs.phalconphp.com/en/latest/reference/install.html#freebsd`

Senior developers might not agree with me on certain subjects or certain techniques and/or recommendations. In general, as a developer, I think you should analyze what is suitable for you and develop a platform according to your (or client) requirements. In addition, most importantly, there is no such thing as "The Perfect Solution". There is always room for improvement.

Installing the required software

We need to install the following software that we are going to use in this book:

- PHP
- Nginx and Apache
- MongoDB
- MySQL
- GIT
- Redis
- Phalcon

Installing PHP

You have probably already installed PHP on your system since you are reading this book. However, just in case you haven't, here are the simple steps to quickly install the latest PHP version (Phalcon is running on PHP version >= 5.3). I recommend you to use the **Personal Package Archive** (**PPA**) from Ondřej Surý (`https://launchpad.net/~ondrej/+archive/ubuntu/php5`) because it has the latest PHP version available on it:

```
$ sudo add-apt-repository ppa:ondrej/php5
$ sudo apt-get update
```

If you don't want to use this step, you can simply install PHP from the official repositories:

```
$ sudo apt-get install php
```

Apache will be installed by default with PHP. However, if you want Nginx instead of Apache, you must install PHP in a certain order.

The following command will **automatically install PHP and Apache.** If you don't need/want to use Apache, please skip using this command:

```
$ sudo apt-get install php5 php5-fpm
```

To avoid Apache installation, execute the following commands in the exact same order:

```
$ sudo apt-get install php5-common
$ sudo apt-get install php5-cgi
$ sudo apt-get install php5 php5-fpm
```

The php5-cgi package fulfills the dependencies that would otherwise be fulfilled by Apache.

Installing Nginx

To install the Nginx web server, we need to execute the following commands:

```
$ sudo add-apt-repository ppa:nginx/stable
$ sudo apt-get update
$ sudo apt-get install nginx
```

Installing MySQL

MySQL is probably the most widely spread RDBMS system with a market share that is greater than 50 percent. Since we are going to use it to develop our project, we need to install it by executing the following command:

```
$ sudo apt-get install mysql-server
```

Downloading the example code

You can download the example code files for all Packt books you have purchased from your account at http://www.packtpub.com. If you purchased this book elsewhere, you can visit http://www.packtpub.com/support and register to have the files e-mailed directly to you.

Installing Redis

Redis is an advanced key-value storage/cache system. We are going to use this mostly for our session and to cache objects to improve the speed of our application. Let's install it by executing the following commands:

```
$ sudo add-apt-repository ppa:chris-lea/redis-server

$ sudo apt-get update

$ sudo apt-get install redis-server

$ sudo apt-get install php5-redis
```

Installing MongoDB

MongoDB is a document database (NoSQL database) system. We will use this to store data that is accessed frequently. Let's install it:

```
$ sudo apt-key adv --keyserver hkp://keyserver.ubuntu.com:80 --recv
  7F0CEB10

$ echo 'deb http://downloads-distro.mongodb.org/repo/ubuntu-upstart
  dist 10gen' | sudo tee /etc/apt/sources.list.d/mongodb.list

$ sudo apt-get update

$ sudo apt-get install -y mongodb-org

$ sudo service mongodb start

$ sudo apt-get install php5-mongo
```

Installing Git

Git is a distributed version control system that we will use to track changes to our application and much more. We will install Git by executing the following command:

```
$ sudo apt-get install git
```

 I strongly recommend that you use the latest versions of all software as much as possible.

Installing Phalcon

Now that we have installed all the required software, we will proceed with the installation of Phalcon. Before we continue, we must install some dependencies:

```
$ sudo apt-get install php5-dev libpcre3-dev gcc make php5-mysql
```

For Windows systems and more details about how to compile the extension on different systems, please check the latest documentation at http://phalconphp.com/en/download.

Now, we can clone the repository and compile our extension:

```
$ git clone --depth=1 git://github.com/phalcon/cphalcon.git
$ cd cphalcon/build
$ sudo ./install
$ echo 'extension=phalcon.so' | sudo tee /etc/php5/mods-available/
  phalcon.ini

$ sudo php5enmod phalcon
$ sudo service php5-fpm restart
```

If everything goes well, you should be able to see Phalcon in the list of PHP installed modules:

```
$ php -m | grep phalcon
```

The Apache and Nginx configuration files

We will use /var/www/learning-phalcon.localhost as the default directory for our project, and we will refer to it as the **root folder**. Please create this folder:

```
$ sudo mkdir -p /var/www/learning-phalcon.localhost/public
```

Of course, if you want, you can use another folder. Let's create a test file in our public folder under the root directory with some PHP content:

```
$ cd /var/www/learning-phalcon.localhost/public
$ echo "<?php date();" > index.php
```

Apache

Let's switch to the default directory where Apache holds the configuration files for the available websites, using the command line: $ cd /etc/apache2/sites-available/. After that, perform the following set of steps:

1. Using your favorite editor, create a file named learning-phalcon.localhost for apache version < 2.4 or learning-phalcon.localhost.conf for apache version >= 2.4:

   ```
   $ vim learning-phalcon.localhost.conf
   ```

2. Now, paste the following content to this file:

```
<VirtualHost *:80>
    DocumentRoot "/var/www/learning-phalcon.localhost"
    DirectoryIndex index.php
    ServerName learning-phalcon.localhost
    ServerAlias www.learning-phalcon.localhost

    <Directory "/var/www/learning-phalcon.localhost/public">
        Options All
        AllowOverride All
        Allow from all
    </Directory>
</VirtualHost>
```

3. Then, switch to the public folder and add a file named .htaccess to it:

```
$ cd /var/www/learning-phalcon.localhost/public
$ vim .htaccess
```

4. Then, add the following content to the .htaccess file:

```
<IfModule mod_rewrite.c>
    RewriteEngine On
    RewriteCond %{REQUEST_FILENAME} !-d
    RewriteCond %{REQUEST_FILENAME} !-f
    RewriteRule ^(.*)$ index.php?_url=/$1 [QSA,L]
</IfModule>
```

5. This will not work unless you have enabled mod_rewrite. To do so, execute this command:

```
$ sudo a2enmod rewrite
```

6. Now that we have configured our virtual host, let's enable it:

```
$ sudo a2ensite learning-phalcon.localhost
$ sudo service apache2 reload
```

The host file

If you open a browser and type http://www.learning-phalcon.localhost/, you'll receive a host not found or connection error. This is because there is no name resolver for this **TLD** (short for **Top Level Domain**). To fix this, we edit our host file and add this name:

```
$ echo "127.0.0.1 learning-phalcon.localhost www.learning-phalcon.
    localhost" | sudo tee /etc/hosts
```

Restart your browser and type the address `http://www.learning-phalcon.localhost/` again. If everything goes well, you should see the current date/time.

Nginx

If you choose to use Nginx (which I recommend, especially because it can serve more concurrent clients with higher throughput, and it serves static content more efficiently) instead of Apache, here is what you need to do:

Locate the `config` folder of Nginx (in Ubuntu, it is installed under `/etc/nginx/`). Create a file named `learning-phalcon.localhost` in your `sites-available` folder (by navigating to `/etc/nginx/sites-available`):

```
$ cd /etc/nginx/sites-available
$ vim learning-phalcon.localhost
```

Now, add the following content to it:

```
server {
    listen 80;
    server_name learning-phalcon.localhost;

    index index.php;
    set $root_path "/var/www/learning-phalcon.localhost/public";
    root $root_path;

    client_max_body_size 10M;

    try_files $uri $uri/ @rewrite;

    location @rewrite {
        rewrite ^/(.*)$ /index.php?_url=/$1;
    }

    location ~ \.php {
        fastcgi_index /index.php;
        fastcgi_pass unix:/var/run/php5-fpm.sock;
        fastcgi_intercept_errors on;
        include fastcgi_params;

        fastcgi_split_path_info ^(.+\.php)(/.*)$;

        fastcgi_param PATH_INFO $fastcgi_path_info;
        fastcgi_param PATH_TRANSLATED
            $document_root$fastcgi_path_info;
```

```
        fastcgi_param SCRIPT_FILENAME
            $document_root$fastcgi_script_name;
        fastcgi_param DOCUMENT_ROOT $realpath_root;
        fastcgi_param SCRIPT_FILENAME $realpath_root/index.php;
    }

    location ~* ^/(css|img|js|flv|swf|download)/(.+)$ {
        root $root_path;
    }

    location ~ /\.ht {
        deny all;
    }
}
```

 In some environments, you might need to edit your php.ini file and set cgi.fix_pathinfo = 0.

Then, save the file and restart Nginx:

$ sudo service nginx restart

Please edit and save your host file (check *The host file* section), then open your browser and type http://www.learning-phalcon.localhost/. At this point, you should see a page that shows the current date/time.

There are many possible methods to install and configure PHP and Apache/Nginx. Feel free to do a simple Google search and choose one that fits you better, if my method is not the optimal one for your needs.

Assuming that everything went well until now, we will go further by learning a little bit about Phalcon's internals.

Understanding the framework's internals

In this section, I will try to make a short introduction to the common parts of the framework. Most of the text presented here is part of the official documentation that you should always read. The idea of this section is to make you familiar with the most common methods and components that will help you to understand quickly how the framework works.

Please note that images in this book might contain the text `http://learning-phalcon.dev`. You need to ignore that and use `http://learning-phalcon.localhost` as suggested in the chapter.

The dependency injection

Probably one of the most powerful characteristics of Phalcon is the **dependency injection (DI)**. If you have no idea about dependency injection, you should read at least the wiki page for this design pattern at `http://en.wikipedia.org/wiki/Dependency_injection`:

> *"Dependency injection is a software design pattern that implements inversion of control for resolving dependencies. An injection is the passing of a dependency (a service or software module) to a dependent object (a client). The service is made part of the client's state. Passing the service to the client, rather than allowing a client to build or find the service, is the fundamental requirement of the pattern.*
>
> *Dependency injection allows a program design to follow the dependency inversion principle.*

The term "Dependency injection" was coined by Martin Fowler.

A real-life example of dependency injection might be the following situation: Suppose you go shopping. At the mall, you will need a bag to put your groceries, but you forgot to take one when you left your home. In this case, you will need to buy a bag. In development, buying this bag can be quite expensive. So, what if your door has a scanner that scans your body for a bag, and will not open unless you have one? This can be called dependency injection.

Phalcon uses the `\Phalcon\DI` component, which is a component that implements the Inversion of Control pattern. This reduces the overall code complexity.

The framework itself or the developer can register services. Phalcon has many built-in components that are available in the DI container, such as the following ones:

- Request and response
- Logger
- Crypt
- Flash
- Router and configuration

- View
- Cache
- Session

Setting up a new component in the DI is as easy as the following code:

```php
<?php

$di = new Phalcon\DI();
// Lazy load
$di['mail'] = function() {
  return new \MyApp\Mail();
};
```

When you need to access the "mail" component, in a controller for example, you can simply call it:

```php
<?php

$mail = $this->getID()->get('mail');
// or
$mail = $this->getDI()->getMail();
```

If you need to create your own DI, Phalcon or the `DiInterface` interface must be implemented to replace the one provided by Phalcon, or you must extend the current one.

These are just a few dummy examples so that you can have an idea about Phalcon's DI by the time we start our project. In the meanwhile, please take your time and read the official documentation that can be found at `http://docs.phalconphp.com/en/latest/reference/di.html`.

The request component

The request component is probably one of the most used components in any framework. It handles any HTTP request (such as GET, POST, or DELETE, among others) and also provides a few shortcuts for the `$_SERVER` variable. Most of the time, we will use the request component in the controllers. The Phalcon documentation (`http://docs.phalconphp.com/en/latest/reference/mvc.html`) states the following:

> *"The controllers provide the "flow" between models and views. Controllers are responsible for processing the incoming requests from the web browser, interrogating the models for data, and passing that data on to the views for presentation."*

In Phalcon, all controllers should extend the \Phalcon\Mvc\Controller component, and the name of the public methods that we want to access via HTTP GET should have the suffix Action. For example:

```php
<?php

class ArticleController extends \Phalcon\Mvc\Controller
{
  // Method for rendering the form to create an article
  public function createAction()
  {
  }

  // Method for searching articles
  public function searchAction()
  {
  }

  // This method will not be accessible via http GET
  public function search()
  {
  }
}
```

Okay. So, how do we use the request component? Easy! Do you remember that we talked about built-in components in the DI section? The request component is one of them. All we need to do is get the DI. Here is an example of how to get and use the request component:

```php
<?php

class ArticleController extends \Phalcon\Mvc\Controller
{
  public function searchAction()
  {
    $request = $this->getDI()->get('request');
    // You can also use $request = $this->request; but I don't
    // recommend it because $this->request can be easily overwritten
    // by mistake and you will spend time to debug ... nothing.

    $request->getMethod(); // Check the request method
    $request->isAjax(); // Checks if the request is an ajax
      request
    $request->get(); // Gets everything, from the request (GET,
        POST, DELETE, PUT)
```

```php
  $request->getPost(); // Gets all the data submitted via POST
    method
  $request->getClientAddress(); // Return the client IP
 }
}
```

These are just a few common methods that are built into the request component. Let's continue with the next important component—Response.

The response component

So, what can this component do? Well, pretty much everything that is response or output related. Using it, we can set headers, do redirects, send cookies, set content, and much more. Here is a list of common methods from this component:

```php
<?php

public function testRedirectAction()
{
  $response = $this->getDI()->get('response');
   // or you can use $this->response directly

  // Redirect the user to another url
  $this->view->disable();
  return $response->redirect('http://www.google.com/', true);
}
```

The `redirect` method accepts three parameters: a location (string), if it is an external redirect (this is a Boolean type which is by default `false`), and a status code (http status code range). The following lines of code is the redirect method:

```php
<?php


/**
 * Redirect by HTTP to another action or URL
 *
 * @param string $location
 * @param boolean $externalRedirect
 * @param int $statusCode
 * @return \Phalcon\Http\ResponseInterface
 */
public function redirect($location, $externalRedirect,
  $statusCode);
```

Another useful method is the `setHeader` method:

```php
<?php

public function testSetHeaderAction()
{
    $this->response->setHeader('APIKEY', 'AWQ23XX258561');
}
```

The preceding example sets a header named `APIKEY` with the value as `AWQ23XX258561`. Sending headers is a common approach when you develop APIs. You can send any type of headers and overwrite current headers using this method.

Content related methods: `setContent()` and `setJsonContent()`. Let's take for example the following code:

```php
<?php

public function testContentAction()
{
    // First, we disable the view if there is any
    $this->view->disable();

    // Set a plain/text or html content
    $this->response->setContent('I love PhalconPHP');

    // OR

    // Set a json content (this will return a json object)
    $this->response->setJsonContent(array(
        'framework' => 'PhalconPHP'
        'versions' => array(
            '1.3.2',
            '1.3.3',
            '2.0.0'
        )
    ));

    // We send the output to the client
    return $this->response->send();
}
```

When you need to send any JSON content, you should set the header as application/json using the built-in method in the response object:

```php
<?php

$this->response->setContentType('application/json', 'UTF-8');
```

Now that we know the basics about response/request components, we might find ourselves in a situation where we may need to log different things, such as errors. For this, we need to check the logger component.

The logger component

In a production environment, we cannot afford to throw errors or blank pages at the client. We will avoid this and log the errors in a log file. You will read more about this in the next chapters. To sum it up, we will implement a custom logger to our DI, catch exceptions, and then log them. For example, perform the following set of steps:

1. Set the custom logger in DI using the following code:

    ```php
    <?php

    $di['logger'] = function() {
      $error_file = __DIR__.'/../logs/'.date("Ymd_error").'.log';
      return new \Phalcon\Logger\Adapter\File($error_file,
        array('mode' => 'a+'));
    };
    ```

2. Create a method that will throw an exception, catch it, and log it, as follows:

    ```php
    <?php

    public function testLoggerAction()
    {
      try {
        $nonExistingComponent = $this->getDI()->get(
            'nonExistingComponent');
        $nonExistingComponent->executeNonExistingMethod();
      } catch (\Exception $e) {
        $this->logger->error($e->getMessage());
        return $this->response->redirect('error/500.html');
      }
    }
    ```

In the preceding example, we try to execute a nonexistent method, and our code will throw an exception that we catch. It will log it and then redirect the user to a friendly error page, `error/500.html`. You will notice that our logger component calls a method named `error`. There are other methods that are implemented, such as, `debug`, `info`, `notice`, `warning`, and so on.

The `logger` component can be transactional. (Phalcon stores the logs temporarily in memory, and later on, it writes the data to the relevant adapter.) For example, consider the following code snippet:

```php
<?php

$this->logger->begin();

$this->logger->error('Ooops ! Error !');
$this->logger->warning('A warning message');

$this->logger->commit();
```

The crypt component

Crypt is a very useful component if someone needs to encrypt data and decrypt it on your side. One situation where you might want to use the crypt component is to send data over the HTTP `get` method or save sensitive information in your database.

This component has many built-in methods such as `encrypt`, `decrypt`, `getAvailableChipers`, `setKey`, `getKey`, and so on. Here is an example of using the crypt component in the HTTP `get` method.

First, we overwrite the DI, and then we pass a key to it in order to avoid setting it every time:

```php
<?php

$di['crypt'] = function () {
  $crypt = new \Phalcon\Crypt();
  $crypt->setKey('0urSup3rS3cr3tK3y!?');

  return $crypt;
};

public function sendActivationAction()
{
  $activation_code = $this->crypt->encryptBase64('1234');
```

```
    $this->view->setVar('activation_code', $activation_code);
}


public function getActivationAction($code)
{
  if ('1234' == $this->crypt->decryptBase64($code)) {
    $this->flash->success('The code is valid ');
  } else {
    $this->flash->error('The code is invalid');
  }
}
```

Of course, you are probably never going to use it this way. The preceding example just demonstrates the power of this component. You might have noticed that there is a new DI method called flash. We are going to talk about it next.

The flash component

This component is used to send notifications to the client and inform him or her about the status of the component's actions. For example, we can send a successful message after a user has completed the registration on our website or submitted a contact form.

There are two kinds of flash messages—direct and session—and both are available in DI. The direct method outputs the message directly and cannot be loaded on a future request. On the contrary, the session method, stores the messages in a session, and they are automatically cleared after they are printed.

Here is a common usage of flash direct and flash session, assuming that you have a page called register, and you post the data on the same page:

```
public function registerAction()
{
  // … code
  if ($errors) {
    $this->flash->warning('Please fix the following errors: ');
    foreach($errors as $error) {
      $this->flash->error($error);
    }
  } else {
    $this->flash->success('You have successfully registered on our
        website');
  }
}
```

In our view, we will render the messages using the `getContent()` method or `content()` in the template engine **Volt** (we'll cover this later in the chapter).

If we need to redirect our user to another page (let's call it `registerSuccess`), then we need to use the flash session method; otherwise, the message will not appear.

```php
<?php


public function registerAction()
{
  // render our template
}
```

The `register` template will contain a form with method `post` and `action` pointing to the `create` method. The `create` method will look something like this:

```php
<?php

public function createAction()
{
  if ($errors) {
    $this->flashSession->warning('Please fix the following errors: ');
    foreach($errors as $error) {
      $this->flashSession->error($error);
    }
  } else {
    $this->flashSession->success('You have successfully registered
        on our website');
  }

  return $this->response->redirect('/register');
}
```

In the preceding example, we set the messages in the session using the `flashSession` method, and we redirect the user back to the register page. In order to render the messages in our view, we need to call the method `flashSession()->output();`.

 The recommended way is to forward the request with the help of dispatcher, not using redirects. If you use redirects, the user will lose all the data that he or she filled in the form.

The router component

The router component helps us to map friendly URLs to our controllers and actions.

By default, if the rewrite module is enabled in your web server, you will be able to access a controller named `Post` and the `read` action like this: `http://www.learning-phalcon.localhost/post/read`. Our code can look like this:

```php
<?php

class PostController extends \Phalcon\Mvc\Controller
{
  public function readAction()
  {
    // get the post
  }
}
```

However, sometimes, this code is not apt if you need to translate the URLs into multiple languages, or if you need to name the URLs in a different way to how they are defined in the code. Here is a usage example for the router component:

```php
<?php

$router = new \Phalcon\Mvc\Router();
// Clear the default routes
$router->clear();

$st_categories = array(
  'entertainment',
  'travel',
  'video'
);

$s_categories = implode('|', $st_categories);

$router->add('#^/('.$s_categories.')[/]{0,1}$#', array(
    'module' => 'frontend',
    'controller' => 'post',
    'action' => 'findByCategorySlug',
    'slug' => 0
));
```

In the preceding example, we map all the categories to the controller `post` and action `findByCategorySlug`. The router component allows us to use regular expressions for our URLs. With `preg_match`, this can be represented as follows

```
$url = 'http://www.learning-phalcon.localhost/video';
preg_match('#^/(entertainment|travel|video)[/]{0,1}$#', $url);
```

By accessing `http://www.learning-phalcon.localhost/video`, the request will be forwarded to the `findByCategorySlug` action from the post controller:

```php
<?php

class PostController extends \Phalcon\Mvc\Controller
{
  public function findByCategorySlug()
  {
    $slug = $this->dispatcher->getParam('slug', array('string',
        'striptags'), null);

    // We access our model (entity) to get all the posts from this
      category
    $posts = Posts::findByCategorySlug($slug);

    if ($posts->count() > 0) {
      $this->view->setVar('posts', $posts);
    } else {
      throw new \Exception('There are no posts', 404);
    }
  }
}
```

The `getParam()` method has three parameters. The first one is the name that we are searching for, the second parameter is an array of filters that can be applied automatically, and the third parameter is the default value in case the requested name does not exist or is not set.

We will discuss models in the next chapter. This was just a simple example of how you can use the router.

The router also supports a precheck of the `request` method. You may be used to check whether the method is POST, DELETE, PUT, or GET, like this:

```php
<?php

if ($_SERVER['REQUEST_METHOD'] == 'post') {
  // process the information
}
```

While this is perfectly correct, it is not very friendly for our code. Phalcon's router has this capability by which you can add the right type of request that you are expecting, without the need to check this in your code:

```php
<?php

// Add a get route for register method within the user controller
$router->addGet('register', 'User::register');

// Add a post route for create method, from the user controller
$router->addPost('create', 'User::create');
```

This is the basic usage of the router. As always, please read the documentation in order to learn everything about this component.

> You can find out more about routing on the official documentation at http://docs.phalconphp.com/en/latest/reference/routing.html.

The config component

This component can handle configuration files of various formats by using adapters. Phalcon has two built-in adapters for it, which are INI and Array. Using INI files is probably never a good idea. Therefore, I recommend you to make use of native arrays.

What kind of data can or needs to be stored in these files? Well, pretty much everything that will be needed globally in our application, such as database connection parameters. In the old days, we used $_GLOBALS (a big security issue), or we used the define() method, and then gradually we started using it globally.

Here is an example of a config file, and how we can use it:

```php
<?php

$st_settings = array(
  'database' => array(
    'adapter'  => 'Mysql',
    'host'     => 'localhost',
    'username' => 'john',
    'password' => 'johndoe',
    'dbname'    => 'test_database',
  ),
  'app' => array(
```

```
      'name' => 'Learning Phalcon'
   )
);

$config = new \Phalcon\Config($st_settings);

// Get our application name:
echo $config->app->name; // Will output Learning Phalcon
```

The `config` object can be converted back to an array by using `toArray()` method:

```php
<?php

$st_config = $config->toArray();
echo $config['app']['name']; // Will output Learning Phalcon
```

Another useful method for this object is the `merge` method. If we have multiple configuration files, we can easily merge them into one object:

```php
<?php

$config = array(
  'database' => array(
    'adapter'  => 'Mysql',
    'host'     => 'localhost',
    'dbname'     => 'test_database',
  ),
  'app' => array(
    'name' => 'Learning Phalcon'
  )
);

$config2 = array(
  'database' => array(
    'username' => 'john',
    'password' => 'johndoe',
  )
```

Now, the `$config` object will have the same content as it did before.

> There are two other adapters that are not implemented yet (YAML and JSON), but you can use them if you clone Phalcon's incubator repository (`https://github.com/phalcon/incubator`). This repository contains a collection of adapters/helpers that might be integrated in Phalcon in the near future.

The view component

This component is used to render our templates. By default, the templates have the `.phtml` extension, and they contain HTML and PHP code. Here are some examples on how to use the view:

1. First, we set up the view in the DI using the following code snippet:

```php
<?php

$di['view'] = function () use ($config) {
  $view = \Phacon\Mvc\View();
  // Assuming that we hold our views directory in the
  configuration file
  $view->setViewsDir($config->view->dir);

  return $view;
};
```

2. Now, we can use this service as follows:

```php
<?php

class PostControler extends \Phalcon\Mvc\Controller
{
  public function listAction()
  {
    // Retrieve posts from DB
    $posts = Post:find();
    $this->view->setVar('pageTitle', 'Posts');
    $this->view->setVar('posts', $posts);
  }
}
```

3. Next, we need to create a view template that must look like this:

```php
<!DOCTYPE html>
<html>
<head>
<meta charset="UTF-8">
<title><?php echo $pageTitle; ?></title>
</head>
<body>
<?php foreach($posts as $post) { ?>
  <p><?php echo $post->getPostTitle(); ?></p>
  <p><?php echo $post->getPostContent(); ?></p>
```

```
<?php } ?>
</body>
</html>
```

Simple, isn't it? This component also supports hierarchical rendering. You can have a base layout, a general template for posts, and a template for a single post. Let's take, for example, the following directory structure:

```
app/views/
- index.phtml
- post/detail.phtml
```

Phalcon will first render `app/views/index.phtml`. Then, when we request for `detailAction()` from the post controller, it will render `app/views/post/details.phtml`. The main layout can contain something similar to this code:

```
<!DOCTYPE html>
<html>
<head>
<meta charset="UTF-8">
<title>Learning Phalcon</title>
</head>
<body>
<?php echo $this->getContent(); ?>
</body>
</html>
```

And, the `details.phtml` template will have the following content:

```
<?php foreach($posts as $post) { ?>
  <p><?php echo $post->getPostTitle(); ?></p>
  <p><?php echo $post->getPostContent(); ?></p>
<?php } ?>
```

This component also allows you to pick different templates to set a render level, disable or enable the view, and much more.

Phalcon has a built-in template engine named Volt. If you are familiar with PHP template engines such as **Smarty** or **Twig**, you will want to use them for sure. Volt is almost identical to Twig, and you will find it very useful—it is inspired by **Jinja** (`http://jinja.pocoo.org/`). You can even use your own template engine, or any other template engine that you can find there.

In order to enable the Volt template engine, we need to make a small modification to our view service, and we need to create a Volt service; here is how to do this:

```php
<?php

$di['voltService'] = function($view, $di) use ($config) {

    $volt = new \Phalcon\Mvc\View\Engine\Volt($view, $di);

    if (!is_dir($config->view->cache->dir)) {
        mkdir($config->view->cache->dir);
    }

    $volt->setOptions(array(
        "compiledPath" => $config->view->cache->dir,
        "compiledExtension" => ".compiled",
        "compileAlways" => false
    ));

    $compiler = $volt->getCompiler();

    return $volt;
};

// First, we setup the view in the DI
$di['view'] = function () use ($config) {
  $view = \Phacon\Mvc\View();
  $view->setViewsDir($config->view->dir);
  $view->registerEngines(array(
    '.volt' => 'voltService'
  ));

  return $view;
};
```

By adding this modification and `voltService`, we can now use this template engine. From the inheritance point of view, Volt acts a little bit differently. We first need to define a main layout with named blocks. Then, the rest of the templates should extend the main layout, and we need to put our content in the same blocks as the main layout. Before we look at some examples, I will tell you a little bit about Volt's syntax, the details are as follows.

- The syntax for outputting data or for echoing content:

  ```
  {{ my_content }}
  ```

- The syntax for defining blocks:

  ```
  {% block body %} Content here {% endblock %}
  ```

- The syntax to extend a template (this should be the first line in your template):

```
{% extends 'layouts/main.volt' %}
```

- The syntax to include a file:

```
{% include 'common/sidebar.volt' %}
```

- The syntax to include a file and pass variables:

```
{% include 'common/sidebar' with{'section':'homepage'} %}
```

 Please note the missing extension. If you pass variables, you *MUST* omit the extension.

- The syntax for control structures (`for`, `if`, `else`):

```
{% for post in posts %}
  {% if post.getCategorySlug() == 'entertainment' %}
    <h3 class="pink">{{ post.getPostTitle() }}</h3>
  {% else %}
    <h3 class="normal">{{ post.getPostTitle() }}</h3>
  {% endif %}
{% endfor %}
```

- The syntax for the loop context:

```
{% for post in posts %}
  {% if loop.first %}
    <h1>{{ post.getPostTitle() }}</h1>
  {% endif %}
{% endif %}
```

- The syntax for assignments:

```
{% set title = 'Learning Phalcon' %}
{% set cars = ['BMW', 'Mercedes', 'Audi'] %}
```

The list is long. Additionally, you can use expressions, comparison operators, logic operators, filters, and so on. Let's write a simple template to see how it works:

```
<!-- app/views/index.volt -->
<!DOCTYPE html>
<html>
<head>
<meta charset="UTF-8">
<title>{% block pageTitle %}Learning Phalcon{% endblock%}</title>
</head>
```

```
<body>
  <div class='header'>{% block header %}Main layout header{%
    endblock%}</div>
  <div class='content'>{% block content %}This is the main layout
    content{% endblock %}</div>
</body>
</html>

<!-- app/views/post/detail.volt -->
{% extends 'index.volt' %}

{% block pageTitle  %}
  {{ post.getPostTitle() }}
{% endblock %}

{% block header %}
  Post layout
{% endblock %}

{% block content %}
  <p>{{ post.getPostContent() }}</p>
{% endblock%}
```

 You can read the full documentation for the view component at `http://docs.phalconphp.com/en/latest/reference/views.html` and for Volt at `http://docs.phalconphp.com/en/latest/reference/volt.html`.

The session component

This component provides object-oriented wrappers to access session data. To start the session, we need to add the service into the DI container:

```php
<?php

$di['session'] = function () {
  $session = new Phalcon\Session\Adapter\Files();
  $session->start();
  return $session;
};
```

The following is a code example for working with session:

```php
<?php

public function testSessionAction()
{
  // Set a session variable
  $this->session->set('username', 'john');

  // Check if a session variable is defined
  if ($this->session->has('username')) {
    $this->view->setVar('username', $this->session->get(
        'username'));
  }

  // Remove a session variable
  $this->session->remove('username');

  // Destroy the session
  $this->session->destroy();
}
```

If you check Phalcon's incubator, there are many available adapters, such as Redis, Database, Memcache, and Mongo. You can also implement your own adapter.

 You can read the official documentation at `http://docs.phalconphp.com/en/latest/reference/session.html`.

The cache component

To improve the performance of some applications, you will need to cache data. For example, we can cache the query results for a post. Why? Imagine 1 million views or posts. Normally, you will query the database for it, but this will mean 1 million queries (you can multiply this by at least 3, if you are using it, and for ORM — this means 3 million queries at least). Why? When you query, the ORM will act like this:

1. It'll check if the table exists, in the information schema:

```sql
SELECT IF(COUNT(*)>0, 1 , 0)
FROM `INFORMATION_SCHEMA`.`TABLES`
WHERE `TABLE_NAME`='user'
```

2. Then, it'll check whether it's executing a "Describe" of the table:

    ```
    DESCRIBE `user`
    ```

3. Then, whether it's executing the actual query:

    ```
    SELECT * FROM user.
    ```

4. If the `user` table has relations, the ORM will repeat each of the preceding steps for each relation.

To solve this problem, we will save the post object into our caching system.

Personally, I use Redis and Igbinary. Redis is probably the most powerful tool, since it stores the data in memory and, saves the data on disk for redundancy. This means that every time you request the data from cache, you will get it from memory. Igbinary (`https://pecl.php.net/package/igbinary`) is a replacement for the standard php serializer. Here is an example cache service:

```php
<?php

$di['redis'] = function () {
    $redis = new \Redis();
    $redis->connect(
        '127.0.0.1',
        6379
    );

    return $redis;
};

$di['cache'] = function () use ($di, $config) {
    $frontend = new \Phalcon\Cache\Frontend\Igbinary(array(
        'lifetime' => 86400
    ));
    $cache = new \Phalcon\Cache\Backend\Redis($frontend, array(
        'redis' => $di['redis'],
        'prefix' => 'learning_phalcon'
    ));

    return $cache;
};
```

The cache component has the following methods that are commonly used:

```php
<?php

// Save data in cache
$this-cache->save('post', array(
  'title' => 'Learning Phalcon',
  'slug' => 'learning-phalcon',
  'content' => 'Article content'
));

// Get data from cache
$post = $this->cache->get('post');

// Delete data from cache
$this->cache->delete('post');
```

Summary

In this chapter, we installed the required software, created the configuration files for the web servers, and you learned a little bit about Phalcon's internals. In the next chapters, we will learn by example, and everything will be much clearer.

Take your time, and before going further, read a little bit more about anything in which you don't have experience.

In the following chapter, we will look at how to set up the MVC structure and the environment for our project.

2
Setting Up the MVC Structure and the Environment for Our Project

In the previous chapter, we summarized the most common parts of Phalcon. Next, we will try to set up the "Hello world" page for our project. In this chapter, we will cover these topics:

- An introduction to MVC—what is MVC?
- The MVC structure
- Creating a configuration file and the Bootstrap
- Preparing the initial DI interface and the router
- Using the router component in a module
- Creating the base layout

What is MVC?

I am pretty sure that if you are reading this book, you are already familiar with the MVC pattern, but for beginners, we will try to explain this in a few words.

MVC is defined as an architectural pattern, and it stands for Model-View-Controller; it is used mostly in web development, but it is widely applied in software that needs a **Graphical User Interface (GUI)**. To make this introduction quick, let's explain these components:

- **Model**: This is usually used as an abstraction layer, and validation for the tables of a database, but it can be used to handle any kind of logic within the application.

- **View**: A view, usually, represents a template (can be an HTML file) that the controller will render.

- **Controller**: In a web application, the controller handles all the HTTP requests and sends an appropriate response. This response can mean rendering a template, outputting JSON data, and so on.

 For the exact definition, I suggest you check out the Wikipedia page of the MVC pattern at `http://code.tutsplus.com/tutorials/mvc-for-noobs--net-10488`).

Let's take a quick look at an example of MVC for a news/blog application by assuming that a user will make a request to `http://www.learning-phalcon.localhost/article/list`. To match this URL, we will need to implement the routing component, but we are going to cover this in the next chapters.

Model

As mentioned earlier, a model is an abstraction layer for a database table and probably, in 99 percent of cases, you will use it for this purpose. In this example, we will extend the `Phalcon\Mvc\Model` component that has some built-in methods, such as the `find` method. By default, this method will return all the records found in a table named `article`.

Let's assume that we have the following MySQL table structure:

```
CREATE TABLE IF NOT EXISTS `article` (
  `id` int(11) NOT NULL AUTO_INCREMENT,
  `article_short_title` varchar(255) COLLATE utf8_unicode_ci NOT NULL,
  `article_long_title` varchar(255) COLLATE utf8_unicode_ci NOT NULL,
  `article_slug` varchar(255) COLLATE utf8_unicode_ci NOT NULL,
  `article_description` text COLLATE utf8_unicode_ci NOT NULL,
  PRIMARY KEY (`id`),
  KEY `id` (`id`)
) ENGINE=InnoDB DEFAULT CHARSET=utf8 COLLATE=utf8_unicode_ci
  AUTO_INCREMENT=1;
```

For this table, our model would look like this:

```
<?php
namespace \App\Core\Models\Article;

class Article extends \Phalcon\Mvc\Model
{
  protected $id;
```

```php
protected $article_short_title;
protected $article_long_title;
protected $article_slug;
protected $article_description;

public function getId()
{
  return $this->id;
}

public function getArticleShortTitle()
{
  return $this->article_short_title;
}

public function getArticleLongTitle()
{
  return $this->article_long_title;
}

public function getArticleSlug()
{
  return $this->article_slug;
}

public function getArticleDescription()
{
  return $this->article_description;
}

public function setId($id)
{
  $this->id = $id;
}

public function setArticleShortTitle($article_short_title)
{
  $this->article_short_title = $article_short_title;
}

public function setArticleLongTitle($article_long_title)
{
  $this->article_long_title = $article_long_title;
}
```

```php
    public function setArticleSlug($article_slug)
    {
      $this->article_slug = $article_slug;
    }

    public function setArticleDescription($article_description)
    {
      $this->article_description = $article_description;
    }
}
```

If we need to overwrite the default find method, we can create one in our model. For example:

```php
public static function find($parameters = null)
{
  return parent::find($parameters);
}
```

View

Let's consider the following PHP/HTML template as our view:

```php
<div class="list">
  <?php foreach ($articles as $article) {?>
    <article>
      <h1><?php echo $article->getArticleShortTitle();?></h1>
      <p><?php echo $article->getArticleLongTitle() ?></p>
      <a href="<?php echo $article->getArticleSlug(); ?>">
        Read more</a>
    </article>
  <?php } ?>
</div>
```

 $article is an instance of our model. This is why we can call our getters from it.

Controller

The controller will handle requests and will send the information to the appropriate method from a model. In this example, the controller will extend the \Phalcon\Mvc\Controller component:

```php
<?php
namespace App\Frontend\Controllers;
```

```
use \App\Core\Models\Article;

class ArticleController extends \Phalcon\Mvc\Controller
{
  public function listAction()
  {
    $articles = Article::find();
    $this->view->setVar('articles', $articles);
  }
}
```

As you can see, we created a public method called `listAction` that calls the `find` method from the model, and it assigns the results to our `view` component. You probably noticed that the namespace of the controller contains the `Frontend` word. This is because we will use a multi-module application. (We will discuss this in the latter sections of this chapter.)

With this, we will close our short introduction to MVC or Phalcon MVC. Next, we will talk about the folder structure of an MVC application.

The MVC structure

This subject (like many other subjects) is quite sensitive. It depends on how much experience you have and how you are used to structure your projects. In a web application, most of the time we have models, views (templates), controllers, and assets (images, JavaScript files, and style sheets). Based on this, I like the following structure, because it's easy to understand where a file resides and what its purpose is.

For a single module application, we can have the following structure:

```
/project
      controllers
              Article.php
              ...
      models
              Article.php
              ...
      views
              article.php
              ...
      public
              assets
                      img
                      js
                      css
              index.php
```

For a multi-module application, we can have the following structure:

```
/project
    modules
            frontend
                    controllers
                            Article.php
                    models
                            Article.php
                    views
                            article.php
            core
            api
            backoffice
    public
            assets
                    img
                    js
                    css
            index.php
```

As you can see, it is quite easy to know exactly what a file is used for and where we can find it. In the end, you should choose the structure that fits your needs but keep in mind that if you are going to work in a team, it should be intuitive enough for any new member.

Creating the structure for our project

Now, we are going to create the structure for our project. In the first chapter, we created the `/var/www/learning-phalcon.localhost` folder. If you have another location, go there and create the following directory structure:

```
YOUR_LOCATION/learning-phalcon.dev/
    modules
            Frontend
            Backoffice
            Core
            Api
    config
    public
    cache
    logs
```

Next, let's create the `index.php` file that will handle our application. This file will be the default file in our web server:

```php
<?php

header('Content-Type: text/html; charset=utf-8');
mb_internal_encoding("UTF-8");
```

```
require_once __DIR__.'/../modules/Bootstrap.php';

$app = new Bootstrap('frontend');
$app->init();
?>
```

In the first two lines, we set the header and internal encoding to UTF-8. This is a good practice if you are going to use special characters / diacritics. In the fourth line, we include a file named `Bootstrap.php`. This file is the Bootstrap of our project, and we will create its content in a few moments. On the next lines, we create a new instance of Bootstrap with a default module (`frontend`), and we initialize it.

We will need to find a way to autoload any file in our application without manually including it. We will make use of the `\Phalcon\Loader` component that will register all our modules in the namespace. In the `config` folder, we will create a new file called `loader.php` with the following content:

```
<?php

$loader = new \Phalcon\Loader();

$loader->registerNamespaces(array(
    'App\Core'       => __DIR__ . '/../modules/Core/',
    'App\Frontend'   => __DIR__ . '/../modules/Frontend/',
    'App\Api'        => __DIR__ . '/../modules/Api/',
    'App\Backoffice' => __DIR__ . '/../modules/Backoffice/',
));

$loader->register();
?>
```

PSR

PSR is a collection of standards used in PHP development, which is supported by a group of people, the **PHP Framework Interop Group**. The standards include these:

- The autoloading standard
- The basic coding standard
- The coding style guide
- Logger interface

The \Phalcon\Loader component is PSR-4 (https://github.com/php-fig/ fig-standards/blob/master/accepted/PSR-4-autoloader.md) compliant, and it helps us to load only the file that we need, when we need them. In this way, we increase the speed of our application. Meanwhile, you can find more information about this component in the official documentation (at http://docs.phalconphp. com/en/latest/reference/loader.html).

Creating the configuration file and the Bootstrap

Almost any application has some constants that will be reused (database credentials, SMTP credentials, and so on). For our application, we will create a global configuration file. This file will be an instance of the \Phalcon\Config component. Switch to the config directory and create it with the following content:

```php
<?php

return new \Phalcon\Config(array(
    'application' => array(
        'name' => 'Learning Phalcon'
    ),
    'root_dir' => __DIR__.'/..//',
    'redis' => array(
        'host' => '127.0.0.1',
        'port' => 6379,
    ),
    'session' => array(
        'unique_id' => 'learning_phalcon',
        'name' => 'learning_phalcon',
        'path' => 'tcp://127.0.0.1:6379?weight=1'
    ),
    'view' => array(
        'cache' => array(
            'dir' => __DIR__.'/../cache/volt/'
        )
    ),
));
```

The `Phalcon\Config` component simplifies the access to the configuration data within our application. By default, data is returned as an object (for example, we have access to the application name using `$config->application->name path`), but it also has a magic method to return data as an array — `$config->toArray()`. If you use `$config->toArray()`, then you will access the application name using the `$config['application']['name']` syntax. Another cool fact about this component is that we can merge another array into it using the `$config->merge($new_config)` syntax.

Now that we have an autoloader and a configuration, let's set up our Bootstrap file. To do this, create a file named `Bootstrap.php` in the `modules` folder with the following content:

```php
<?php
    class Bootstrap extends \Phalcon\Mvc\Application
    {
        private $modules;
        private $default_module = 'frontend';

        public function __construct($default_module)
        {
            $this->modules = array(
                'core' => array(
                    'className' => 'App\Core\Module',
                    'path' => __DIR__ . '/Core/Module.php'
                ),
                'api' => array(
                    'className' => 'App\Api\Module',
                    'path' => __DIR__ . '/Api/Module.php'
                ),
                'frontend' => array(
                    'className' => 'App\Frontend\Module',
                    'path' => __DIR__ . '/Frontend/Module.php'
                ),
                'backoffice' => array(
                    'className' => 'App\Backoffice\Module',
                    'path' => __DIR__ . '/Backoffice/Module.php'
                ),
            );

            $this->default_module = $default_module;
        }
```

```php
    private function _registerServices()
    {
        $default_module = $this->default_module;
        $di             = new \Phalcon\DI\FactoryDefault();
        $config         = require __DIR__.'/../config/config.php';
        $modules        = $this->modules;

        include_once __DIR__.'/../config/loader.php';
        include_once __DIR__.'/../config/services.php';
        include_once __DIR__.'/../config/routing.php';

        $this->setDI($di);
    }

    public function init()
    {
        $debug = new \Phalcon\Debug();
        $debug->listen();

        $this->_registerServices();
        $this->registerModules($this->modules);

        echo $this->handle()->getContent();
    }
}
```

Our Bootstrap file extends \Phalcon\Mvc\Application (http://docs.
phalconphp.com/en/latest/reference/applications.html) that gives us access
to the registerModules() method. The class constructor registers all our modules
and sets the default module. The _registerServices() method initializes the
DI and includes the required files for our application. Finally, the init() method
initializes the application. Here, we make use of the \Phalcon\Debug component,
because we need to be able to debug the application at any time. This should not be
enabled in a production environment.

Until now, we created the folder structure, the configuration file, the autoloader, and
the Bootstrap. We will go further by creating the services, routing, and the frontend
modules files.

Preparing the initial DI interface and the router

In the Bootstrap, we don't have two files: `services.php` and `routing.php`. The `services.php` file will hold the information about global services that our application will use, and the `routing.php` file will hold information about our routes. Let's start by creating the `services.php` file in our `config` folder with the following content:

```php
<?php
use \Phalcon\Logger\Adapter\File as Logger;

$di['session'] = function () use ($config) {

    $session = new \Phalcon\Session\Adapter\Redis(array(
        'uniqueId' => $config->session->unique_id,
        'path' => $config->session->path,
        'name' => $config->session->name
    ));

    $session->start();

    return $session;
};

$di['security'] = function () {
    $security = new \Phalcon\Security();
    $security->setWorkFactor(10);

    return $security;
};

$di['redis'] = function () use ($config) {
    $redis = new \Redis();
    $redis->connect(
        $config->redis->host,
        $config->redis->port
    );

    return $redis;
};
```

```php
$di['url'] = function () use ($config, $di) {
    $url = new \Phalcon\Mvc\Url();

    return $url;
};

$di['voltService'] = function($view, $di) use ($config) {

    $volt = new \Phalcon\Mvc\View\Engine\Volt($view, $di);

    if (!is_dir($config->view->cache->dir)) {
        mkdir($config->view->cache->dir);
    }

    $volt->setOptions(array(
        "compiledPath" => $config->view->cache->dir,
        "compiledExtension" => ".compiled",
        "compileAlways" => true
    ));

    return $volt;
};

$di['logger'] = function () {
    $file = __DIR__."/../logs/".date("Y-m-d").".log";
    $logger = new Logger($file, array('mode' => 'w+'));

    return $logger;
};

$di['cache'] = function () use ($di, $config) {

    $frontend = new \Phalcon\Cache\Frontend\Igbinary(array(
        'lifetime' => 3600 * 24
    ));

    $cache = new \Phalcon\Cache\Backend\Redis($frontend, array(
        'redis' => $di['redis'],
        'prefix' => $config->application->name.':'
    ));

    return $cache;
};
```

The `$di` variable is available because we initialized it in the `_registerServices()` method from the Bootstrap. `$di` is an instance of `\Phalcon\DI\FactoryDefault()`. Let's try to understand each component that we set:

- `$di['session']` is available by default, but we overwrite it because we want to use Redis to store our session.

- `$di['security']` is available by default, but we overwrite it because we want to set a higher work factor than the default one. We will use this component to encrypt our passwords.

- `$di['redis']` connects to the Redis server. We pass the parameters from our configuration file. The `\Redis` class is already available, because we installed it in the first chapter (`php5-redis`).

- `$di['url']` is available by default. The reason why we overwrite this is for backwards compatibility with older versions of Phalcon. In the past, I wasn't able to access it without being defined. Since Phalcon 1.3, it works as expected.

- `$di['voltService']` is a custom DI component that we will use for the Volt template engine (you will learn about Volt soon).

- `$di['logger']` is a custom DI component, and it uses `\Phalcon\Logger\Adapter\File`. We will use this to log different errors/warnings.

- `$di['cache']` is also a custom DI component that uses Igbinary as frontend cache and redis for backend. You will need to install Igbinary from PECL, if you don't have it, by issuing the following command: `sudo pecl install igbinary`. Note that you might need to reinstall `php5-redis` after installing Igbinary.

Since we are going to use some components that are not available by default in Phalcon, we will need to install them from `phalcon/incubator` (`https://github.com/phalcon/incubator`). **Incubator** is a collection of components developed by the community, which may or may not be included in Phalcon's core. One of the components that we need right now is the `\Phalcon\Cache\Backend\Redis`.

We will use **Composer** (`https://getcomposer.org/`) to manage our package dependency. To install composer, execute the following command in the `learning-phalcon.localhost` folder:

```
$ curl -s http://getcomposer.org/installer | php
```

Now, you should have a new file named `composer.phar` in your root folder. Next, let's install `phalcon/incubator` by executing the following command:

```
$ php composer.phar require phalcon/incubator dev-master
```

This will install other dependencies such as Swift Mailer, so it might take a few minutes to finish. If you check the folder structure, you will see that a new directory named vendor has been created. This is the default installation folder for composer, and all the packages will reside here.

However, this is not enough. In order to autoload the files from vendor, we need to make a small modification to our public/index.php file by adding the autoloader from composer. The new index.php file should look like this:

```php
<?php
header('Content-Type: text/html; charset=utf-8');
mb_internal_encoding("UTF-8");

require_once __DIR__.'/../vendor/autoload.php';
require_once __DIR__.'/../modules/Bootstrap.php';

$app = new Bootstrap('frontend');
$app->init();
```

Using the router component in a module

We will continue this chapter by creating the routes for our application. To do this, switch to the config directory, and create a file named routing.php with the following content:

```php
<?php

$di['router'] = function() use ($default_module, $modules, $di,
$config) {

    $router = new \Phalcon\Mvc\Router(false);
    $router->clear();

    $moduleRouting = __DIR__.'/../apps/'.ucfirst($default_module).'/
Config/routing.php';

    if (file_exists($moduleRouting) && is_file($moduleRouting)) {
        $router = include $moduleRouting;
    } else {
        $router->add('#^/(|/)$#', array(
            'module' => $default_module,
            'controller' => 'index',
            'action' => 'index',
        ));
```

```
$router->add('#^/([a-zA-Z0-9\_]+)[/]{0,1}$#', array(
    'module' => $default_module,
    'controller' => 1,
));

$router->add('#^/{0,1}([a-zA-Z0-9\_]+)/([a-zA-Z0-9\_]+)
    (/.*)*$#', array(
    'module' => $default_module,
    'controller' => 1,
    'action' => 2,
    'params' => 3,
));
    }

    return $router;
};
```

In this file, we make use of the \Phalcon\Mvc\Router component. We check whether there is any routing information for the module and we load it; otherwise, we create the default routing rules. If you've been following us until now, you should have the following directory structure:

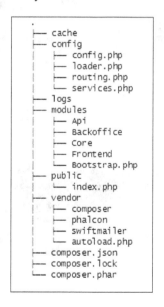

In the first chapter, we already created and enabled the configuration files for the web server. In addition, we edited the host file, and www.learning-phalcon.localhost is pointing to our local host (127.0.0.1). Let's try to access http://www.learning-phalcon.localhost in our browser

Please use `http://`. Otherwise, Chrome and probably other browsers will fail to access this URL, because `.dev` is not a registered Top Level Domain.

If you managed to access the application, you should see an error page similar to the following screenshot:

Let's fix this error by creating the files needed for our `Frontend` module. Go to the `modules/Frontend` folder, and create a file named `Module.php` with the following content:

```php
<?php
namespace App\Frontend;

use Phalcon\Mvc\ModuleDefinitionInterface;

class Module implements ModuleDefinitionInterface
{
    /**
     * Registers the module auto-loader
     */
    public function registerAutoloaders(\Phalcon\DiInterface di =
null) {}

    /**
     * Registers the module-only services
     *
     * @param Phalcon\DI $di
     */
    public function registerServices(\Phalcon\DiInterface $di)
    {
        $config = include __DIR__ . "/Config/config.php";
        $di['config'] = $config;
        include __DIR__ . "/Config/services.php";
    }
}
```

Now, copy this file into each module and change the namespace. For example, the `Module.php` file that resides in the `Api` module should have the `App\Api` namespace. Now, your modules directory structure should be like this:

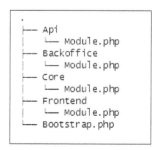

```
.
├── Api
│   └── Module.php
├── Backoffice
│   └── Module.php
├── Core
│   └── Module.php
├── Frontend
│   └── Module.php
└── Bootstrap.php
```

If you refresh the page, you will get another error that says `Phalcon\DI\Exception:`
`Service 'view' was not found in the dependency injection container.`
This happens because each module will have its own `config` folder, and we need
to create the files there. Go to the `modules/Frontend/` directory and create a new
folder named `Config` with C in uppercase.

 We use the uppercase because it's more easy to read and load
within the namespace.

Now, in `modules/Frontend/Config/` create a file named `config.php` with the
following content:

```php
<?php
$config = require __DIR__.'/../../../config/config.php';
$module_config = array(
    'application' => array(
        'controllersDir' => __DIR__ . '/../Controllers/',
        'modelsDir' => __DIR__ . '/../Models/',
        'viewsDir' => __DIR__ . '/../Views/',
        'baseUri' => '/',
        'cryptSalt' => '5up3r5tr0n6p@55',
        'publicUrl' => 'http://www.learning-phalcon.localhost'
    ));

$config->merge($module_config);
return $config;
```

In the first line, we assign the content of the global configuration file to the `$config`
variable. Then, we set the module configuration, and we merge this information into
our global `$config` variable. Next, let's create the routing and services files in the
same folder (`modules/Frontend/Config/`):

`services.php`:

```php
<?php

$di['dispatcher'] = function () use ($di) {
    $eventsManager = $di->getShared('eventsManager');

    $dispatcher = new \Phalcon\Mvc\Dispatcher();
    $dispatcher->setEventsManager($eventsManager);
    $dispatcher->setDefaultNamespace('App\Frontend\Controllers');
```

```
        return $dispatcher;
    };

    $di['url']->setBaseUri(''.$config->application->baseUri.'');

    $di['view'] = function () {

        $view = new \Phalcon\Mvc\View();
        $view->setViewsDir(__DIR__ . '/../Views/Default/');
        $view->registerEngines(array(
            ".volt" => 'voltService'
        ));

        return $view;
    };
```

In the `services.php` file, we overwrite the DI's URL and dispatcher components, and we create a custom view service that will use voltService that we declared in the global services file (`config/services.php`).

`routing.php`:

```php
<?php
$router = new \Phalcon\Mvc\Router(false);
$router->clear();

$router->add('/', array(
    'module' => 'frontend',
    'controller' => 'index',
    'action' => 'index'
));

return $router;
```

We need the `routing.php` file here, because we are going to create custom routes for our Frontend module. The next thing that we need is a controller. It is a good practice in general to create a base file and all the other files to extend the base. This way you will avoid code duplication. Of course, you can use traits of other methods, but for this project, we will use a base file most of the time.

So, let's create the `Controllers` directory in `modules/Frontend/` and a blank base controller in `modules/Frontend/Controllers/` directory:

```
$ cd modules/Frontend/
$ mkdir Controllers
$ touch Controllers/BaseController.php
```

Now, put the following content in `BaseController.php` file:

```php
<?php
namespace App\Frontend\Controllers;

class BaseController extends \Phalcon\Mvc\Controller
{

}
```

Next, create another file here named `IndexController.php` with the following content:

```php
<?php
namespace App\Frontend\Controllers;

class IndexController extends BaseController
{
    public function indexAction()
    {

    }
}
```

If you check the `routing.php` file, you will notice that the default route goes to index controller → index action. In Phalcon, the standard is that any controller should have the `Controller` suffix, and any public action that matches a route should have the Action suffix.

Let's take a look at our directory structure from `modules/Frontend`. It should be exactly like this:

```
.
├── Config
│   ├── config.php
│   ├── routing.php
│   └── services.php
├── Controllers
│   ├── BaseController.php
│   └── IndexController.php
└── Module.php
```

If you try to refresh the page at `http://www.learning-phalcon.localhost`, you will see a blank page. This is perfectly normal. Next, let's copy the `Controllers` and `Config` folders from our `Frontend` module into each remaining module (`Api`, `Core`, and `Backoffice`). After we copy the files, we need to change the namespace and replace anything related to frontend with the new module name.

For example, after we copy the files into the `Api` module, we need to do the following:

1. Replace the `App\Frontend\Controllers` namespace with `App\Api\Controllers` in the `Controllers/` folder.

2. Replace the word "`frontend`" with the word "`api`" in `Config/routing.php`.

3. Replace `\App\Frontend\Controllers` with `App\Api\Controllers` in `services.php`.

4. Append the module name in lowercase to the `baseUri` key from the `config.php` file. The result should be `'baseUri' => '/api/'`.

After you finish, the new directory structure should be this:

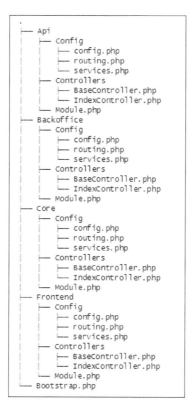

Create the base layout

Now, it's time to focus a little bit on the layout (templates). We are going to use twitter-bootstrap for CSS and jQuery. Then, we are going to create first view in order to close this chapter.

Navigate to `public/folder` and create a folder named `assets`. Then, go to `assets` and create a folder named `default`:

```
$ cd public
$ mkdir -p assets/default
```

I am using Bower (`http://bower.io/`) as a package manager for my assets. It is what composer is for php packages.

If you don't have Bower installed and you don't want to use it, you will need to create a folder named `bower_components` in your `public/default/assets` folder and clone twitter-bootstrap repository from GitHub. You will also need to download jQuery and unzip it into the `bower_components` folder.

```
$ cd public/default/assets/bower_components
$ git clone https://github.com/twbs/bootstrap.git
```

If you have Bower, then just go to the `public/default/assets` folder and install twitter Bootstrap:

```
$ cd public/default/assets
$ bower install bootstrap
```

This will install jQuery automatically because Bootstrap requires jQuery, and Bower is smart enough to check for dependencies.

In the near future, we will also need some custom JavaScript, CSS files, and images. We need to create these directories in the public/assets/default folder, and we will also create two empty files named `lp.js` and `lp.css`. The folder structure of your public folder should be like this:

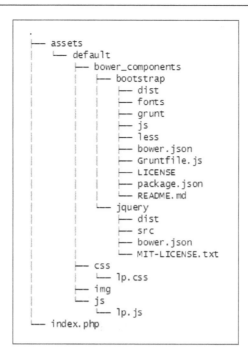

```
.
├── assets
│   └── default
│       ├── bower_components
│       │   ├── bootstrap
│       │   │   ├── dist
│       │   │   ├── fonts
│       │   │   ├── grunt
│       │   │   ├── js
│       │   │   ├── less
│       │   │   ├── bower.json
│       │   │   ├── Gruntfile.js
│       │   │   ├── LICENSE
│       │   │   ├── package.json
│       │   │   └── README.md
│       │   └── jquery
│       │       ├── dist
│       │       ├── src
│       │       ├── bower.json
│       │       └── MIT-LICENSE.txt
│       ├── css
│       │   └── lp.css
│       ├── img
│       └── js
│           └── lp.js
└── index.php
```

Let's get back to our `frontend` module. Navigate to `modules/Frontend` and create a folder named Views. Then, in the `Views` folder, create another one named Default:

```
$ cd modules/Frontend
$ mkdir -p Views/Default
```

Remember that we are using Volt (`http://docs.phalconphp.com/en/latest/reference/volt.html`) as our template engine. We already discussed Volt's syntax in the first chapter, and as we move forward, we will dig more into this subject, but at the right moment. For now, we just want to finish our project structure and render a dummy layout for our fronted module.

This way we can ensure that we did everything as expected until now. In the dependency injection from `services.php`, we assigned the file extension .volt to our template engine. Therefore, all the views that we are going to create will have the extension .volt. Let's create the main layout. Navigate to `modules/Frontend/Views/Default` and create a new file named `layout.volt` with the following content:

```
<!DOCTYPE html>
<html lang="en">
<head>
<meta charset="utf-8">
<meta http-equiv="X-UA-Compatible" content="IE=edge">
```

```
<meta name="viewport" content="width=device-width, initial-scale=1">
<title>{% block pageTitle %}Learning Phalcon{% endblock %}</title>

{{ stylesheetLink('../assets/default/bower_components/bootstrap/dist/
css/bootstrap.min.css') }}
{{ stylesheetLink('../assets/default/css/lp.css') }}

<!--[if lt IE 9]>
        <script src="https://oss.maxcdn.com/html5shiv/3.7.2/html5shiv.
min.js"></script>
        <script src="https://oss.maxcdn.com/respond/1.4.2/respond.min.
js"></script>
<![endif]-->
</head>
<body>
    {% block body %}
    <h1>Main layout</h1>
    {% endblock %}

        {{ javascriptInclude("../assets/default/bower_components/jquery/
dist/jquery.min.js") }}
        {{ javascriptInclude("../assets/default/bower_components/
bootstrap/dist/js/bootstrap.min.js") }}
        {{ javascriptInclude("../assets/default/js/lp.js") }}
        {% block javascripts %} {% endblock %}
</body>
</html>
```

As we mentioned earlier, we are not going to talk about volt's syntax for now. There is one more step that needs to be performed in order to render the templates. We need to create a new folder named index; then, in the index folder, we also need to create a file named index.volt. This will match IndexController → IndexAction.

```
$ cd modules/Frontend/Views/Default
$ mkdir index
$ cd index
$ touch index.volt
```

The content of the index.volt file is this:

```
{% extends 'layout.volt' %}
{% block body %}
I did it !
{% endblock %}
```

The final directory structure for our frontend module should be this:

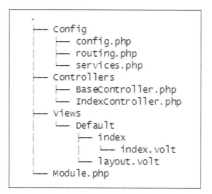

```
├── config
│   ├── config.php
│   ├── routing.php
│   └── services.php
├── Controllers
│   ├── BaseController.php
│   └── IndexController.php
├── Views
│   └── Default
│       ├── index
│       │   └── index.volt
│       └── layout.volt
└── Module.php
```

Now, let's try to refresh the page `http://www.learning-phalcon.localhost`. If you see a page like the one in the following screenshot, then you have made it!

Summary

In this chapter, we learned the basics of MVC, created the folder structure for our project, and learned a little bit about how to use the DI component, routing component, and the view component. We also created the views and rendered the first page from the Frontend module.

In the next chapters, we will learn about Phalcon's ORM and ODM, and we will continue to add features until we have a fully functional online newspaper website.

3
Learning Phalcon's ORM and ODM

Now that you have learned a little bit about Phalcon's internals and we have our project structure, we can move forward to a more serious thing—databases. In this chapter, we will cover these topics:

- The main differences between SQL and NoSQL databases
- Learning how to connect to a database
- ORM/ODM CRUD operations (create, read, update, and delete) and transactions
- Understanding the drawbacks of an ORM in general, and how we can improve performance using caching methods

The main differences between SQL and NoSQL databases

MySQL is good! It is a powerful RDBMS with a big market share, supported by a large community. It is open source (though enterprise flavors exist), and almost every PHP application uses it as the main database system.

But once in a while, you will notice that MySQL isn't good enough for your needs. Maybe you have heard people talk about MongoDB, CouchDB, Cassandra, and so on. We will use MongoDB in our project, so I am going to talk about it.

In general, you will use a NoSQL system, such as MongoDB, when you want to develop real-time analytics, cache, and logs; store big data, such as comments or likes; and handle many other situations.

A few of the differences between a SQL and NoSQL database are as follows:

- NoSQL is *not* relational
- NoSQL is not reliable; or better said, it is not safe to use in a complex system, because it does not support transactions
- A relational database requires a structure with defined attributes to hold the data, but a NoSQL database usually allows free-flow operations

Later in our project, we will use MongoDB mainly for logging and comments. We have already installed MongoDB in the first chapter.

Let's look at a few usage examples:

SQL	MongoDB
`SELECT a,b FROM users`	`$db->users->find([], ["a" => 1, "b" => 1]);`
`SELECT * FROM users WHERE age=33`	`$db->users->find(["age" => 33]);`

On the official PHP website, you can check out the full SQL-to-MongoDB mapping chart (`http://php.net/manual/ro/mongo.sqltomongo.php`).

Connecting to the database

In the previous chapter, we added a global configuration file and configuration files per module. In order to be able to connect to a database, we need to add some lines to our configuration file first.

Let's recall our directory structure:

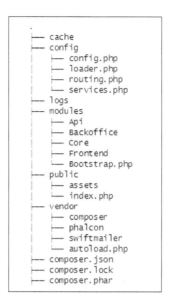

```
.
├── cache
├── config
│   ├── config.php
│   ├── loader.php
│   ├── routing.php
│   └── services.php
├── logs
├── modules
│   ├── Api
│   ├── Backoffice
│   ├── Core
│   ├── Frontend
│   └── Bootstrap.php
├── public
│   ├── assets
│   └── index.php
├── vendor
│   ├── composer
│   ├── phalcon
│   ├── swiftmailer
│   └── autoload.php
├── composer.json
├── composer.lock
├── composer.phar
```

In order to connect to a database, we need to create it. Create a database named `learning_phalcon`. You can do this quickly with the help of the following command line:

```
$ mysql -u YOURUSERNAME -p -e 'create database learning_phalcon;'
```

Open the global configuration file (`config/config.php`), and add these lines:

```
'database' => array(
    'adapter'  => 'Mysql',
    'host'     => 'localhost',
    'username' => 'Input your username here',
    'password' => 'Input your password here',
    'dbname'   => 'learning_phalcon',
),
```

Now that we have the configuration parameters for our database, we must create a service. Open the global services file (`config/service.php`) and add the following lines:

```
$di['db'] = function () use ($config) {

    return new \Phalcon\Db\Adapter\Pdo\Mysql(array(
        "host" => $config->database->host,
```

```
            "username" => $config->database->username,
            "password" => $config->database->password,
            "dbname" => $config->database->dbname,
            "options" => array(
                \PDO::MYSQL_ATTR_INIT_COMMAND => "SET NAMES 'UTF8'",
                \PDO::ATTR_CASE => \PDO::CASE_LOWER,
                \PDO::MYSQL_ATTR_USE_BUFFERED_QUERY => true,
                \PDO::ATTR_PERSISTENT => true
            )
        ));
    };
```

We can now save and close this file. Next, we are going to create a table named `article` in our database, and we'll insert one sample record into this table:

```
USE learning_phalcon;


CREATE TABLE IF NOT EXISTS `article` (
`id` int(11) NOT NULL AUTO_INCREMENT,
`article_short_title` varchar(255) COLLATE utf8_unicode_ci NOT NULL,
`article_long_title` varchar(255) COLLATE utf8_unicode_ci NOT NULL,
`article_slug` varchar(255) COLLATE utf8_unicode_ci NOT NULL,
`article_description` text COLLATE utf8_unicode_ci NOT NULL,
PRIMARY KEY (`id`),
KEY `id` (`id`)
) ENGINE=InnoDB DEFAULT CHARSET=utf8 COLLATE=utf8_unicode_ci AUTO_
INCREMENT=1 ;


INSERT INTO `learning_phalcon`.`article` (
`id` ,
`article_short_title` ,
`article_long_title` ,
`article_slug` ,
`article_description`
)
VALUES (
NULL , 'Test article short title', 'Test article long title', 'test-
article-short-title', 'Test article description'
);
```

To test the database connection, we will use our `Frontend` and `Core` modules. In the `Core` module, we are going to create a model for the article table. Based on the previous chapter, the directory structure of the `Frontend` module should look like this:

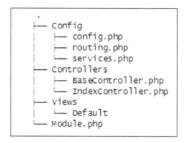

For the `Core` module, the structure should look like this:

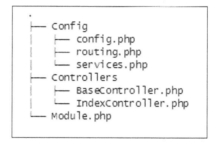

We will create the model for the `article` table in a new folder, named `Models`. Create the `Models` directory in `modules/Core`:

```
$ cd modules/Core
$ mkdir Models
```

In the `Models` directory, create two new files: `Base.php` and `Article.php`. We'll now look at these files:

- The content of `Base.php` is as follows:

```php
<?php
namespace App\Core\Models;

class Base extends \Phalcon\Mvc\Model
{

}
```

- The content of `Article.php` is this:

```php
<?php
namespace App\Core\Models;

class Article extends \Phalcon\Mvc\Model
{
    protected $id;
    protected $article_short_title;
    protected $article_long_title;
    protected $article_slug;
    protected $article_description;

    public function setId($id)
    {
        $this->id = $id;
        return $this;
    }

    public function setArticleShortTitle($article_short_title)
    {
        $this->article_short_title = $article_short_title;
        return $this;
    }

    public function setArticleLongTitle($article_long_title)
    {
        $this->article_long_title = $article_long_title;
        return $this;
    }

    public function setArticleSlug($article_slug)
    {
        $this->article_slug = $article_slug;
        return $this;
    }

    public function setArticleDescription(
      $article_description)
    {
        $this->article_description = $article_description;
        return $this;
    }
```

```php
    public function getId()
    {
        return $this->id;
    }

    public function getArticleShortTitle()
    {
        return $this->article_short_title;
    }

    public function getArticleLongTitle()
    {
        return $this->article_long_title;
    }

    public function getArticleSlug()
    {
        return $this->article_slug;
    }

    public function getArticleDescription()
    {
        return $this->article_description;
    }
}
```

Personally, I like to work in the cleanest manner possible. We are going to use an intermediate file – a manager – to handle all of the heavy logic. This means that you are not going to use the models in the controller, and you are not going to alter the models by adding queries or other kind of data. The models should be as clean as possible. On the other hand, some people prefer to move the heavy logic to models. It's your choice, but in this book we are going to use managers. This being said, let's create the manager for the article:

1. Go to modules/Core/ and create a folder named Managers:

```
$ cd modules/Core/
$ mkdir Managers
```

2. Create two new files named BaseManager.php and ArticleManager.php, and add the following content:

    ○ The BaseManager.php file will be placed under modules/Core/Managers/:

    ```php
    <?php
    namespace App\Core\Managers;
    ```

```
class BaseManager extends \Phalcon\Mvc\User\Module
{
}
```

o The `ArticleManager.php` file will be placed under `modules/Core/Managers/`:

```php
<?php
namespace App\Core\Managers;

use App\Core\Models\Article;

class Article extends Base
{
    public function find($parameters = null)
    {
        return Article::find($parameters);
    }
}
```

The new directory structure of the `Core` module should now look like this:

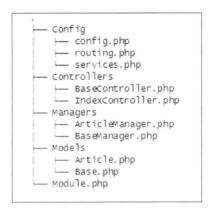

```
.
├── Config
│   ├── config.php
│   ├── routing.php
│   └── services.php
├── Controllers
│   ├── BaseController.php
│   └── IndexController.php
├── Managers
│   ├── ArticleManager.php
│   └── BaseManager.php
├── Models
│   ├── Article.php
│   └── Base.php
└── Module.php
```

All good so far! Let's try to make use of this manager to list the records from our `Article` table. For that, we need to declare it as a service first. To do so, perform the following steps:

1. Open the global services file (`config/service.php`), and add the following content:

```php
$di['core_article_manager'] = function() {
    return new App\Core\Managers\ArticleManager();
};
```

We will use the `frontend` module to carry out this test.

2. Navigate to the `Frontend` directory, edit the `modules/Frontend/Config/routing.php` file, and add this content:

```php
$router->add('#^/articles[/]{0,1}$#', array(
    'module' => 'frontend',
    'controller' => 'article',
    'action' => 'list'
));

$router->add('#^/articles/([a-zA-Z0-9\-]+)[/]{0,1}$#', array(
    'module' => 'frontend',
    'controller' => 'article',
    'action' => 'read',
    'slug' => 1
));
```

The first routing pattern will point any request made at `http://www.learning-phalcon.localhost/articles` to the `frontend` module, the `article` controller, and the `listAction` action.

The second pattern will point to a different action within the article controller, named `readAction` and will pass the slug parameter to this action.

3. Next, we will create the `article` controller and the template. Navigate to `modules/Frontend/Controllers`, and create a file named `ArticleController.php` with the following content:

```php
<?php
namespace App\Frontend\Controllers;

class ArticleController extends BaseController
{
    public function listAction()
    {
        $article_manager = $this->getDI()->get(
            'core_article_manager');
        $this->view->articles = $article_manager->find();
    }
}
```

In `listAction`, we get the `article` manager from DI, and assign the result of the `find()` method to a view variable named `articles`.

4. Now let's create a template for this action. Navigate to `modules/Frontend/Views/Default,` and create a new directory named `article`:

```
$ cd modules/Frontend/Views/Default
$ mkdir article
```

5. In the `article` folder, create a file named `list.volt` and add the following content to it:

```
{% extends 'layout.volt' %}
{% block body %}
    <ul>
    {% for article in articles %}
        <li><a href="{{ url('article/' ~ article.
            getArticleSlug()) }}">{{
                article.getArticleShortTitle() }}</a></li>
    {% endfor %}
    </ul>
{% endblock %}
```

The `Frontend` directory structure should look like this:

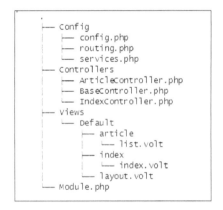

If you did everything by the book, you're all set. You can now go to `http://www.learning-phalcon.localhost/articles`, and you should be able to see our test article as shown here:

Great job! You are now connected to the database, and you have the first model and manager. We will continue this chapter with data manipulation, validations, and simple queries over MySQL and MongoDB.

ORM/ODM operations (create, update, delete, transactions, and validations)

Before we continue, let's make our article table a little more complex, by adding a few columns. We will add three more columns: is_published, created_at, and updated_at.

The is_published field will be a Boolean type (in MySQL, it will have a value of 0 or 1), and the created_at and updated_at fields will have the datetime type. They will hold information about when our article was created and when it was updated. You can alter the article table and add these fields using the following code:

```
ALTER TABLE `article` ADD `is_published` BOOLEAN NOT NULL DEFAULT FALSE ,
ADD `created_at` DATETIME NOT NULL ,
ADD `updated_at` DATETIME NULL DEFAULT NULL ;
```

We also need to make modifications to our Article model and add the getters and setters for these new fields. Open the modules/Core/Models/Article.php file and add the following content:

```
    protected $is_published;
    protected $created_at;
    protected $updated_at;

    public function setIsPublished($is_published)
    {
        $this->is_published = $is_published;
        return $this;
    }

    public function setCreatedAt($created_at)
    {
        $this->created_at = $created_at;
        return $this;
    }

    public function setUpdatedAt($updated_at)
    {
        $this->updated_at = $updated_at;
```

```
        return $this;
    }

    public function getIsPublished()
    {
        return $this->is_published;
    }

    public function getCreatedAt()
    {
        return $this->created_at;
    }

    public function getUpdatedAt()
    {
        return $this->created_at;
    }
```

Since most of the CRUD actions that we will use will be handled by the Backoffice module, we are going to set up this module as we did with the Frontend. The actual development of this module will be done later in the book. For now, we will enable a quick and simple CRUD operation for the Article table.

Let's review our Backoffice directory structure. At this point, you should have the following structure:

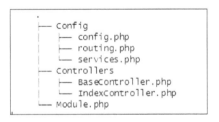

For this to be functional, we will need to:

- Add routing information
- Create the controller and the actions
- Create the views

Adding the routing information

Edit the `config/routing.php` global routing file by adding the following content:

```php
foreach ($modules as $moduleName => $module){
    if ($default_module == $moduleName) {
    continue;
}

$moduleRouting = __DIR__.'/../modules/'.ucfirst(
    $moduleName).'/Config/routing.php';
    include $moduleRouting;
}
```

Delete (or overwrite) the routing file from the `Backoffice` module `modules/Backoffice/Config/routing.php`, and add a new one with the following content:

```php
<?php

$router->add('#^/backoffice(|/)$#', array(
    'module' => 'backoffice',
    'controller' => 'index',
    'action' => 'index',
));

$router->add('#^/backoffice/([a-zA-Z0-9\_]+)[/]{0,1}$#', array(
    'module' => 'backoffice',
    'controller' => 1,
));

$router->add('#^/backoffice[/]{0,1}([a-zA-Z0-9\_]+)/([a-zA-Z0-9\_]+)
(/.*)*$#', array(
    'module' => 'backoffice',
    'controller' => 1,
    'action' => 2,
    'params' => 3,
));
```

Creating the controller and the actions

Navigate to `modules/Backoffice/Controllers/`, and create a new file named `ArticleController.php` with the following content:

```php
<?php
namespace App\Backoffice\Controllers;

class ArticleController extends BaseController
```

```
{
    public function indexAction()
    {
        return $this->dispatcher->forward(['action' => 'list']);
    }

    public function listAction()
    {
        $article_manager      = $this->getDI()->get(
            'core_article_manager');
        $this->view->articles = $article_manager->find();
    }
}
}
```

Creating the views

Copy the views from `Frontend`. We will adapt them for our Backoffice module in *Chapter 7, The Backoffice Module (Part 1)*:

```
$ cd modules/Backoffice
$ cp -r ../Frontend/Views .
```

Now let's modify the views a bit so that we can have a nice `Backoffice` module. Go to `modules/Backoffice/Views/`, open the `layout.volt` file, and make the following change.

Look for this line:

```
<title>{% block pageTitle %}Learning Phalcon{% endblock %}</title>
```

Replace it with the following line:

```
<title>{% block pageTitle %}Backoffice - Learning Phalcon{% endblock %}</title>
```

Create a new file named `lp.backoffice.css` in `public/assets/default/css/`, and add the following content to it:

```
body               { padding-top: 50px; }
.sub-header        { padding-bottom: 10px; border-bottom: 1px solid
#eee; }
.navbar-fixed-top { border: 0; }
.sidebar           { display: none; }

@media (min-width: 768px) {
```

```
.sidebar {position: fixed;top: 51px;bottom: 0;left: 0;z-index:
1000;display: block;padding: 20px;overflow-x: hidden;overflow-y:
auto;background-color: #f5f5f5;border-right: 1px solid #eee;}
}

.nav-sidebar           { margin-right: -21px; margin-bottom: 20px;
margin-left: -20px; }
.nav-sidebar > li > a { padding-right: 20px; padding-left: 20px; }
.nav-sidebar > .active > a,
.nav-sidebar > .active > a:hover,
.nav-sidebar > .active > a:focus { color: #fff; background-color:
#428bca; }

.main { padding: 20px; }
@media (min-width: 768px) {
   .main { padding-right: 40px; padding-left: 40px; }
}
.main .page-header { margin-top: 0; }
```

Then we include the preceding file in our `layout.volt` file. We do this by looking for this line:

```
{{ stylesheetLink('../assets/default/css/lp.css') }}
```

We replace it with the following line:

```
{{ stylesheetLink('../assets/default/css/lp.backoffice.css') }}
```

In the same `layout.volt` file, remove the following code snippet:

```
{% block body %}
<h1>I did it !</h1>
{% endblock %}
```

Add the following content between the `<body>` and `</body>` tags:

```
<nav class="navbar navbar-inverse navbar-fixed-top"
    role="navigation">
  <div class="container-fluid">
    <div class="navbar-header">
      <button type="button" class="navbar-toggle collapsed"
          data-toggle="collapse" data-target="#navbar"
             aria-expanded="false" aria-controls="navbar">
        <span class="sr-only">Toggle navigation</span>
        <span class="icon-bar"></span>
        <span class="icon-bar"></span>
        <span class="icon-bar"></span>
      </button>
```

```
      <a class="navbar-brand" href="#">Learning Phalcon</a>
    </div>
    <div id="navbar" class="navbar-collapse collapse">
      <ul class="nav navbar-nav navbar-right">
        <li><a href="#">Sign out</a></li>
      </ul>
    </div>
  </div>
</nav>

<div class="container-fluid">
  <div class="row">
    <div class="col-sm-3 col-md-2 sidebar">
      <ul class="nav nav-sidebar">
        <li class="active"><a href="{{ url('article/list')
}}">Articles <span class="sr-only">(current)</span></a></li>
        <li><a href="#">Other menu item</a></li>
      </ul>
    </div>
    <div class="col-sm-9 col-sm-offset-3 col-md-10 col-md-offset-2
main">
      {% block body %}
      <h1 class="page-header">Dashboard</h1>
      <h2 class="sub-header">Section title</h2>
      <div class="table-responsive">

      </div>
      {% endblock %}
    </div>
  </div>
</div>
```

We are done editing our layout.volt file, but we need to make one more change. Open `modules/Backoffice/Views/Default/article/list.volt`, and replace its content with the following code:

```
{% extends 'layout.volt' %} {% block body %}
<h1 class="page-header">Articles</h1>
<h2 class="sub-header">List</h2>
<div class="table-responsive">

    <table class="table table-striped">
        <thead>
            <tr>
                <th>#</th>
```

```
            <th>Title</th>
            <th>Is published</th>
            <th>Created at</th>
            <th>Updated at</th>
            <th>Options</th>
        </tr>
    </thead>
    <tbody>
    {% for article in articles %}
        <tr>
            <td>{{ article.getId() }}</td>
            <td>{{ article.getArticleShortTitle() }}</td>
            <td>{{ article.getIsPublished() }}</td>
            <td>{{ article.getCreatedAt() }}</td>
            <td>{{ article.getUpdatedAt() }}</td>
            <td>
                <a href="{{ url('article/edit/' ~ article.getId())
                    }}">Edit</a> |
                <a href="{{ url('article/delete/' ~ article.
                    getId()) }}">Delete</a> |
            </td>
        </tr>
    {% endfor %}
    </tbody>
</table>

</div>
{% endblock %}
```

After all of these changes, the new directory structure should look like what is shown in the following screenshot:

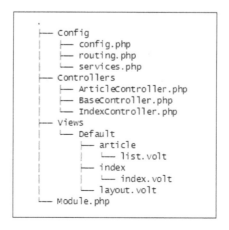

Let's open `http://www.learning-phalcon.localhost/backoffice/article/` `list` in a browser. If everything goes well, you should be able to see the new `Backoffice` layout and our test article in a list exactly like this:

Now that we have a UI, you can start learning about Phalcon's ORM. You need to know that Phalcon provides three ways of working with databases:

- Using ORM
- Using PHQL
- Using raw SQL

We will learn about all of these in this chapter. Let's start with ORM.

CRUD operations using ORM

By using the ORM, there is virtually no need to write any SQL in your code. Everything is OOP, and it is using the models to perform operations. The first, and the most basic, operation is retrieving data. In the old days, you would do this:

```
$result = mysql_query("SELECT * FROM article");
```

The class that our models are extending is `\Phalcon\Mvc\Model`. This class has some very useful methods built in, such as `find()`, `findFirst()`, `count()`, `sum()`, `maximum()`, `minimum()`, `average()`, `save()`, `create()`, `update()`, and `delete()`.

CRUD – reading data

We have already used the `find()` method in our `article` manager when calling `Article::find()`. By default, this method will return all the records from the `article` table, sorting them in a natural order. It also accepts an array with parameters. The following code examples will explain this:

```
$article_slug = "test-article-short-title";

$result = Article::find(
    [
        "article_slug = :article_slug:",
        "bind" => ["article_slug" => $article_slug]
        "order" => "created_at DESC",
        "limit" => 1
    ]
);
```

In the preceding example, we are searching for records that contain the `test-article-short-title` article slug. We bind the data order by the `created_at` field in a descending order, and limit the number of rows returned to one. The first key of the parameters array should always be the condition. Binding parameters is good practice in order to avoid SQL injections. I recommend that you always use it.

The result of `Article::find()` is an array of objects. This means that if we need to iterate between the results, we can do it like this:

```
foreach ($result as $article) {
    echo $article->getTitle();
}
```

Let's add two new records to our `article` table, so that you can see live what it is happening:

```
INSERT INTO `learning_phalcon`.`article` (`id` ,`article_short_title`
,`article_long_title` ,`article_slug` ,`article_description` ,`is_
published` ,`created_at` ,`updated_at`)
VALUES (NULL ,  'Test article short title 2',  'Test article long
title 2',  'test-article-short-title-2',  'Test article description
2',  '0',  '2014-12-14 05:13:26', NULL);

INSERT INTO `learning_phalcon`.`article` (`id` ,`article_short_title`
,`article_long_title` ,`article_slug` ,`article_description` ,`is_
published` ,`created_at` ,`updated_at`)
VALUES (NULL ,  'Test article short title 3',  'Test article long
title 3',  'test-article-short-title-3',  'Test article description
3',  '0',  '2014-12-14 05:13:26', NULL);
```

If you access `http://www.learning-phalcon.localhost/backoffice/article/` `list` now, you should be able to see the new records, as shown in this screenshot:

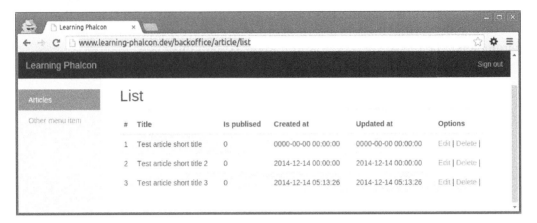

Next, we are going to make some sorting tests. For reference, the default order shown in the preceding screenshot is a natural one, and the IDs are 1, 2, and 3. Keep this in mind, because we will refer to these IDs in the next few lines.

Open the `article` controller `modules/Backoffice/Controllers/` `ArticleController.php`, and then remove the following line:

```
$this->view->articles = $article_manager->find();
```

Now add the following line, which will order the articles by creation date in descending order:

```
$articles = $article_manager->find([
    'order' => 'created_at DESC'
]);
$this->view->articles = $articles;
```

If you refresh the page at `http://www.learning-phalcon.localhost/` `backoffice/article/list`, you will see that the records are ordered differently. The order that you should see is this: 3, 2, and 1.

Feel free to practice and try to order by different columns and by adding limits.

Another useful method is `findFirst()`. This method accepts the same parameters as `find()`, except that the result will be an instance of the `Article` model; this means that you don't need to iterate between records:

```
$article = Article::findFirst();
echo $article->getTitle();
```

Some of the helpful methods are the magic methods, `findBy*()` and `findFirstBy*()`. For example, if you need to search articles by slug, you can do it like this with these magic methods:

```
$articles = Article::findByArticleSlug('test-article-short-title');
foreach ($articles as $article) {
    echo $article->getId();
}


$article = Article:;findFirstByArticleSlug('test-article-short-title');
echo $article->getId();
```

CRUD – creating data

Creating data with the help of ORM is easier than it sounds. We are going to make use of the model. Remember what I told you—that I like to keep the models as clean as possible. This is why most of the time, we will create and make use of managers. Open the `article` manager in `modules/Core/Managers/ArticleManager.php`, and add the following code:

```
public function create($data)
{
    $article = new Article();
    $article->setArticleShortTitle(
        $data['article_short_title']);
    $article->setArticleLongTitle(
        $data['article_long_title']);
    $article->setArticleDescription(
        $data['article_description']);
    $article->setArticleSlug($data['article_slug']);
    $article->setIsPublished(0);
    $article->setCreatedAt(new \Phalcon\Db\RawValue('NOW()'));

    if (false === $article->create()) {
        foreach ($article->getMessages() as $message) {
            $error[] = (string) $message;
        }
        throw new \Exception(json_encode($error));
    }
    return $article;
}
```

Next, we will add a dummy `createAction` method to our controller. Open `modules/Backoffice/Controllers/ArticleController.php`, and add the following content:

```
    public function createAction()
{
  $this->view->disable();
  $article_manager = $this->getDI()->
    get('core_article_manager');

        try {
            $article = $article_manager->create([]);
            echo $article->getArticleShortTitle(), " was created.";
        } catch (\Exception $e) {
            echo $e->getMessage();
        }
    }
}
```

Upon accessing `http://www.learning-phalcon.localhost/backoffice/article/create`, you will see some errors, similar to the ones shown in this screenshot:

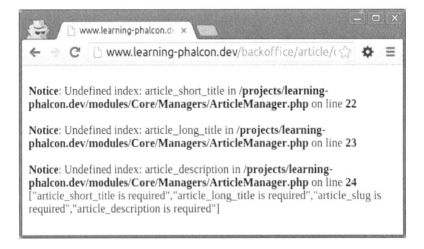

This is perfectly normal, since we didn't pass any parameters to our `create()` method. Modify the `createAction` method by adding these parameters to the create method:

```
$article = $article_manager->create([
    'article_short_title' => 'Test article short title 5',
    'article_long_title' => 'Test article long title 5',
    'article_description' => 'Test article description 5',
    'article_slug' => 'test-article-short-title-5'
]);
```

If we refresh the page at http://www.learning-phalcon.localhost/backoffice/article/create, we should see a success message similar to what is shown here:

 Each time you refresh this page, a new record will be inserted into the database. You can access http://www.learning-phalcon.localhost/backoffice/article/list to see the new records.

Let's quickly analyze the create() method:

We instantiate the Article model and assign values to it using the setters that we wrote for it. Then, we call the built-in create() method to create the data. If there are any errors, we read them and throw an exception with those errors (JSON-encoded), otherwise we return the newly created object.

 You can also use the save() method instead of create().

If you have a big table (tens of columns), you might want to use the built-in assign() method when you create the object, instead of assigning it via setters for each column. You can do this using a key-value array, where the keys are the names of the columns, like this for example:

```
$article = $article_manager->create([
    'article_short_title' => 'Test article short title 5',
    'article_long_title' => 'Test article long title 5',
    'article_description' => 'Test article description 5',
    'article_slug' => 'test-article-short-title-5'
]);

// create() method from manager:

$article = new Article();
$article->assign($data);
$article->create();
```

You might wonder what's with `\Phalcon\Db\RawValue('NOW()')` assigned to `created_at`. Well, whenever you need to assign database-driver-specific / driver built-in data, you will need to use `\Phalcon\Db\RawValue()`.

In our example, we are using it to call the `NOW()` MySQL function, which returns the current date and time. If you are working with date-sensitive data, I recommend that you use the PHP date and not rely on any database timestamp.

CRUD – updating data

Updating data is as easy as creating it. The only thing that we need to do is find the record that we want to update. Open the `article` manager and add the following code:

```php
public function update($id, $data)
{
    $article = Article::findFirstById($id);

    if (!$article) {
        throw new \Exception('Article not found', 404);
    }

    $article->setArticleShortTitle($data[
'article_short_title']);
    $article->setUpdatedAt(new \Phalcon\Db\RawValue('NOW()'));

    if (false === $article->update()) {
        foreach ($article->getMessages() as $message) {
            $error[] = (string) $message;
        }
        throw new \Exception(json_encode($error));
    }
    return $article;
}
```

As you can see, we are passing a new variable, `$id`, to the `update` method and searching for an article that has its ID equal to the value of the `$id` variable. For the sake of an example, this method will update only the article title and the `updated_at` field for now.

Next, we will create a new dummy method as we did for the article, `create`.
Open `modules/Backoffice/Controllers/ArticleController.php` and
add the following code:

```
public function updateAction($id)
{
    $this->view->disable();

    $article_manager = $this->getDI()->get(
      'core_article_manager');

    try {
        $article = $article_manager->update($id, [
            'article_short_title' => 'Modified article 1'
        ]);
        echo $article->getId(), " was updated.";
    } catch (\Exception $e) {
        echo $e->getMessage();
    }
}
```

If you access `http://www.learning-phalcon.localhost/backoffice/article/`
`update/1` now, you should be able to see the **1 was updated.** response. Going back
to the article list, you will see the new title, and the **Updated** column will have a
new value.

CRUD – deleting data

Deleting data is easier, since we don't need to do more than calling the built-in
`delete()` method. Open the `article` manager, and add the following code:

```
public function delete($id)
{
    $article = Article::findFirstById($id);

    if (!$article) {
        throw new \Exception('Article not found', 404);
    }

    if (false === $article->delete()) {
        foreach ($article->getMessages() as $message) {
            $error[] = (string) $message;
        }
```

```
                   throw new \Exception(json_encode($error));
        }

        return true;
    }
```

We will once again create a dummy method to delete records. Open `modules/Backoffice/Controllers/ArticleControllers.php`, and add the following code:

```
    public function deleteAction($id)
{
  $this->view->disable();
  $article_manager = $this->getDI()->get('core_article_manager');

        try {
            $article_manager->delete($id);
            echo "Article was deleted.";
        } catch (\Exception $e) {
            echo $e->getMessage();
        }
    }
```

To test this, simply access `http://www.learning-phalcon.localhost/backoffice/article/delete/1`. If everything went well, you should see the **Article was deleted.** message. Going back to, article list, you won't be able to see the article with ID `1` anymore.

These are the four basic methods: create, read, update, and delete. Later in this book, we will use these methods a lot.

 If you need/want to, you can use the Phalcon Developer Tools to generate CRUD automatically. Check out `https://github.com/phalcon/phalcon-devtools` for more information.

Using PHQL

Personally, I am not a fan of PHQL. I prefer using ORM or Raw queries. But if you are going to feel comfortable with it, feel free to use it. PHQL is quite similar to writing raw SQL queries. The main difference is that you will need to pass a model instead of a table name, and use a models manager service or directly call the \Phalcon\Mvc\ Model\Query class. Here is a method similar to the built-in find() method:

```
public function find()
{
    $query = new \Phalcon\Mvc\Model\Query("SELECT * FROM App\Core\
Models\Article", $this->getDI());
    $articles = $query->execute();
return $articles;
}
```

To use the models manager, we need to inject this new service. Open the global services file, config/service.php, and add the following code:

```
$di['modelsManager'] = function () {
    return new \Phalcon\Mvc\Model\Manager();
};
```

Now let's rewrite the find() method by making use of the modelsManager service:

```
public function find()
{
    $query = $this->modelsManager->createQuery(
        "SELECT * FROM App\Core\Models\Article");
    $articles = $query->execute();

    return $articles;
}
```

If we need to bind parameters, the method can look like this one:

```
public function find()
{
    $query = $this->modelsManager->createQuery(
        "SELECT * FROM App\Core\Models\Article WHERE id = :id:");
    $articles = $query->execute(array(
        'id' => 2
    ));
    return $articles;
}
```

We are not going to use PHQL at all in our project. If you are interested in it, you can find more information in the official documentation at `http://docs.phalconphp.com/en/latest/reference/phql.html`.

Using raw SQL

Sometimes, using raw SQL is the only way of performing complex queries. Let's see what a raw SQL will look like for a custom `find()` method and a custom `update()` method :

```php
<?php

use Phalcon\Mvc\Model\Resultset\Simple as Resultset;

class Article extends Base
{
    public static function rawFind()
    {

        $sql     = "SELECT * FROM robots WHERE id > 0";
        $article = new self();

        return new Resultset(null, $article,
            $article->getReadConnection()->query($sql));
    }

    public static function rawUpdate()
    {
        $sql = "UPDATE article SET is_published = 1";
        $this->getReadConnection()->execute($sql);
    }
}
```

As you can see, the `rawFind()` method returns an instance of `\Phalcon\Mvc\Model\Resultset\Simple`. The `rawUpdate()` method just executes the query (in this example, we will mark all the articles as published). You might have noticed the `getReadConnection()` method. This method is very useful when you need to iterate over a large amount of data or if, for example, you use a master-slave connection. As an example, consider the following code snippet:

```php
<?php
class Article extends Base
{
```

```
    public function initialize()
    {
        $this->setReadConnectionService('a_slave_db_connection_
service'); // By default is 'db'
        $this->setWriteConnectionService('db');
    }
}
```

 Working with models might be a complex thing. We cannot cover everything in this book, but we will work with many common techniques to achieve this part of our project. Please spare a little time and read more about working with models at http://docs.phalconphp.com/en/latest/reference/models.html.

Database transactions

If you need to perform multiple database operations, then in most cases you need to ensure that every operation is successful, for the sake of data integrity. A good database architecture in not always enough to solve potential integrity issues. This is the case where you should use transactions. Let's take as an example a virtual wallet that can be represented as shown in the next few tables.

The User table looks like the following:

ID	NAME
1	John Doe

The Wallet table looks like this:

ID	USER_ID	BALANCE
1	1	5000

The Wallet transactions table looks like the following:

ID	WALLET_ID	AMOUNT	DESCRIPTION
1	1	5000	Bonus credit
2	1	-1800	Apple store

How can we create a new user, credit their wallet, and then debit it as the result of a purchase action? This can be achieved in three ways using transactions:

- Manual transactions
- Implicit transactions
- Isolated transactions

A manual transactions example

Manual transactions are useful when we are using only one connection and the transactions are not very complex. For example, if any error occurs during an update operation, we can roll back the changes without affecting the data integrity:

```php
<?php
class UserController extends Phalcon\Mvc\Controller
{
    public function saveAction()
    {
        $this->db->begin();

        $user = new User();
        $user->name = "John Doe";

        if (false === $user->save() {
            $this->db->rollback();
            return;
        }

        $wallet = new Wallet();
        $wallet->user_id = $user->id;
        $wallet->balance = 0;

        if (false === $wallet->save()) {
            $this->db->rollback();
            return;
        }

        $walletTransaction = new WalletTransaction();
        $walletTransaction->wallet_id = $wallet->id;
        $walletTransaction->amount = 5000;
        $walletTransaction->description = 'Bonus credit';
```

```php
        if (false === $walletTransaction1->save()) {
            $this->db->rollback();
            return;
        }

        $walletTransaction1 = new WalletTransaction();
        $walletTransaction1->wallet_id = $wallet->id;
        $walletTransaction1->amount = -1800;
        $walletTransaction1->description = 'Apple store';

        if (false === $walletTransaction1->save()) {
            $this->db->rollback();
            return;
        }

        $this->db->commit();
    }
}
```

An implicit transactions example

Implicit transactions are very useful when we need to perform operations on related tables / exiting relationships:

```php
<?php
class UserController extends Phalcon\Mvc\Controller
{
    public function saveAction()
    {
        $walletTransactions[0] = new WalletTransaction();
        $walletTransactions[0]->wallet_id = $wallet->id;
        $walletTransactions[0]->amount = 5000;
        $walletTransactions[0]->description = 'Bonus credit';

        $walletTransactions[1] = new WalletTransaction();
        $walletTransactions[1]->wallet_id = $wallet->id;
        $walletTransactions[1]->amount = -1800;
        $walletTransactions[1]->description = 'Apple store';

        $wallet = new Wallet();
        $wallet->user_id = $user->id;
        $wallet->balance = 0;
        $wallet->transactions = $walletTransactions;
```

```php
        $user = new User();
        $user->name = "John Doe";
        $user->wallet = $wallet;
    }
}
```

An isolated transactions example

Isolated transactions are always executed in a separate connection, and they require a transaction manager:

```php
<?php

use Phalcon\Mvc\Model\Transaction\Manager as TxManager,
    Phalcon\Mvc\Model\Transaction\Failed as TxFailed;

class UserController extends Phalcon\Mvc\Controller
{
    public function saveAction()
    {
      try {
    $manager     = new TxManager();
    $transaction = $manager->get();


    $user = new User();
    $user->setTransaction($transaction);
    $user->name = "John Doe";

    if ($user->save() == false) {
        $transaction->rollback("Cannot save user");
    }

    $wallet = new Wallet();
    $wallet->setTransaction($transaction);
    $wallet->user_id = $user->id;
    $wallet->balance = 0;

    if ($wallet->save() == false) {
        $transaction->rollback("Cannot save wallet");
    }
```

```
$walletTransaction = new WalletTransaction();
$walletTransaction->setTransaction($transaction);;
$walletTransaction->wallet_id = $wallet->id;
$walletTransaction->amount = 5000;
$walletTransaction->description = 'Bonus credit';

if ($walletTransaction1->save() == false) {
    $transaction->rollback("Cannot create transaction");
}

$walletTransaction1 = new WalletTransaction();
$walletTransaction1->setTransaction($transaction);
$walletTransaction1->wallet_id = $wallet->id;
$walletTransaction1->amount = -1800;
$walletTransaction1->description = 'Apple store';

if ($walletTransaction1->save() == false) {
    $transaction->rollback("Cannot create transaction");
}

$transaction->commit();

    } catch(TxFailed $e) {
    echo "Error: ", $e->getMessage();
    }
}
```

ODM/MongoDB

We will not discuss ODM too much. It mostly supports the same actions as ORM. CRUD operations can be done in the same way as we did with ORM. Of course, we can't use transactions here, since MongoDB is not a transactional database.

Another important thing is that we need to declare the variables as public, not protected, as we did with the article model. This is the case in Phalcon version 1.3.4, but maybe in version 2.0, things will change.

A big difference is in the parameters that we pass to a find() method. Suppose we used something like the following code for ORM:

```
Article::find([
    'article_slug' => 'test-article-title'
]);
```

For the ODM, we need to do it like this:

```
Article::find([
    [
        'article_slug' => 'test-article-title'
    ]
]);
```

 Please read more about these differences at `http://docs.phalconphp.com/en/latest/reference/odm.html` and `http://php.net/manual/ro/mongo.sqltomongo.php`.

Because we will be using MongoDB later, for now, we will just set up the connection. Open the `config/services.php` global services file, and add the following code:

```
$di['mongo'] = function() {
    $mongo = new MongoClient();
    return $mongo->selectDB("bitpress");
};

$di['collectionManager'] = function(){
    return new Phalcon\Mvc\Collection\Manager();
};
```

ORM – drawbacks and caching

If you are developing a small-to-medium project, or if you are working with a big team of developers (more than three), using an ORM—in general—is a good idea. This is because firstly, it forces you to follow some rules, and secondly, the development will be much faster.

Let's take as an example the SELECT * FROM article query . Using a raw query, the MySQL log will return you this:

```
141214 23:35:53    572 Connect  root@localhost on
       572 Query   select @@version_comment limit 1
       572 Query   SELECT DATABASE()
       572 Init DB  learning_phalcon
       572 Query   SELECT * FROM article
       572 Quit
```

By using the ORM and the `find()` method, your MySQL log will look like the following:

```
141214 23:37:26    490 Query  SELECT IF(COUNT(*)>0, 1 , 0) FROM
`INFORMATION_SCHEMA`.`TABLES` WHERE `TABLE_NAME`='article'
     490 Query  DESCRIBE `article`
     490 Query  SELECT `article`.`id`, `article`.`article_short_
title`, `article`.`article_long_title`, `article`.`article_
slug`, `article`.`article_description`, `article`.`is_published`,
`article`.`created_at`, `article`.`updated_at` FROM `article` ORDER BY
`article`.`created_at` DESC
```

The ORM first checks whether the table exists. Then it executes the `describe` operation of the table, and after that, it executes the query we need. I am not saying that the ORM's logic is not right. I am just trying to point out the number of operations needed to finish a job. Things are quite messy when you have relations across multiple tables, and you can end up with hundreds of queries returning data for just 10 records.

To avoid querying the database server every time, we can use the automatic caching method. Phalcon accepts a parameter named `cache`, which can be passed in the `find()` method. To enable the cache, we need a `modelsCache` service. Open the `config/services.php` global services file and add the following code:

```
$di['modelsCache'] = $di['cache'];
```

Now let's modify the `listAction` function from `modules/Backoffice/ Controllers/ArticleController.php` by adding a cache key. The final function is as follows:

```
public function listAction() {
    $article_manager = $this->getDI()->get(
        'core_article_manager');

    $articles = $article_manager->find([
        'order' => 'created_at DESC',
        'cache' => [
            'key' => 'articles',
            'lifetime' => 3600
        ]
    ]);

    $this->view->articles = $articles;
}
```

The cache key contains two parts: `key` is the key name, and `lifetime` represents the time in seconds. That's it! For the next hour, your database will not be queried again. This is a simple example, and I recommend that you pay attention to what kind of data are you caching and for how long. Also, invalidating the cache can become a complex and very hard job. We will work on caching in the upcoming chapters, where you will be able to see more interesting things.

> As always, please take some time to read the official documentation at `http://docs.phalconphp.com/en/latest/reference/models-cache.html`, so that you can learn more about caching data.

Summary

In this chapter, you learned about ORM and ODM in general and how to use the main built-in methods to perform CRUD operations. You also learned about database transactions and ORM caching, and how to use PHQL or raw SQL queries.

In the next chapter, we will start developing our database architecture, and you will learn more about ORM. We will create forms and implement validations. We will also develop a CLI application to help us test our code faster.

4
Database Architecture, Models, and CLI Applications

Now that we know the basics of Phalcon's ORM and ODM, we can create the database architecture and most of the models needed for our project. We will also create some CLI tasks in order to help us work faster. Because there is a large amount of code, when referring to some of the parts in *Chapter 1, Getting Started with Phalcon*, I will use the abbreviation **CSC** (**check source code**).

We will cover the following topics in the chapter:

- The database architecture
- Models
- CLI applications

The database architecture

The main goal of this book is to learn by example and we are achieving this by developing an online news/magazine website. We will assume the following tables as mandatory:

- `User`
- `UserGroup`
- `UserProfile`
- `Article`
- `ArticleCategory`
- `ArticleTranslation`

- `ArticleCategoryArticle`
- `Hashtag`
- `ArticleHashtagArticle`

These are basic tables, and we will add a few more in the later chapters. I like to use singular terms as part of the naming convention, but it's a matter of choice. To work faster, I recommend tools such as PhpMyAdmin or MySQL Workbench. Let's start with the first table.

The User table

The `User` table will hold basic information about a user:

```
CREATE TABLE IF NOT EXISTS `user` (
  `id` int(11) NOT NULL AUTO_INCREMENT,
  `user_first_name` varchar(16) COLLATE utf8_unicode_ci NOT NULL,
  `user_last_name` varchar(16) COLLATE utf8_unicode_ci NOT NULL,
  `user_email` varchar(32) COLLATE utf8_unicode_ci NOT NULL,
  `user_password` varchar(128) COLLATE utf8_unicode_ci NOT NULL,
  `user_group_id` int(11) DEFAULT NULL,
  `user_is_active` tinyint(1) NOT NULL DEFAULT '0',
  `user_created_at` datetime NOT NULL,
  `user_updated_at` datetime DEFAULT NULL,
  PRIMARY KEY (`id`),
  UNIQUE KEY `idx_email` (`user_email`),
  KEY `idx_user_group_id` (`user_group_id`),
  KEY `idx_is_active` (`user_is_active`)
) ENGINE=InnoDB DEFAULT CHARSET=utf8 COLLATE=utf8_unicode_ci AUTO_
INCREMENT=1 ;
```

The `group_id` and `profile_id` fields will have a relation to the `UserGroup` and `UserProfile` tables. After we have created these tables, we will also create the relations.

The UserGroup table

The `UserGroup` table will hold information about user groups, and each user will be part of one of the available groups. We are not going to use one-to-many relationship between users and groups, but if you need them, feel free to implement them:

```
CREATE TABLE IF NOT EXISTS `user_group` (
  `id` int(11) NOT NULL AUTO_INCREMENT,
  `user_group_name` varchar(16) COLLATE utf8_unicode_ci NOT NULL,
  `user_group_created_at` datetime NOT NULL,
  `user_group_updated_at` datetime DEFAULT NULL,
  PRIMARY KEY (`id`)
) ENGINE=InnoDB DEFAULT CHARSET=utf8 COLLATE=utf8_unicode_ci AUTO_
INCREMENT=1 ;
```

The UserProfile table

`UserProfile` is useful if you want a profile for the user. We are going to hold information about the user's location and date of birth:

```
CREATE TABLE IF NOT EXISTS `user_profile` (
  `id` int(11) NOT NULL AUTO_INCREMENT,
  `user_profile_user_id` int(11) NOT NULL,
  `user_profile_location` varchar(64) COLLATE utf8_unicode_ci NOT NULL,
  `user_profile_birthday` date NOT NULL,
  `user_profile_created_at` datetime NOT NULL,
  `user_profile_updated_at` datetime DEFAULT NULL,
  PRIMARY KEY (`id`),
  UNIQUE KEY `idx_user_profile_user_id` (`user_profile_user_id`)
) ENGINE=InnoDB DEFAULT CHARSET=utf8 COLLATE=utf8_unicode_ci AUTO_
INCREMENT=1 ;
```

For simplicity, the user location field will be free text, not a location based on coordinates. Now that we have all the user tables, let's create the relations/constraints between them:

```
ALTER TABLE `user_profile`
  ADD CONSTRAINT `user_profile_ibfk_1` FOREIGN KEY (`user_profile_user_
id`) REFERENCES `user` (`id`) ON DELETE CASCADE ON UPDATE NO ACTION;
```

```
ALTER TABLE `user`
  ADD CONSTRAINT `user_ibfk_2` FOREIGN KEY (`user_profile_id`) REFERENCES
`user_profile` (`id`) ON UPDATE NO ACTION,
  ADD CONSTRAINT `user_ibfk_1` FOREIGN KEY (`user_group_id`) REFERENCES
`user_group` (`id`) ON UPDATE NO ACTION;
```

Finally, your database structure should look like what is shown in the following screenshot:

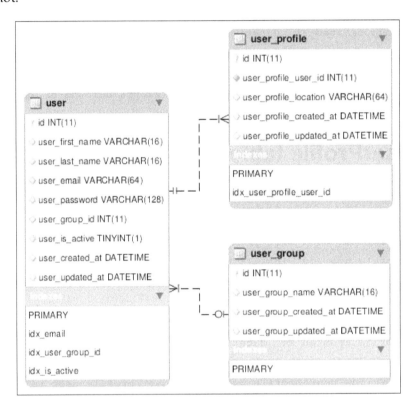

Models

Now that we have the user architecture, before we continue with the rest of the database, let's create the models and a simple CLI task to register a new user.

If you have already installed the Phalcon Developer Tools, you can use them to generate models, or you can manually create them. You can also find them in the source code for this chapter.

Using the model generator will not create relations between tables. You have to manually create them.

All our models will extend the `Base` models created in the previous chapter. Next, I will show you a few lines of code containing the important parts of the models, excluding the getters, setters, and protected variables.

The User model

The `User` model will be located under the `App\Core\Models` namespace in the `apps/Core/Models/` directory:

```php
<?php
namespace App\Core\Models;

class User extends Base {
  public static function find($parameters = array()) {
    return parent::find($parameters);
  }

  public static function findFirst($parameters = array()) {
    return parent::findFirst($parameters);
  }

  public function initialize() {
    $this->hasOne('id', 'App\Core\Models\UserProfile',
      'user_profile_user_id', array(
        'alias' => 'profile',
        'reusable' => true
    ));

    $this->hasOne('user_group_id', 'App\Core\Models\UserGroups',
      'id', array(
      'alias' => 'group',
      'reusable' => true
    ));
  }
}
```

The `initialize()` method acts like a constructor, so here we will put most of the code that we need to execute when the model is loaded.

In the preceding example, we created relations between the models in the `initialize()` method. We have already talked about relations, but you can always read more on the official website at `http://docs.phalconphp.com/en/latest/reference/models.html#relationships-between-models`.

The model contains two other methods for quick access (`find` and `findFirst`). Remember that Phalcon's ORM supports calls using magic methods, for example, if you want to find a user by ID, you can use `findFirstById()`; if you want to find the first user by e-mail, you can use `findFirstByEmail()`; and so on.

The `find()` and `findFirst()` methods are automatically created if you generate the model using the Phalcon Developer Tools.

The UserGroup model

`UserGroup` will be located under the `App\Core\Models` namespace in the `apps/Core/Models/` directory:

```php
<?php
namespace App\Core\Models;

class UserGroup extends Base{
  public static function find($parameters = array()){
    return parent::find($parameters);
  }
  public static function findFirst($parameters = array()){
    return parent::findFirst($parameters);
  }
  public function initialize(){
    $this->hasMany('id', 'App\Core\Models\User', 'group_id',
      array(
        'alias' => 'users'
    ));
  }
}
```

This model has a 1-n relationship with users, which means that when you invoke `$group->users`, the command will return the names of all the users assigned to the users group.

The UserProfile model

The `UserProfile` model will be located under the `App\Core\Models` namespace in the `apps/Core/Models/` directory:

```php
<?php
namespace App\Core\Models;

class UserProfile extends Base
{
    public static function find($parameters = array())
    {
        return parent::find($parameters);
    }

    public static function findFirst($parameters = array())
    {
        return parent::findFirst($parameters);
    }

    public function initialize()
    {
        $this->hasOne('user_profile_user_id', 'App\Core\Models\User',
          'id', array(
            'alias' => 'user',
            'reusable' => true
        ));
    }
}
```

The `UserProfile` model has a 1-1 relationship with the user, which means that a profile is tightly coupled to a single user.

We're all set. Let's take a look at our `modules\Core\Models` directory structure. It should look like this:

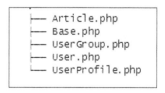

```
├── Article.php
├── Base.php
├── UserGroup.php
├── User.php
└── UserProfile.php
```

`Article.php` is in the list because we created it in the previous chapter. We can now go forward and create a CLI task to register a new user.

In general, you develop CLI applications to be used within cron jobs, to create utilities, and so on. We are going to develop a few tasks in this book for different situations. One of them is for registering a new user via command line.

Registering a new user

Create a new directory named `Task` in the `modules\` folder:

```
$ cd modules
$ mkdir Task
```

Go to the `Task` directory, create a new file named `BaseTask.php`, and append the following content to it:

```php
<?php

class BaseTask extends \Phalcon\CLI\Task
{
    public function consoleLog($s_message, $color = 'green',
      $endline = true)
    {
        $start       = "\033[";
        $end         = "\033[0m\n";
        $bash_color = '0;32';
        $colors = array(
            'green'  => '0;32',
            'red'    => '0;31',
            'yellow' => '0;33',
            'blue'   => '0;34',
            'grey'   => '0;30',
        );
        if (isset($colors[$color])) {
            $bash_color = $colors[$color];
        }
        echo $start, $bash_color, 'm', $s_message;
        if ($endline) echo $end;
    }

    public function countdown($time)
    {
        for ($i=1;$i<=$time;$i++) {
            sleep(1);
            $this->consoleLog(($time-$i).' seconds left ...', 'red');
        }
```

```
    }

    public function quit($s_message)
    {
        $this->consoleLog($s_message, 'red');
        exit;
    }

    public function log($s_message, $log_file='/tmp/app.log')
    {
        error_log(PHP_EOL.$s_message.PHP_EOL, 3, $log_file);
    }

    protected function confirm($message='Are you sure you want to
      process it')
    {
        echo "\033[0;31m".$message.' [y/N]: '."\033[0m";

        $confirmation = trim( fgets( STDIN ) );
        if ($confirmation !== 'y') {
            exit (0);
        }
    }
}
```

 I wrote the content of this file a few years ago to "prettify" my command-line scripts a bit. If you are not happy with it, please feel free to remove it or change it.

Next, we are going to need a bootstrap for our CLI application, but before we do that, we need to install some dependencies. Assuming that you have installed Composer (http://getcomposer.org), edit composer.json and add this content:

```
{
    "require": {
        "phalcon/incubator": "dev-master",
        "crada/php-apidoc": "@dev"
    }
}
```

Update Composer by using the following command:

```
$ php composer.phar update
```

Go back to the `modules\` folder and create a new file named `cli.php`.

We will try to split and explain the contents of the following code:

```php
#!/usr/bin/env php
<?php
umask(0022);
set_time_limit(1200);
require_once __DIR__.'/../vendor/autoload.php';

use Phalcon\DI\FactoryDefault\CLI as CliDI;
use Phalcon\CLI\Console as ConsoleApp;
use Crada\Apidoc\Extractor;
```

In these first lines, we include the autoloader generated by Composer and make use of Phalcon's DI and CLI and the `Extractor` helper, which will be needed to parse annotation comments for the methods:

```php
class Cli
{
    private $arguments;
    private $params;
    private $console;

    public function __construct($argv)
    {
        $di = new CliDI();

        include __DIR__ .'/../config/loader.php';
        $config  = include __DIR__ . '/../config/config.php';

        $di->set('config', $config);

        include __DIR__ . '/../config/services.php';

        $console = new ConsoleApp();
        $console->setDI($di);

        foreach ($argv as $k => $arg) {
            if ($k == 1) {
                $this->arguments['task'] = $arg;
            } elseif ($k == 2) {
                $this->arguments['action'] = $arg;
            } elseif ($k >= 3) {
                $this->params[] = $arg;
```

```
            }
        }

        if (count($this->params) > 0) {
            $this->arguments['params'] = $this->params;
        }

        $this->console = $console;
    }
```

The preceding class constructor will set up the DI for us and load the configuration files needed to run the tasks. It will also read any argument assigned to a task:

```
public function readTasks() {
   if ($handle = opendir(__DIR__.'/Task/')) {

      require_once __DIR__.'/Task/BaseTask.php';
      $util = new BaseTask();
      $util->consoleLog('Learning Phalcon CLI','grey');
      $util->consoleLog(str_repeat('-', 80),'grey');

      while (false !== ($entry = readdir($handle))) {
         if ($entry != '.' && $entry != '..' && $entry !=
            'BaseTask.php' && preg_match("/\.php$/",$entry)) {
         $entries[] = $entry;
                  }
               }

            asort($entries);

            $charCountActionName = 0;

            foreach ($entries as $entry) {
                $task = str_replace('Task.php', '', $entry);

                require_once __DIR__.'/Task/'.$entry;
                $tmp_className = str_replace('.php','',$entry);
                $tmp = new $tmp_className();

                $taskName = PHP_EOL.strtolower(preg_replace('/\
                   B([A-Z])/', '_$1', $task));
                $taskDescription = '';
```

```php
$util->consoleLog(str_pad($taskName,
  25).$taskDescription, 'yellow');
$st_classMethods = get_class_methods($tmp);
asort($st_classMethods);
foreach ($st_classMethods as $value) {
  if (preg_match('/Action/', $value)) {
    $theActionName = str_pad(str_replace('Action',
      '', $value), 6);
    if (strlen($theActionName) >
      $charCountActionName) {

        $charCountActionName = strlen(
          $theActionName);
    }
  }
}
foreach ($st_classMethods as $value) {
  if (preg_match('/Action/', $value)) {
    $theActionName = str_replace('Action', '',
      $value);
    $theActionDescription = '';
    $annotations = Extractor::getMethodAnnotations(
      $tmp_className, $value);
    if (count($annotations) > 0) {
      foreach ($annotations as $key =>
        $st_values) {

        if ($key == 'Description') {
          $theActionDescription .= implode(', ', $st_values);
        }
      }
    }
    $util->consoleLog(str_pad($theActionName,
    $charCountActionName + 5)."\033[
      0;28m".$theActionDescription, 'green');
    }
  }
}
closedir($handle);
  }
}
```

We use the `readTask` method to read the annotation from each task and to list the tasks available in our application. By executing $ php modules/cli.php in your terminal, you will understand the purpose of this method better:

```php
public function getArguments()
{
    return $this->arguments;
}

public function getConsole()
{
    return $this->console;
}
}
```

Finally, we need to initialize our newly created class. We do this with the help of the next few lines:

```php
try {
    $cli       = new Cli($argv);
    $arguments = $cli->getArguments();

    if (0 === count($arguments)) {
        $cli->readTasks();
    } else {
        $console = $cli->getConsole();
        $console->handle($arguments);
    }
} catch (\Phalcon\Exception $e) {
    echo $e->getMessage();
}
```

...

We need to register the new task folder. Open the `config/loader.php` file and add this content:

```php
$loader->registerDirs(array(
    __DIR__ . '/../modules/Task/'
));
```

We're now ready to create our first task. Let's create a test task just to be sure that our code is working. Go to the `modules/Task/` folder and create a new file named `UserTask.php` with the following content:

```php
<?php
class UserTask extends BaseTask
{
```

```
    /**
     * @Description("Test action")
     */
    public function testAction()
    {
        $this->consoleLog('OK');
    }
}
```

Execute the task from your project root folder:

```
$ php modules/cli.php user test
```

You should see something similar to the following screenshot:

```
vagrant@thex:/projects/learning-phalcon.dev-(git/ master )$ php modules/cli.php
Learning Phalcon CLI
- - - - - - - - - - - - - - - - - - - - - - - - - - - - - - - - - - - - - - - - - - - - -

user
test        Test action
vagrant@thex:/projects/learning-phalcon.dev-(git/ master )$ php modules/cli.php user test
OK
vagrant@thex:/projects/learning-phalcon.dev-(git/ master )$
```

So far, we have the database structure and the models for the `user*` tables. We also have a working CLI application and a dummy test task. We can move forward with the user task.

Next, we are going to develop a user registration process that can be accessed from a CLI. The first thing we need to do is implement a registration method in our manager. This manager does not exist yet, but we will create it in `modules/Core/Managers/`, where `ArticleManager.php` resides (from the previous chapter).

Go to `modules/Core/Managers/` and create a new file named `UserManager.php` with the following content:

```php
<?php
namespace App\Core\Managers;

use \App\Core\Models\User;
use \App\Core\Models\UserGroup;
use \App\Core\Models\UserProfile;

class UserManager extends BaseManager
{
    public function find($parameters = null)
```

```
    {
        return User::find($parameters);
    }

    /**
     * Create a new user
     *
     * @param   array                       $data
     * @return  string|\App\Core\Models\User
     */
    public function create($data)
    {
        $security = $this->getDI()->get('security');

        $user = new User();
        $user->setUserFirstName($data['user_first_name']);
        $user->setUserLastName($data['user_last_name']);
        $user->setUserEmail($data['user_email']);
        $user->setUserPassword($security->hash($data[
        'user_password']));
        $user->setUserIsActive($data['user_is_active']);

        if (false === $user->create()) {
            foreach ($user->getMessages() as $message) {
                $error[] = (string) $message;
            }

            throw new \Exception(json_encode($error));

        }

        return $user;
    }
}
```

Note that we are using the security service to hash the user's password.
The hash method uses the bcrypt algorithm.

After this, we need to register the newly created manager. To do this, open the
service file located at `config/service.php` and add the following content:

```
$di['core_user_manager'] = function () {
    return new \App\Core\Managers\UserManager();
};
```

Now we can implement the user creation task. Open `modules/Task/UserTask.php` and append the following content:

```php
/**
 * @Description("Create a new user")
 * @Example("php modules/cli.php user create F_NAME L_NAME
   EMAIL@DOMAIN.TLD PASSWORD IS_ACTIVE")
 */
public function createAction($params = null) {
  if (!is_array($params) || count($params) < 5) {
    $this->quit('Usage: php modules/cli.php user create F_NAME
      L_NAME EMAIL@DOMAIN.TLD PASSWORD IS_ACTIVE');
  }

  $this->confirm('You will create a user with the following data:
    '.implode(' | ', $params));

  $manager = $this->getDI()->get('core_user_manager');

  try {
    $user = $manager->create(array(
      'user_first_name' => $params[0],
      'user_last_name' => $params[1],
      'user_email' => $params[2],
      'user_password' => $params[3],
      'user_is_active' => $params[4],
    ));

    $this->consoleLog(sprintf(
      "User %s %s has been created. ID: %d",
      $user->getUserFirstName(),
      $user->getUserLastName(),
      $user->getId()
    ));

  } catch (\Exception $e) {
    $this->consoleLog("There were some errors creating the
      user: ","red");
    $errors = json_decode($e->getMessage(), true);
    foreach ($errors as $error) {
      $this->consoleLog("  - $error", "red");
    }
  }
}
```

In the first two lines of the `createAction()` method, we just make a simple validation of parameters and ask the developer for a confirmation of the input. You can now execute the task:

```
$ php modules/cli.php user create john doe john.doe@john.tld P@ss0rd!1
```

But you will get an error similar to the one shown in this screenshot:

```
vagrant@thex:/projects/learning-phalcon.dev-(git/ master )$ php modules/cli.php user create john doe john.doe@john.tld P@ss0rd! 1
You will create a user with the following data: john | doe | john.doe@john.tld | P@ss0rd! | 1 [y/N]: y
There were some errors creating the user:
  - user_created_at is required
vagrant@thex:/projects/learning-phalcon.dev-(git/ master )$
```

The `user_created_at is required` exception is thrown, because in our `create()` method from the user manager, we didn't add this field—and we are not going to add it. Instead, we are going to use Phalcon's "timestampable" behavior.

Open the `User` model (`modules/Core/Models/User.php`) and add the following code to the `initialize()` method:

```php
$this->addBehavior(new Timestampable(array(
  'beforeValidationOnCreate' => array(
    'field' => 'user_created_at',
    'format' => 'Y-m-d H:i:s'
  ),
  'beforeValidationOnUpdate' => array(
    'field' => 'user_updated_at',
    'format' => 'Y-m-d H:i:s'
  ),
)));
```

 Add this behavior to all the models where we are using `*_created_at` and `*_updated_at`. Also, don't forget to make use of `use \Phalcon\Mvc\Model\Behavior\Timestampable;`.

Now, you can execute the user creation task again. If everything goes OK, you should see something similar to the following screenshot:

```
vagrant@thex:/projects/learning-phalcon.dev-(git/ master )$ php modules/cli.php user create john doe john.doe@john.tld P@ss0rd! 1
You will create a user with the following data: john | doe | john.doe@john.tld | P@ss0rd! | 1 [y/N]: y
User john doe has been created. ID: 1
vagrant@thex:/projects/learning-phalcon.dev-(git/ master )$
```

We now have a functional CLI application for a user and a user manager, but the user has no profile and no group. We will modify the `create()` method from the user manager to be able to assign groups and create a profile. Because the user_group table is empty, we need to insert some data:

```
INSERT INTO `user_group` (`id`, `user_group_name`, `user_group_
created_at`, `user_group_updated_at`) VALUES
(1, 'User', '2015-01-13 00:00:00', NULL);
```

Here, we created a new group named `User`. This will be the default group. Next, we will modify the `create()` method from the user manager to be able to assign an existing group to a user. The new `create()` method will look like this:

```
public function create($data, $user_group_name = 'User') {
    $security = $this->getDI()->get('security');

    $user = new User();
    $user->setUserFirstName($data['user_first_name']);
    $user->setUserLastName($data['user_last_name']);
    $user->setUserEmail($data['user_email']);
    $user->setUserPassword($security->hash($data['user_password']));
    $user->setUserIsActive($data['user_is_active']);

    $user_group_id = $this->findFirstGroupByName($user_group_name)-
>getId();
    $user->setUserGroupId($user_group_id);

    if (false === $user->create()) {
        foreach ($user->getMessages() as $message) {
            $error[] = (string) $message;
        }

        throw new \Exception(json_encode($error));

    }
    return $user;
}
```

We also need to create the `findFirstGroupByName()` method. Append the following content to the `UserManager.php` file:

```
public function findFirstGroupByName($user_group_name) {
    return UserGroup::findFirstByUserGroupName($user_group_name);
}
```

Before we run the `user create` task again, we need to ensure data integrity, avoiding duplicate e-mails. Because of the database structure, we are not allowed to insert duplicate records (the `email` column is unique), and the `create()` method will throw a SQL exception similar to `SQLSTATE[23000]: Integrity constraint violation: 1062 Duplicate entry 'john.doe@john.tld' for key 'idx_email'`.

To avoid this, we will make use of the built-in validators. In this case, we will implement two of them: a uniqueness validator and an e-mail validator, both for the `user_email` column. We achieve this by adding the following code to the user model in the `modules/Core/Models/User.php` file:

```php
public function validation() {
  $this->validate(new \Phalcon\Mvc\Model\Validator\Email(array(
    "field" => "user_email",
    "message" => "Invalid email address"
  )));

  $this->validate(new \Phalcon\Mvc\Model\Validator\Uniqueness(
    array(
    "field" => "user_email",
    "message" => "The email is already registered"
  )));

  return $this->validationHasFailed() != true;
}
```

Now that we have a validator, we can be sure that an e-mail has the correct format and it does exist in our database. Let's execute the same task to see what happens:

```
$ php modules/cli.php user create john doe john.doe@john.tld P@ss0rd!1
```

If you did everything well, you should see a response similar to the one presented in the following screenshot:

Now, execute the task again by changing the e-mail address and checking whether the group ID has been assigned to the new user. Let's call it me@me.com:

```
$ php modules/cli.php user create john doe me@me.com P@ss0rd! 1
```

If you get a response similar to the one shown in the following screenshot, it means that you have done a great job!:

```
vagrant@thex:/projects/learning-phalcon.dev-(git/ master )$ php modules/cli.php user create john doe me@me.com P@ssOrd! 1
You will create a user with the following data: john | doe | me@me.com | P@ssOrd! | 1 [y/N]: y
User john doe has been created. ID: 16
vagrant@thex:/projects/learning-phalcon.dev-(git/ master )$
```

 You can read more about validating data integrity at http://docs.phalconphp.com/en/latest/reference/models.html#validating-data-integrity.

Creating a user profile

What we need to do next is repeat almost the same process to create a user profile. The final create() method in UserManager.php should look like this:

```php
public function create($data, $user_group_name = 'User') {
    $security = $this->getDI()->get('security');

    $user = new User();
    $user->setUserFirstName($data['user_first_name']);
    $user->setUserLastName($data['user_last_name']);
    $user->setUserEmail($data['user_email']);
    $user->setUserPassword($security->hash($data['user_password']));
    $user->setUserIsActive($data['user_is_active']);

    $user_group_id = $this->findFirstGroupByName($user_group_name)
      ->getId();
    $user->setUserGroupId($user_group_id);

    $profile = new UserProfile();
    $profile->setUserProfileLocation($data['user_profile_location']);
    $profile->setUserProfileBirthday($data['user_profile_birthday']);

    $user->profile = $profile;

    return $this->save($user);
}
```

To avoid code repetition, we will create a save() method in the BaseManager file. Open modules/Core/Managers/BaseManager.php and append the following code:

```php
public function save($object, $type = 'save') {
    switch($type) {
        case 'save':
```

```
      $result = $object->save();
      break;
   case 'create':
      $result = $object->create();
      break;
   case 'update':
      $result = $object->update();
      break;
}

if (false === $result) {
   foreach ($object->getMessages() as $message) {
      $error[] = (string) $message;
   }

   throw new \Exception(json_encode($error));
}

   return $object;
}
```

One last change we need to make is in the UserTask.php file. Open it and update the createAction() method by replacing the $user = $manager->create ... block of code with the following code:

```
$user = $manager->create(array(
   'user_first_name' => $params[0],
   'user_last_name' => $params[1],
   'user_email' => $params[2],
   'user_password' => $params[3],
   'user_is_active' => $params[4],
   'user_profile_location' => $params[5],
   'user_profile_birthday' => $params[6],
));
```

We can try to execute the task again and test whether the new user has been created and a profile has also been created:

```
$ php modules/cli.php user create john doe other@email.com P@ss0rd! 1
Barcelona 1985-03-25
```

You should see something like this:

If you check out the records in the database, you should get a profile linked to the user, as follows:

```
mysql> select * from user u join user_profile up on (up.user_profile_user_id = u.id)\G;
*************************** 1. row ***************************
                    id: 12
       user_first_name: john
        user_last_name: doe
            user_email: other@email.com
         user_password: $2a$12$ZKRJSZb/bztk0YEEmJnBxelgL3qixjHqYD.RjiRJmDAlanLx864Ea
         user_group_id: 1
         user_is_active: 1
        user_created_at: 2015-01-15 10:53:39
        user_updated_at: NULL
                    id: 4
    user_profile_user_id: 12
    user_profile_location: Barcelona
  user_profile_created_at: 2015-01-15 10:53:39
  user_profile_updated_at: NULL
1 row in set (0.00 sec)
```

Remember that when you create or update a record using the ORM, it is not mandatory to use the setters. Phalcon has a method named `assign()` that accepts the `key => value` array, where the key is the column name as defined in the table structure, for example, our `create()` method can also look like this:

```
public function create($data, $user_group_name = 'User') {
  $security = $this->getDI()->get('security');

  $user = new User();
  $user->assign(array(
    'user_first_name' => $data['user_first_name'],
    'user_last_name'  => $data['user_last_name'],
    'user_email'      => $data['user_email'],
    'user_password'   => $security->hash($data['user_password']),
    'user_is_active'  => $data['user_is_active']
  ));

  $user_group_id = $this->findFirstGroupByName($user_group_name)
    ->getId();
  $user->setUserGroupId($user_group_id);

  $profile = new UserProfile();
  $profile->assign(array(
    'user_profile_location' => $data['user_profile_location'],
    'user_profile_birthday' => $data['user_profile_birthday'],
  ));
```

```
    $user->profile = $profile;

    return $this->save($user);
}
```

We are ready to go further with this project by creating the rest of our database structure. Let's start with the `Article` table. First, drop the existing table from your database, and then create a new one:

```
DROP TABLE IF EXISTS `article`;
CREATE TABLE IF NOT EXISTS `article` (
   `id` int(11) NOT NULL AUTO_INCREMENT,
   `article_user_id` int(11) NOT NULL,
   `article_is_published` tinyint(1) NOT NULL DEFAULT '0',
   `article_created_at` datetime NOT NULL,
   `article_updated_at` datetime DEFAULT NULL,
   PRIMARY KEY (`id`),
   KEY `id` (`id`),
   KEY `article_user_id` (`article_user_id`)
) ENGINE=InnoDB  DEFAULT CHARSET=utf8 COLLATE=utf8_unicode_ci AUTO_
INCREMENT=1 ;

ALTER TABLE `article`
   ADD CONSTRAINT `fk_user_id` FOREIGN KEY (`article_user_id`)
REFERENCES `user` (`id`) ON DELETE CASCADE ON UPDATE NO ACTION;
```

For simplicity, an article will be assigned to a user through the `article_user_id` column.

 If you want to implement more complex things, such as "blameable" behavior, you can read an interesting article here `http://blog.phalconphp.com/post/47652831003/tutorial-creating-a-blameable-behavior-with`.

As you can see, we eliminated all the text fields from the `article` table. This is because we are going to create another table named `article_translation`. In this way, we will be able to create multilingual articles/website content. The `article_translation` table is as follows:

```
CREATE TABLE IF NOT EXISTS `article_translation` (
   `id` int(11) NOT NULL AUTO_INCREMENT,
   `article_translation_article_id` int(11) NOT NULL,
   `article_translation_short_title` varchar(255) COLLATE utf8_unicode_
ci NOT NULL,
```

```
  `article_translation_long_title` varchar(255) COLLATE utf8_unicode_
ci NOT NULL,
  `article_translation_slug` varchar(255) COLLATE utf8_unicode_ci NOT
NULL,
  `article_translation_description` text COLLATE utf8_unicode_ci NOT
NULL,
  `article_translation_lang` char(2) COLLATE utf8_unicode_ci DEFAULT
'en',
  PRIMARY KEY (`id`),
  KEY `id` (`id`),
  KEY `article_translation_article_id` (`article_translation_article_
id`)
) ENGINE=InnoDB DEFAULT CHARSET=utf8 COLLATE=utf8_unicode_ci AUTO_
INCREMENT=1 ;

ALTER TABLE `article_translation`
  ADD CONSTRAINT `fk_article_id` FOREIGN KEY (`article_translation_
article_id`) REFERENCES `article` (`id`) ON DELETE CASCADE ON UPDATE
NO ACTION;
```

The `article_lang` column will accept the two-letter ISO code for languages (ISO 639-1). Any news item, blog, or magazine has two major factors: **categories** and **hashtags/keywords**. We are going to create many-to-many relationship between articles and categories and between articles and hashtags. First, let's create the tables:

```
CREATE TABLE IF NOT EXISTS `category` (
  `id` smallint(5) NOT NULL AUTO_INCREMENT,
  `category_is_active` tinyint(1) NOT NULL DEFAULT '1',
  `category_created_at` datetime NOT NULL,
  `category_updated_at` datetime DEFAULT NULL,
  PRIMARY KEY (`id`),
  KEY `category_is_active` (`category_is_active`),
  KEY `category_created_at` (`category_created_at`),
  KEY `category_updated_at` (`category_updated_at`)
) ENGINE=InnoDB  DEFAULT CHARSET=utf8 COLLATE=utf8_unicode_ci AUTO_
INCREMENT=1 ;

CREATE TABLE IF NOT EXISTS `category_translation` (
  `category_translation_category_id` smallint(5) NOT NULL,
  `category_translation_name` varchar(64) COLLATE utf8_unicode_ci NOT
NULL,
  `category_translation_slug` varchar(128) COLLATE utf8_unicode_ci NOT
NULL,
  `category_translation_lang` char(2) COLLATE utf8_unicode_ci NOT
NULL,
```

```
   PRIMARY KEY (`category_translation_category_id`),
   UNIQUE KEY `category_translation_slug` (`category_translation_
slug`),
   KEY `category_translation_lang` (`category_translation_lang`)
) ENGINE=InnoDB DEFAULT CHARSET=utf8 COLLATE=utf8_unicode_ci;

ALTER TABLE `category_translation`
   ADD CONSTRAINT `category_translation_ibfk_1` FOREIGN KEY (`category_
translation_category_id`) REFERENCES `category` (`id`) ON DELETE
CASCADE ON UPDATE NO ACTION;
```

 If you check out the code from incubator (https://github.com/ phalcon/incubator/tree/master/Library/Phalcon/Mvc/ Model/Behavior), you will see that there is a nice solution for a nested set, if you ever need to implement it.

Because we will use a many-to-many relationship, we need to create an intermediate table between articles and categories:

```
CREATE TABLE IF NOT EXISTS `article_category_article` (
   `article_id` int(11) NOT NULL,
   `category_id` smallint(5) NOT NULL,
   KEY `idx_article_id` (`article_id`),
   KEY `idx_category_id` (`category_id`)
) ENGINE=InnoDB DEFAULT CHARSET=utf8 COLLATE=utf8_unicode_ci;

ALTER TABLE `article_category_article`
   ADD CONSTRAINT `article_category_article_ibfk_2` FOREIGN KEY
(`category_id`) REFERENCES `category` (`id`) ON DELETE CASCADE ON
UPDATE NO ACTION,
   ADD CONSTRAINT `article_category_article_ibfk_1` FOREIGN KEY
(`article_id`) REFERENCES `article` (`id`) ON DELETE CASCADE ON UPDATE
NO ACTION;
```

Having made these tables, let's create the models and the managers. The Article model already exists; remove it and create a new one with the new getters and setters. The next code samples will not contain the getters and setters, so you have to create them manually or check out the source code for this chapter.

The Category model

The `Category` model can be seen with the `modules/Core/Models/Category.php` file. The following code contains an important method — `initialize()`. Here, we create a relation between models and add certain kinds of behavior for the date and time fields:

```php
<?php
namespace App\Core\Models;

class Category extends Base
{
    public function initialize()
    {
        /*
         * @param string $fields
         * @param string $intermediateModel
         * @param string $intermediateFields
         * @param string $intermediateReferencedFields
         * @param string $referencedModel
         * @param string $referencedFields
         * @param  array $options
         * @return \Phalcon\Mvc\Model\Relation
         */
        $this->hasManyToMany(
            "id",
            "App\Core\Models\ArticleCategoryArticle",
            "category_id",
            "article_id",
            "App\Core\Models\Article",
            "id",
            array('alias' => 'articles')
        );

    $this->hasMany('id', 'App\Core\Models\CategoryTranslation',
      'category_translation_category_id', array(

            'alias' => 'translations',
            'foreignKey' => true
        ));

        $this->addBehavior(new Timestampable(array(
            'beforeValidationOnCreate' => array(
                'field' => 'category_created_at',
                'format' => 'Y-m-d H:i:s'
            ),
```

```php
        'beforeValidationOnUpdate' => array(
            'field' => 'category_updated_at',
            'format' => 'Y-m-d H:i:s'
        ),
    )));
    }
}
```

The Category translation model

The Category translation model makes use of `\Phalcon\Utils\Slug` to generate slugs. It uses the `Uniqueness` validator to ensure the uniqueness of the newly generated slug. This verification is made by interrogating the database:

```php
<?php
namespace App\Core\Models;

use \Phalcon\Mvc\Model\Validator\Uniqueness;
use \Phalcon\Utils\Slug;

class CategoryTranslation extends Base{
  public function initialize() {
    $this->belongsTo('category_translation_category_id',
      'App\Core\Models\Category', 'id', array(
      'foreignKey' => true,
      'reusable' => true,
      'alias' => 'category'
        ));
    }

    public function validation()
    {
        $this->validate(new Uniqueness(array(
            "field" => "category_translation_slug",
            "message" => "Category slug should be unique"
        )));

        return $this->validationHasFailed() != true;
    }

    public function beforeValidation()
    {
        if ($this->category_translation_slug == '') {
```

```
        $this->category_translation_slug = Slug::generate($this-
>category_translation_name).'-'.$this->category_translation_category_
id;
    }
  }
}
```

We make use of `\Phalcon\Utils\Slug` to generate slugs for `category`. The same
applies to the Article translation model.

The Article translation model

This model, like the Category translation model, is validating the slug field to be
unique and makes use of `\Phalcon\Utils\Slug` to generate a slug. This model is
defined as follows. We'll be referencing the model from the `modules/Core/Models/
ArticleTranslation.php` file:

```php
<?php
namespace App\Core\Models;

use \Phalcon\Mvc\Model\Validator\Uniqueness;
use \Phalcon\Utils\Slug;

class ArticleTranslation extends Base
{
    public function initialize()
    {
        $this->belongsTo('article_translation_article_id',
          'App\Core\Models\Article', 'id', array(
            'foreignKey' => true,
            'reusable' => true,
            'alias' => 'article'
        ));
    }

    public function validation()
    {
        $this->validate(new Uniqueness(array(
            "field" => "article_translation_slug",
            "message" => "Article slug should be unique"
        )));

        return $this->validationHasFailed() != true;
    }
```

```php
    public function beforeValidation()
    {
        if ($this->article_translation_slug == '') {
            $this->article_translation_slug = Slug::generate($this->article_translation_short_title).'-'.$this->article_translation_article_id;
        }
    }
}
```

The Article model

The Article model is similar to the Category model, with the difference being in the relations and the names of the fields. We'll be referencing the model from the `modules/Core/Models/Article.php` file:

```php
<?php
namespace App\Core\Models;

use \Phalcon\Mvc\Model\Behavior\Timestampable;

class Article extends Base
{
  public function initialize() {
    $this->hasMany('id', 'App\Core\Models\ArticleTranslation',
      'article_translation_article_id', array(
        'alias' => 'translations',
        'foreignKey' => true
    ));

    $this->hasOne('article_user_id', 'App\Core\Models\User', 'id',
      array(
        'alias' => 'user',
        'reusable' => true
    ));

    $this->hasManyToMany(
      "id",
      "App\Core\Models\ArticleCategoryArticle",
      "article_id",
      "category_id",
      "App\Core\Models\Category",
      "id",
      array(
```

```
              'alias' => 'categories'
    ));

    $this->addBehavior(new Timestampable(array(
      'beforeValidationOnCreate' => array(
        'field' => 'article_created_at',
        'format' => 'Y-m-d H:i:s'
      ),
      'beforeValidationOnUpdate' => array(
        'field' => 'article_updated_at',
        'format' => 'Y-m-d H:i:s'
      ),
    )));
  }
}
```

The Article-Category-Article model

The Article-Category-Article model is an intermediate table and model used in a many-to-many relationship between articles and categories. We'll be referencing this model from the `modules/Core/Models/Article.php` file:

```php
<?php
namespace App\Core\Models;

class ArticleCategoryArticle extends Base
{
    public function initialize()
    {
        $this->belongsTo('category_id', 'App\Core\Models\Category',
    'id', array('alias' => 'category')
        );

        $this->belongsTo('article_id', 'App\Core\Models\Article',
    'id', array('alias' => 'article')
        );
    }
}
```

The final relations between articles and categories are presented here:

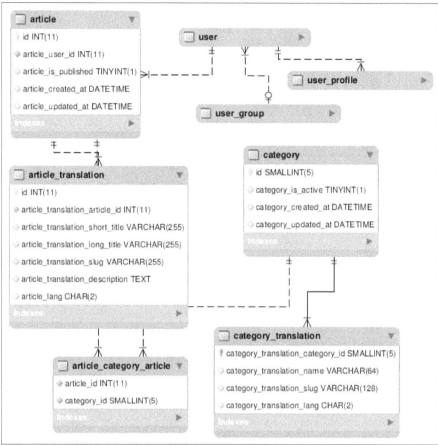

We have the models. Now, let's continue by creating the managers and a simple task to create an article. The article manager already exists, but we are going to change the `create()` method. Before this, we will need to write the category manager with a `create()` method and enable it.

Create a file named `CategoryManager.php` in `modules/Core/Managers/` and add this content:

```php
<?php
namespace App\Core\Managers;

use \App\Core\Models\Category;
use \App\Core\Models\CategoryTranslation;
```

```php
class CategoryManager extends BaseManager
{
    /**
     * Create method
     * @param array $input_data
     * @throws \Exception
     * @return \App\Core\Models\Category
     */
    public function create(array $input_data)
    {
        $default_data = array(
            'translations' => array(
                'en' => array(
                    'category_translation_name' => 'Category name',
                    'category_translation_slug' => '',
                    'category_translation_lang' => 'en',
                )
            ),
            'category_is_active' => 0
        );

        $data = array_merge($default_data, $input_data);

        $category = new Category();
        $category->setCategoryIsActive($data['category_is_active']);

        $categoryTranslations = array();

        foreach ($data['translations'] as $lang => $translation) {
            $tmp = new CategoryTranslation();
            $tmp->assign($translation);
            array_push($categoryTranslations, $tmp);
        }

        $category->translations = $categoryTranslations;

        return $this->save($category, 'create');
    }
}
```

We will also need to register the new manager. Open `config/service.php` and add the following code:

```php
$di['core_category_manager'] = function () {
    return new \App\Core\Managers\CategoryManager();
};
```

The `$default_data` array is meant to always remember the structure of the input that we need to use. We can test everything now by creating a task. Let's name it the `Article` task. Create the new file in `modules/Tasks/ArticleTask.php` and add this code:

```php
<?php
class ArticleTask extends BaseTask
{
    /**
     * @Description("Create a new category with the default data as it
is defined in the manager->create() method")
     * @Example("php modules/cli.php article createCategory")
     */
    public function createCategoryAction()
    {
        $manager = $this->getDI()->get('core_category_manager');

        try {
            $category = $manager->create(array());
            $this->consoleLog(sprintf(
                "The category has been created. ID: %d",
                $category->getId()
            ));

        } catch (\Exception $e) {
            $this->consoleLog("There were some errors creating the
                category: ","red");
            $errors = json_decode($e->getMessage(), true);

            if (is_array($errors)) {
                foreach ($errors as $error) {
                    $this->consoleLog("  - $error", "red");
                }
            } else {
                $this->consoleLog("  - $errors", "red");
            }
        }
    }
}
```

This task will create a new category and generate a slug for it. Execute this task:

```
$ php modules/cli.php article createCategory
```

You should see something similar to the following screenshot:

```
vagrant@thex:/projects/learning-phalcon.dev-(git/ master )$ php modules/cli.php article createCategory
The category has been created. ID: 18
vagrant@thex:/projects/learning-phalcon.dev-(git/ master )$
```

We have pretty much everything we need to create a new article. Let's go back to our `ArticleManager.php` file and replace the existing `create()` method with this one:

```php
    public function create($input_data)
{
  $default_data = array(
    'article_user_id' => 1,
    'article_is_published' => 0,
    'translations' => array(
      'en' => array(
        'article_translation_short_title' => 'Short title',
        'article_translation_long_title' => 'Long title',
        'article_translation_description' => 'Description',
        'article_translation_slug' => '',
        'article_translation_lang' => 'en',
      )
    ),
    'categories' => array()
  );
  $data = array_merge($default_data, $input_data);
  $article = new Article();
  $article->setArticleUserId($data['article_user_id']);
  $article->setArticleIsPublished(
    $data['article_is_published']);
  $articleTranslations = array();
  foreach ($data['translations'] as $lang => $translation) {
    $tmp = new ArticleTranslation();
    $tmp->assign($translation);
    array_push($articleTranslations, $tmp);
  }
  $article->translations = $articleTranslations;
  return $this->save($article, 'create');
}
```

The `createAction()` method from `ArticleTask.php`, which will enable us to create the new article, is given as follows:

```
public function createAction()
{
    $manager = $this->getDI()->get('core_article_manager');

    try {
        $article = $manager->create(array(
            'article_user_id' => 12
        ));
        $this->consoleLog(sprintf(
            "The article has been created. ID: %d",
            $article->getId()
        ));

    } catch (\Exception $e) {
        $this->consoleLog("There were some errors creating the
          article: ","red");
        $this->consoleLog($e->getMessage(),"yellow");
        $errors = json_decode($e->getMessage(), true);

        if (is_array($errors)) {
            foreach ($errors as $error) {
                $this->consoleLog("  - $error", "red");
            }
        } else {
            $this->consoleLog("  - $errors", "red");
        }
    }
}
```

Pay attention to this code:

```
$article = $manager->create(array(
    'article_user_id' => 12
));
```

In this case, I have assigned a user ID that I already have in the database. Check your database and add the specific user ID. Normally, this will be the ID of the authenticated user.

You can now run the task and you should see something similar to the next screenshot:

```
$ php modules/cli.php article create
```

```
vagrant@thex:/projects/learning-phalcon.dev-(git/ master )$ php modules/cli.php article create
The article has been created. ID: 13
vagrant@thex:/projects/learning-phalcon.dev-(git/ master )$ █
```

The newly created article does not have any category assigned to it.

We will close this chapter with a small summary, and you will learn more about models when we develop the API module. In the meantime, I recommend that you try and develop the `hashtag` and `article_hashtag_article` tables, tasks, and models. There is no point in writing about this here, because it's the same thing as we did for categories (only the names have been changed). Also, you have it in the source code of this chapter.

 As always, please spare some time to read the official documentation at `http://docs.phalconphp.com/en/latest/reference/models.html`, where you can learn more about working with models.

Summary

In this chapter, we created the database structure for our project, and you learned how to create a CLI application. We created models and managers and saw how relations between tables work. You also learned about model behavior ("timestampable"), model validations, and the storage of related records.

The next chapter will be about developing an API module, and we will have the chance to discover more techniques of working with models, searching for data, authenticating users, and much more.

5
The API Module

An **Application Programming Interface** (**API**) is the most common way of exposing services to third parties, and lately, most of the software out there is driven by APIs. Why? Because, by having an API for your application, not only is it easy to implement a fully functional HTML + JS frontend, but you can also use it if you develop a mobile application, for example. In this chapter, we will implement most of the functionalities needed for our project, covering topics such as these:

- Using APIs—recommended practices
- Enabling SSL on our local machine
- Creating the module structure
- Writing a fully functional REST module with Phalcon PHP
- Securing an API
- Documenting the API

Using APIs – recommended practices

If you are completely new to APIs, I recommend that you read at least the basics about developing an API. In the simplest way, an API response can be created with plain PHP, like this:

```
$data = [
  'name' => 'John Doe',
  'age' => 50
];

echo json_encode($data);
```

Next, we are going to talk about some general rules that you should follow when developing an API, which are discussed as follows:

- Use plural nouns instead of verbs, use concrete names, and make use of HTTP verbs (GET, POST, PUT, and DELETE) to operate on them:

  This format is bad:

  ```
  GET /getAllArticles
  GET /getArticle
  POST /newArticle
  ```

  This format is good:

  ```
  GET /articles (Retrieve all articles)
  GET /article/12 (Retrieve article with id 12)
  POST /article (Create a new article)
  PUT /article/12 (Update article with id 12)
  DELETE /article/12 (Delete article with id 12)
  ```

- Use verbs when the response does not involve a resource:

  ```
  GET /search?title=Learning+Phalcon
  ```

   Always version your API. In this way, when you make changes to your application, you ensure backward compatibility. Some examples are given here:

  ```
  https://learning-phalcon.localhost/api/v1
  https://api.learning-phalcon.localhost/v1/
  ```

- Always use a secure connection (HTTPS), as you can see in the preceding information box.

- Allow data filtering and sorting:

  ```
  GET /articles?author=John
  GET /articles?author=John&sort=created_at
  ```

- Use camelCase instead of snake_case. I know that using snake case it would be easier to read, and I agree with you. But since (I assume that) you are going to represent your data in JSON format, you should use the JavaScript naming conventions. Anyway, this is a recommendation. After many years, I still cannot get used to camel case for these situations. In this book, I will use snake case.

If a business decision does not force you to expose XML format, go with JSON. From my point of view, XML is kind of dead.

These are just a few general rules. You are going to learn about a few more, later in this chapter.

> If you don't know much about APIs, please check out resources such as
> `https://blog.apigee.com/taglist/restful`, `http://www.vinaysahni.com/best-practices-for-a-pragmatic-restful-api`, or *Web API design*, an e-book by Brian Mulloy (38 pages).

Enabling SSL on our local machine

We will take into account one of the API rules: always use a secure connection. Assuming that you are using Nginx, this can be done in four easy steps:

1. Create a directory, `/etc/nginx/ssl`:

   ```
   $ sudo mkdir /etc/nginx/ssl
   ```

2. Generate a new certificate using the following command:

   ```
   $ sudo openssl req -x509 -nodes -days 365 -newkey rsa:2048 -keyout /etc/nginx/ssl/nginx.key -out /etc/nginx/ssl/nginx.crt
   ```

   At this point you will be asked to provide some information about the new certificate, as shown in the following diagram:

```
vagrant@thex:/projects/learning-phalcon.dev-(git/ master )$ sudo openssl req -x509 -nodes -days 365 -newkey rsa:2048 -keyout /etc/
nginx/ssl/nginx.key -out /etc/nginx/ssl/nginx.crt
Generating a 2048 bit RSA private key
.....................................+++
.............+++
writing new private key to '/etc/nginx/ssl/nginx.key'
-----
You are about to be asked to enter information that will be incorporated
into your certificate request.
What you are about to enter is what is called a Distinguished Name or a DN.
There are quite a few fields but you can leave some blank
For some fields there will be a default value,
If you enter '.', the field will be left blank.
-----
Country Name (2 letter code) [AU]:ES
State or Province Name (full name) [Some-State]:Barcelona
Locality Name (eg, city) []:Barcelona
Organization Name (eg, company) [Internet Widgits Pty Ltd]:MyCompany Ltd
Organizational Unit Name (eg, section) []:MyCompany
Common Name (e.g. server FQDN or YOUR name) []:learning-phalcon.dev
Email Address []:calin@learning-phalcon.dev
vagrant@thex:/projects/learning-phalcon.dev-(git/ master )$
```

3. Open the `learning-phalcon.localhost` configuration file (`/etc/nginx/sites-available/learning-phalcon.localhost`) and enable SSL:

```
server {
  listen 80;
  listen 443 ssl;

  ssl_certificate /etc/nginx/ssl/nginx.crt;
  ssl_certificate_key /etc/nginx/ssl/nginx.key;

  #....rest of the code
}
```

4. Then reload the Nginx configuration:

```
$ sudo service nginx reload
```

Now you can try to access `https://learning-phalcon.localhost/`. In any browser that you are using, you will get a warning saying that the server certificate is not trusted. This is normal because it has not been signed by any authority. On Chrome, you should click on the **Advanced** link (seen in the following screenshot) and then on the **Proceed to learning-phalcon.localhost (unsafe)** link (shown in the next screenshot). Other browsers will have similar links:

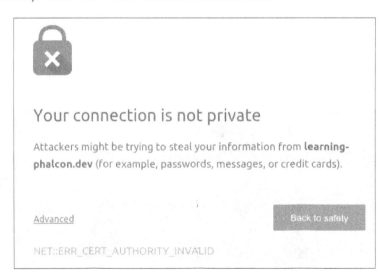

After you click on **Advanced**, a new page will open and it should look like the following screenshot:

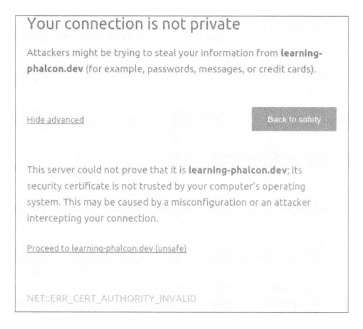

Note that your connection is not actually secured. The purpose of this was for us to be able to access our project via HTTPS.

Creating the module structure

We have already created the basic structure in the previous chapters. The directory structure should look like this:

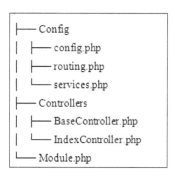

This is okay. What we need to do here is enable the routing and add some methods to BaseController so that we can move forward. Let's start this process by performing the following steps:

1. Open the routing.php file from the api module, delete its content, and put in this code:

```php
<?php
$versions = [
    'v1' => '/api/v1',
    'v2' => '/api/v2'
];
$router->removeExtraSlashes(true);

// Articles group
$articles = new \Phalcon\Mvc\Router\Group(array(
    'module' => 'api',
    'controller' => 'articles'
));

$articles->setPrefix($versions['v1'].'/articles');
$articles->addGet('', array(
    'module' => 'api',
    'controller' => 'articles',
    'action' => 'list'
));

$router->mount($articles);
```

2. Next, we add an array with the available versions of our API, and we tell the router to remove extra slashes. Therefore, a request to /api/v1/articles will be the same as a request to /api/v1/articles/.

3. After that, we make use of the router's capability of grouping and create a new group for the articles.

4. Finally, we mount the articles group onto the router.

There are a few things that we need to fix regarding the routing system. They are as follows:

1. We'll be putting in new content in the global routing file (config/routing.php), like the following:

```php
<?php

$di['router'] = function () use ($default_module, $modules,
    $di, $config) {
```

```php
$router = new \Phalcon\Mvc\Router(false);
$router->clear();

$moduleRouting = __DIR__.'/../modules/'.ucfirst(
  $default_module).'/Config/routing.php';

if (file_exists($moduleRouting) && is_file(
  $moduleRouting)) {
  include $moduleRouting;
} else {
  $router->add('#^/(|/)$#', array(
    'module' => $default_module,
    'controller' => 'index',
    'action' => 'index',
  ));

  $router->add('#^/([a-zA-Z0-9\_]+)[/]{0,1}$#', array(
    'module' => $default_module,
    'controller' => 1,
  ));

  $router->add('#^/{0,1}([a-zA-Z0-9\_]+)/([a-zA-Z0-9\_]+)
    (/.*)*$#', array(
    'module' => $default_module,
    'controller' => 1,
    'action' => 2,
    'params' => 3,
  ));
}

foreach ($modules as $moduleName => $module) {
  if ($default_module == $moduleName) {
    continue;
  }

  $moduleRouting = __DIR__.'/../modules/'.ucfirst(
    $moduleName).'/Config/routing.php';

  if (file_exists($moduleRouting) && is_file(
    $moduleRouting)) {
    include $moduleRouting;
  }
}

return $router;
};
```

2. Delete the `modules/App/Core/Config/routing.php` file—we are not going to have any routes for the core module. This module is more like a library.

3. Finally, replace the content of `modules/Frontend/Config/routing.php` with this content:

```php
<?php
$router->add('/', array(
    'module' => 'frontend',
    'controller' => 'index',
    'action' => 'index'
));

$router->add('#^/articles[/]{0,1}$#', array(
    'module' => 'frontend',
    'controller' => 'article',
    'action' => 'list'
));

$router->add('#^/articles/([a-zA-Z0-9\-]+)[/]{0,1}$#',
    array(
    'module' => 'frontend',
    'controller' => 'article',
    'action' => 'read',
    'slug' => 1
));
```

The new router group uses a controller named `Articles`, which does not exist. Now, let's continue with further processes:

1. Let's create `ArticlesController.php` with the following content:

```php
<?php
namespace App\Api\Controllers;

class ArticlesController extends BaseController {
    public function listAction() {
        $this->view->disable();
        echo __METHOD__;
    }
}
```

The following screenshot shows the output after running the
`ArticlesController.php` file:

Now, if you access `https://learning-phalcon.localhost/api/v1/articles`, you should see the same content as shown in the preceding
screenshot.

2. Next, let's modify our base controller. Open `BaseController.php` and
append this content:

```php
<?php
namespace App\Api\Controllers;

use \Phalcon\Http\Response;

class BaseController extends \Phalcon\Mvc\Controller {
  protected $statusCode = 200;

  protected $headers    = [
    'Access-Control-Allow-Origin' => '*',
    'Access-Control-Allow-Headers' => 'X-Requested-With,
      content-type, access-control-allow-origin, accept,
        apikey',
    'Access-Control-Allow-Methods' => 'GET, PUT, POST,
      DELETE, OPTIONS',
    'Access-Control-Allow-Credentials' => 'true'
  ];

  protected $payload = '';

  protected $format = 'json';

  protected function initResponse($status = 200) {
    $this->statusCode = $status;
    $this->headers    = array();
    $this->payload    = '';
  }
```

```php
    protected function _getContent($payload) {
      return json_encode($payload);
    }

    protected function output() {
      $payload     = $this->getPayload();
      $status      = $this->getStatusCode();
      $description = $this->getHttpCodeDescription($status);
      $headers     = $this->getHeaders();

      $response = (new Response())
        ->setStatusCode($status, $description)
        ->setContentType('application/json', 'UTF-8')
        ->setContent(json_encode($payload,
          JSON_PRETTY_PRINT))
      ;

      foreach ($headers as $key => $value) {
        $response->setHeader($key, $value);
      }

      $this->view->disable();

      return $response;
    }

    protected function render($st_output, $statusCode = 200){
      $this->initResponse();

      $this->setStatusCode($statusCode);
      $this->setPayload($st_output);

      return $this->output();
    }
}
```

 Note that we have left out some methods. For a complete class, check out the source code for this chapter.

3. Now, let's edit the `listAction()` function in `ArticlesController.php`. The new `listAction()` function will look like this:

```
public function listAction() {
  try {
    $st_output = [
      'method' => __METHOD__
    ];

    return $this->render($st_output);
  } catch (\Exception $e) {
    return $this->render($e->getMessage(), 500);
  }
}
```

We can now reopen `https://learning-phalcon.localhost/api/v1/articles` and check the result. You should see JSON-encoded text, as shown in this screenshot:

We have the basics. Let's move forward with our project and develop its API.

Writing a fully functional REST module with Phalcon PHP

Before starting, I recommend that you use a RESTful client that will help you test things faster. Personally, I prefer DHC (it's a Chrome extension), which can be found at `https://chrome.google.com/webstore/detail/dhc-resthttp-api-client/aejoelaoggembcahagimdiliamlcdmfm?hl=en`.

We are going to develop the CRUD operations for `Articles`, `Categories`, `Hashtags` and `Users`. Let's start with `Articles`.

Articles

We have already created the controller, so by executing a GET method on
`https://learning-phalcon.localhost/api/v1/articles`, you should get a
response. Let's implement the article manager for the articles listing so that we can
retrieve real data.

First of all, we will make some changes to the `Article` model and overwrite the
`toArray()` method. Open `modules/Core/Models/Article.php` and append the
following code:

```php
public function getTranslations($arguments = null) {
    return $this->getRelated('translations', $arguments);
}

public function getCategories($arguments = null) {
    return $this->getRelated('categories', $arguments);
}

public function getHashtags($arguments = null) {
    return $this->getRelated('hashtags', $arguments);
}

public function getUser($arguments = null) {
    return $this->getRelated('user', $arguments);
}

public function toArray($columns = null) {
    $output = parent::toArray($columns);

    $output['article_translations'] = $this->getTranslations([
        'columns' => [
            'article_translation_short_title',
            'article_translation_long_title',
            'article_translation_slug',
            'article_translation_description',
            'article_translation_lang'
        ]
    ])->toArray();

    $output['article_categories'] = $this->getCategories()
        ->filter(function($category){
        return $category->toArray(['id','category_translations']);
    });
```

```
$output['article_hashtags'] = $this->getHashtags([
  'columns' => [
    'id',
    'hashtag_name'
  ]
])->filter(function($hashtag){
  return $hashtag->toArray();
});

$output['article_author'] = $this->getUser([
  'columns' => [
    'user_first_name',
    'user_last_name',
    'user_email'
  ]
])->toArray();

return $output;
}
```

As you can see, we append everything related to the article: translations, information about the author, categories, and hashtags.

As the categories have translations, we will also overwrite the `toArray()` method from the category model. Open `modules/Core/Models/Category.php` and add the following code:

```
public function getTranslations($arguments = null) {
  return $this->getRelated('translations', $arguments);
}

public function toArray($columns = null) {
  $output = parent::toArray($columns);

  $output['category_translations'] = $this->getTranslations([
    'columns' => [
      'category_translation_name',
      'category_translation_slug',
      'category_translation_lang'
    ]
  ])->toArray();

  return $output;
}
```

All we have to do now is implement a new method in the Article manager. We call that method from the Article controller, and we should have our first call ready.

Open `modules/Core/Managers/ArticleManager.php` and append the following code:

```php
public function restGet(array $parameters = null, array $options =
  null, $page = 1, $limit = 10) {
  $articles = $this->find($parameters);

  $result = $articles->filter(function($article){
    return $article->toArray();
  });

  $paginator = new \Phalcon\Paginator\Adapter\NativeArray([
    'data'  => $result,
    'limit' => $limit,
    'page'  => $page
  ]);

  $data = $paginator->getPaginate();

  if ($data->total_items > 0) {
    return $data;
  }

  if (isset($parameters['bind']['id'])) {
    throw new \Exception('Not Found', 404);
  } else {
    throw new \Exception('No Content', 204);
  }
}
```

You will see that the method name is `restGet`. I like to append the `rest` prefix to my methods that are strictly used for APIs. It is a personal preference; you can use any naming conventions for your projects.

The restGet() method will throw exceptions. If we request a list of articles and the request is successful but we don't have the articles in the database, we use HTTP code 204. In simple words, it means, *Your request was okay, but I have no content.* We use HTTP 404 (not found) if we try to get an article by ID but that article does not exist in our database.

The final step is to call this method from our controller. Open modules/Api/ Controllers/ArticlesController.php and update the listAction() method with the following code:

```
public function listAction() {
  try {
    $manager = $this->getDI()->get('core_article_manager');
    $page    = $this->request->getQuery('p', 'int', 0);

    $st_output = $manager->restGet([], [], $page);

    return $this->render($st_output);
  } catch (\Exception $e) {
    return $this->render([
      'code' => $e->getCode(),
      'message' => $e->getMessage()
    ], $e->getCode());
  }
}
```

That's it! From your favorite API client, make a GET request to http://learning-phalcon.localhost/api/v1/articles, or do it from the command line with CURL:

```
$ curl -i -X GET \
 'http://learning-phalcon.localhost/api/v1/articles'
```

If you did everything well, you should be able to see a response similar to what is presented in the following screenshot:

```
vagrant@thex:/projects/learning-phalcon.dev-(git/ master )$ curl -i -X GET 'http://learning-phalcon.dev/api/v1/articles'
HTTP/1.1 200 OK
Server: nginx
Date: Sun, 01 Feb 2015 23:35:06 GMT
Content-Type: application/json; charset=UTF-8
Transfer-Encoding: chunked
Connection: keep-alive
Access-Control-Allow-Headers: Authorization

{
    "items": [
        {
            "id": "6",
            "article_user_id": "12",
            "article_is_published": "0",
            "article_created_at": "2015-01-15 00:00:00",
            "article_updated_at": null,
            "article_translations": [
                {
                    "article_translation_short_title": "Learning Phalcon",
                    "article_translation_long_title": "This is an article about PhalconPHP Framewrok",
                    "article_translation_slug": "learning-phalcon",
                    "article_translation_description": "Lorem Ipsum is simply dummy text of the printing and typesetting industry.
",
                    "article_translation_lang": "en"
                }
            ],
            "article_categories": [
                {
                    "id": "9",
                    "category_translations": [
                        {
                            "category_translation_name": "Tech",
                            "category_translation_slug": "tech",
                            "category_translation_lang": "en"
                        }
                    ]
                }
            ],
            "article_hashtags": [
                {
                    "id": "1",
                    "hashtag_name": "phalcon"
                }
            ],
            "article_author": {
                "user_first_name": "John",
                "user_last_name": "Doe",
                "user_email": "john.doe@learning-phalcon.dev"
            }
        }
    ],
    "before": 1,
    "first": 1,
    "next": 1,
    "last": 1,
    "current": 1,
    "total_pages": 1,
    "total_items": 1
}vagrant@thex:/projects/learning-phalcon.dev-(git/ master )$
```

We now have all of the information needed to render the most common data for an article. Consider, for example, if you are going to get this data with jQuery, it is easy:

```
$.get('http://learning-phalcon.localhost/api/v1/articles',
function(data){
    // render a list with articles
});
```

You can also append the page number in your request like this: `http://learning-phalcon.localhost/api/v1/articles?p=2`.

Let's continue with our CRUD operations as follows:

1. We will now create a service to retrieve a single article. Open the `routing.php` file from the `api` module, and append the following route to the `$articles` group:

```
$articles->addGet('/{id}', array(
    'module' => 'api',
    'controller' => 'articles',
    'action' => 'get'
));
```

2. Then, we add the `get()` method to `ArticlesController.php`:

```
public function getAction($id) {
    try {
        $manager = $this->getDI()->get('core_article_manager');

        $st_output = $manager->restGet([
            'id = :id:',
            'bind' => [
                'id' => $id
            ],
        ]);

        return $this->render($st_output);
    } catch (\Exception $e) {
        return $this->render([
            'code' => $e->getCode(),
            'message' => $e->getMessage()
        ], $e->getCode());
    }
}
```

That's it! You can now request an article that exists in your database, and you should get exactly the same structure. Also, the `items` key will contain only this article. In my case, it was the article with the ID equal to 6:

```
$ curl -i -X GET  'http://learning-phalcon.localhost/api/v1/articles/6'
```

If you request a non-existing article, you should get a response similar to what is shown in this screenshot:

```
vagrant@thex:/projects/learning-phalcon.dev-(git/ master )$ curl -i -X GET  'http://learning-phalcon.dev/api/v1/articles/158'
HTTP/1.1 404 Not Found
Server: nginx
Date: Mon, 02 Feb 2015 00:08:31 GMT
Content-Type: application/json; charset=UTF-8
Transfer-Encoding: chunked
Connection: keep-alive


{
    "code": 404,
    "message": "Not Found"
}vagrant@thex:/projects/learning-phalcon.dev-(git/ master )$
```

Next, we are going to implement the `update` method for an article as follows:

1. First, we need to add the routing information. Open `modules/Api/Config/routing.php` and append the following code:

    ```
    $articles->addPut('/{id}', array(
        'module' => 'api',
        'controller' => 'articles',
        'action' => 'update'
    ));
    ```

     Note that we use PUT, the recommended method for updating resources.

2. Create a new method named `updateAction()` in `ArticlesController.php` with the following code:

    ```
    public function updateAction($id) {
      try {
        $manager = $this->getDI()->get('core_article_manager');

        if ($this->request->getHeader('CONTENT_TYPE') ==
          'application/json') {
          $data = $this->request->getJsonRawBody(true);
        } else {
          $data = [$this->request->getPut()];
        }

        if (count($data[0]) == 0) {
          throw new \Exception('Please provide data', 400);
        }

        $result = $manager->restUpdate($id, $data);
    ```

```
    return $this->render($result);
  } catch (\Exception $e) {
    return $this->render([
      'code' => $e->getCode(),
      'message' => $e->getMessage()
    ], $e->getCode());
  }
}
```

In `updateAction()`, we check whether the content-type header is of the `application/json` type. If it is, we call `getJsonRawBody()` from the request object. The `true` Boolean parameter means that we force decoding as an array. If the data is received via a form, we will make use of the `getPut()` method.

3. Submitting data as a JSON body is the best approach from my point of view. Using jQuery, you can do this very simply, as follows:

```
var data = [{ "article_is_published" : 1 }];
$.ajax({
  type: "PUT",
  url: "/api/v1/articles/6",
  processData: false,
  contentType: 'application/json',
  data: JSON.stringify(data),
  success: function(response) {
    console.log(response);
  }
});
```

Now, let's see how our `restUpdate()` method looks. Open `ArticleManager.php` and add the following code:

```
public function restUpdate($id, $data) {
  $article = Article::findFirstById((int)$id);

  if (!$article) {
    throw new \Exception('Not found', 404);
  }

  $article->setArticleIsPublished($data[0][
    'article_is_published']);

  if (false === $article->update()) {
    foreach ($article->getMessages() as $message) {
      throw new \Exception($message->getMessage(), 500);
```

```
        }
    }
    return $article->toArray();
}
```

As you can see, for now, we are going to update only one field:
article_is_published. If the article has been successfully updated, you will
get the new update article as a response (check out the following screenshot).
Now let's test this:

```
$ curl -i -X PUT -H "Content-Type:application/json" -d '[{"article_is_pu
blished": 0}]' 'http://learning-phalcon.localhost/api/v1/articles/6'
```

```
^[[Avagrant@thex:/projects/learning-phalcon.dev-(git/ master )$ curl -i -X PUT -H "Content-Type:application/json" -d '[{"article_i
blished": 0}]' 'http://learning-phalcon.dev/api/v1/articles/6'
HTTP/1.1 200 OK
Server: nginx
Date: Mon, 02 Feb 2015 02:00:54 GMT
Content-Type: application/json; charset=UTF-8
Transfer-Encoding: chunked
Connection: keep-alive
Access-Control-Allow-Headers: Authorization

{
    "id": "6",
    "article_user_id": "12",
    "article_is_published": 0,
    "article_created_at": "2015-01-15 00:00:00",
    "article_updated_at": "2015-02-02 03:00:54",
    "article_translations": [
        {
            "article_translation_short_title": "Learning Phalcon",
            "article_translation_long_title": "This is an article about PhalconPHP Framewrok",
            "article_translation_slug": "learning-phalcon",
            "article_translation_description": "Lorem Ipsum is simply dummy text of the printing and typesetting industry.",
            "article_translation_lang": "en"
        }
    ],
    "article_categories": [
        {
            "id": "9",
            "category_translations": [
                {
                    "category_translation_name": "Tech",
                    "category_translation_slug": "tech",
                    "category_translation_lang": "en"
                }
            ]
        }
    ],
    "article_hashtags": [
        {
            "id": "1",
            "hashtag_name": "phalcon"
        }
    ],
    "article_author": {
        "user_first_name": "John",
        "user_last_name": "Doe",
        "user_email": "john.doe@learning-phalcon.dev"
    }
}vagrant@thex:/projects/learning-phalcon.dev-(git/ master )$
```

If we don't provide any data, we will get a `400 Bad Request` message, like this:

```
vagrant@thex:/projects/learning-phalcon.dev-(git/ master )$ curl -i -X PUT -H "Content-Type:application/json" 'http://learning-pha
lcon.dev/api/v1/articles/6'
HTTP/1.1 400 Bad Request
Server: nginx
Date: Mon, 02 Feb 2015 02:04:25 GMT
Content-Type: application/json; charset=UTF-8
Transfer-Encoding: chunked
Connection: keep-alive

{
    "code": 400,
    "message": "Please provide data"
}vagrant@thex:/projects/learning-phalcon.dev-(git/ master )$
```

Well done! So far, we have exposed a service with three methods: GET for a list of articles, GET for a single article, and PUT for updating an article.

We will continue developing the remaining two methods: DELETE (for deleting) and POST (for creation). Let's start with the easier one, which is DELETE. To do so, let's perform the following steps:

1. Open the API routing file and append the following code:

```
$articles->addDelete('/{id}', array(
  'module' => 'api',
  'controller' => 'articles',
  'action' => 'delete'
));
```

2. Next, we create a method named `deleteAction()` in `ArticlesController.php`:

```
public function deleteAction($id) {
  try {
    $manager = $this->getDI()->get('core_article_manager');

    $st_output = $manager->restDelete($id);

    return $this->render($st_output);
  } catch (\Exception $e) {
    return $this->render([
      'code' => $e->getCode(),
      'message' => $e->getMessage()
    ], $e->getCode());
  }
}
```

3. Finally, create the `restDelete()` method in `ArticlesManager.php`:

```
public function restDelete($id) {
  $article = Article::findFirstById((int)$id);

  if (!$article) {
    throw new \Exception('Not found', 404);
  }

  if (false === $article->delete()) {
    foreach ($article->getMessages() as $message) {
      throw new \Exception($message->getMessage(), 500);
    }
  }

  return true;
}
```

Before testing, we must make a small change to the `Articles.php` model by adding `\Phalcon\Mvc\Model\Relation::ACTION_CASCADE` to the foreign key for translations, otherwise, we will get an error message saying **Record is referenced by model App\\Core\\Models\\ArticleTranslation**. This change is needed because of the existing relation between articles and translations. When we delete an article, its translation will be automatically deleted.

Open `modules/Core/Models/Article.php` file and replace the relation for translations with the following code snippet:

```
$this->hasMany('id', 'App\Core\Models\ArticleTranslation',
  'article_translation_article_id', array(
  'alias' => 'translations',
  'foreignKey' => array(
    'action' => \Phalcon\Mvc\Model\Relation::ACTION_CASCADE
  )
));
```

We can now test our code, and the result should be similar to what is shown in the following screenshot. If the article was not found, you will receive a 404 error instead of 200:

```
$ curl -i -X DELETE 'http://learning-phalcon.localhost/api/v1/articles/1'
```

```
vagrant@thex:/projects/learning-phalcon.dev-(git/ master )$ curl -i -X DELETE 'http://learning-phalcon.dev/api/v1/articles/14'
HTTP/1.1 200 OK
Server: nginx
Date: Mon, 02 Feb 2015 02:33:32 GMT
Content-Type: application/json; charset=UTF-8
Transfer-Encoding: chunked
Connection: keep-alive
Access-Control-Allow-Headers: Authorization

truevagrant@thex:/projects/learning-phalcon.dev-(git/ master )$
```

That's it! You can delete articles by simply making a DELETE request to the right URL.

Now, let's continue with the implementation of POST (to create an article). To do so, perform the following steps:

1. Open modules/Api/Config/routing.php and add this code:

```
$articles->addPost('', array(
  'module' => 'api',
  'controller' => 'articles',
  'action' => 'create'
));
```

2. Implement a createAction() method in ArticlesController.php:

```php
public function createAction() {
  try {
    $manager    = $this->getDI()->get(
      'core_article_manager');

    if ($this->request->getHeader('CONTENT_TYPE') ==
      'application/json') {
      $data = $this->request->getJsonRawBody(true);
    } else {
      $data = $this->request->getPost();
    }

    if (count($data) == 0) {
      throw new \Exception('Please provide data', 400);
    }

    $st_output = $manager->restCreate($data);

    return $this->render($st_output);
  } catch (\Exception $e) {
    return $this->render([
      'code' => $e->getCode(),
      'message' => $e->getMessage()
    ], $e->getCode());
  }
}
```

3. The manager (`ArticleManager.php`) will contain a new method named `restCreate()`, but we will also update the `create()` method:

```php
public function restCreate($data) {
  $result = $this->create($data);

  return $result->toArray();
}


public function create($input_data) {
  $default_data = array(
    'article_user_id' => 1,
    'article_is_published' => 0,
    'translations' => array(
      'en' => array(
        'article_translation_short_title' => 'Short title',
        'article_translation_long_title' => 'Long title',
        'article_translation_description' => 'Description',
        'article_translation_slug' => '',
        'article_translation_lang' => 'en',
      )
    ),
    'categories' => array(),
    'hashtags' => array(),
  );

  $data = array_merge($default_data, $input_data);

  $article = new Article();
  $article->setArticleIsPublished($data[
    'article_is_published']);

  $articleTranslations = array();

  foreach ($data['translations'] as $lang => $translation){
    $tmp = new ArticleTranslation();
    $tmp->assign($translation);
    array_push($articleTranslations, $tmp);
  }

  if (count($data['categories']) > 0) {
    $article->categories = Category::find([
```

```
      "id IN (".implode(',', $data['categories'])."")"
    ])->filter(function($category){
      return $category;
    });
  }

  if (count($data['hashtags']) > 0) {
    $article->hashtags = Hashtag::find([
      "id IN (".implode(',', $data['hashtags'])."")"
    ])->filter(function($hashtag){
      return $hashtag;
    });
  }

  $user = User::findFirstById((int) $data[
    'article_user_id']);

  if (!$user) {
    throw new \Exception('User not found', 404);
  }

  $article->setArticleUserId($data['article_user_id']);

  $article->translations = $articleTranslations;

  return $this->save($article, 'create');
}
```

Let's test the new code. Create a JSON body content and the POST method data
to /api/v1/articles as follows:

```
$ curl -i -X POST -H "Content-Type:application/json" -d '{"article_
user_id":12,"article_is_published":1,"translations":{"en":{"artic
le_translation_short_title":"Test API create","article_translation_
long_title":"Test API create","article_translation_description":"Test
API create description","article_translation_slug":"test-api-
create","article_translation_lang":"en"}},"categories":[9,16],"hashta
gs":[1]}' 'http://learning-phalcon.localhost/api/v1/articles'
```

Don't forget to replace the user ID, and the IDs of the categories and hashtags that you have in your database. The result should be a newly created article, similar to the following screenshot:

```
vagrant@thex:/projects/learning-phalcon.dev-(git/ master )$ curl -i -X POST -H "Content-Type:application/json" -d '{"article_user_id":12,"articl
e_is_published":1,"translations":{"en":{"article_translation_short_title":"Test API create","article_translation_long_title":"Test API create","
article_translation_description":"Test API create description","article_translation_slug":"test-api-create","article_translation_lang":"en"}},"c
ategories":[9,16],"hashtags":[1]}' 'http://learning-phalcon.dev/api/v1/articles'
HTTP/1.1 200 OK
Server: nginx
Date: Mon, 02 Feb 2015 03:27:07 GMT
Content-Type: application/json; charset=UTF-8
Transfer-Encoding: chunked
Connection: keep-alive
Access-Control-Allow-Headers: Authorization

{
    "id": "23",
    "article_user_id": 12,
    "article_is_published": 1,
    "article_created_at": "2015-02-02 04:27:07",
    "article_updated_at": null,
    "article_translations": [
        {
            "article_translation_short_title": "Test API create",
            "article_translation_long_title": "Test API create",
            "article_translation_slug": "test-api-create",
            "article_translation_description": "Test API create description",
            "article_translation_lang": "en"
        }
    ],
    "article_categories": [
        {
            "id": "9",
            "category_translations": [
                {
                    "category_translation_name": "Tech",
                    "category_translation_slug": "tech",
                    "category_translation_lang": "en"
                }
            ]
        },
        {
            "id": "16",
            "category_translations": [
                {
                    "category_translation_name": "Category name",
                    "category_translation_slug": "category-name-16",
                    "category_translation_lang": "en"
                }
            ]
        }
    ],
    "article_hashtags": [
        {
            "id": "1",
            "hashtag_name": "phalcon"
        }
    ],
    "article_author": {
        "user_first_name": "John",
        "user_last_name": "Doe",
        "user_email": "john.doe@learning-phalcon.dev"
    }
}vagrant@thex:/projects/learning-phalcon.dev-(git/ master )$
```

Following the same rule as followed in `Articles`, you should try to develop the rest of the endpoints (categories, hashtags, and users). If you don't feel comfortable with it, you can always check out the source code for this chapter.

Securing an API

In general, when you put something online, it is not secure anymore. Virtually anything can be hacked. What can you do in this case? Well, if you are not a billionaire who can afford huge investments in human resources and security software and hardware, all that you can do is try to make the attackers' life a bit rough and always monitor your stuff.

There are hundreds of books about security and securing an API. We will try to implement a few basic security methods that can help you avoid a disaster.

So what are these methods? Here is a list:

- Always use SSL
- Add an API key for extra protection
- Limit the number of requests per second from the same IP
- Limit access to resources, such as DELETE, PUT, POST, for authenticated users

Using SSL

There is no need to elaborate on SSL. Using a secure connection is how you need to go about it. SSL certificates are quite cheap these days. For example, the guys from `http://www.namecheap.com` sell the multi-domain SSL certificate for 80 EUR per year.

Adding an API key for extra protection

We will create a white list of API keys in our global configuration. We will append an APIKEY header to all our requests and check it against the values from config. If the API key does not match, the server will respond with a `403 Forbidden` error. If you use this key in a JavaScript environment, everyone will be able to see it, but at least you can take control and change the API key in a second. Let's implement the protection:

1. Open the `config/config.php` global configuration file and append this code to the `$config` array:

   ```
   'apiKeys' => array(

   '6y825Oei113X3vbz78Ck7Fh7k3xF68Uc0lki41GKs2Z73032T4z8m1I81648JcrY'
   )
   ```

2. Create a new directory named `Listeners` in `modules/Core/`, and create a new file named `ApiListener.php` with the following content:

```php
<?php
namespace App\Core\Listeners;

class ApiListener extends \Phalcon\Mvc\User\Plugin{
  public function beforeExecuteRoute($event, $dispatcher) {
    $hasValidKey = $this->checkForValidApiKey();

    if (false === $hasValidKey) {
      return false;
    }
  }

  private function checkForValidApiKey() {
    $apiKey = $this->request->getHeader('APIKEY');

    if (!in_array($apiKey, $this->config->apiKeys->
      toArray())) {
      $this->response->setStatusCode(403, 'Forbidden');
      $this->response->sendHeaders();
      $this->response->send();
      $this->view->disable();

      return false;
    }

    return true;
  }
}
```

3. Finally, inject this service into `dispatcher`. Open `modules/Api/service.php` and replace the `$di['dispatcher']` array with this:

```php
$di['dispatcher'] = function () use ($di) {
  $eventsManager = $di->getShared('eventsManager');

  $apiListener = new \App\Core\Listeners\ApiListener();
  $eventsManager->attach('dispatch', $apiListener);

  $dispatcher = new Phalcon\Mvc\Dispatcher();
  $dispatcher->setEventsManager($eventsManager);
  $dispatcher->setDefaultNamespace(
    "App\Api\Controllers");

  return $dispatcher;
};
```

If you make a request using the following command line, you will notice that all you get is a 403 Forbidden error:

```
$ curl -i -X GET 'http://learning-phalcon.localhost/api/v1/articles/6'
```

The 403 Forbidden error is as presented in the following screenshot:

```
vagrant@thex:/projects/learning-phalcon.dev-(git/ master )$ curl -i -X GET 'http://learning-phalcon.dev/api/v1/articles/6'
HTTP/1.1 403 Forbiden
Server: nginx
Date: Mon, 02 Feb 2015 11:01:04 GMT
Content-Type: text/html; charset=utf-8
Transfer-Encoding: chunked
Connection: keep-alive

vagrant@thex:/projects/learning-phalcon.dev-(git/ master )$
```

This happened because you didn't provide the APIKEY header. All you need to do is provide the correct header with the correct key, and you will get the article:

```
$ curl -i -X GET -H "APIKEY:6y825Oei113X3vbz78Ck7Fh7k3xF68Uc01ki41GK
s2Z73032T4z8m1I81648JcrY" 'http://learning-phalcon.localhost/api/v1/
articles/6'
```

This is it! Of course, this method can be improved, but that is beyond the scope of this book. Additionally, you can map API keys with clients and/or IP addresses, and so on.

Limiting the number of requests per second from the same IP

We will use a simple solution from Redis for limiting the number of requests per second from the same IP. Let's assume that we want a limit of five requests per second from the same IP:

1. Open ApiListener.php and add the following method:

```php
private function checkIpRateLimit() {
    $ip   = $this->request->getClientAddress();
    $time = time();
    $key  = $ip.':'.$time;

    $redis   = $this->getDI()->get('redis');
    $current = $redis->get($key);

    if ($current != null && $current > 5) {

        $this->response->setStatusCode(429, 'Too Many Requests');
        $this->response->sendHeaders();
        $this->response->send();
```

```
        $this->view->disable();

        return false;
    } else {
        $redis->multi();
        $redis->incr($key, 1);
        $redis->expire($key, 5);
        $redis->exec();
    }

        return true;
    }
```

2. Then, update the `beforeExecuteRoute()` method with the following code:

```
public function beforeExecuteRoute($event, $dispatcher) {
    $hasValidKey = $this->checkForValidApiKey();
    $ipRateLimit = $this->checkIpRateLimit();

    if (false === $hasValidKey || false === $ipRateLimit) {
        return false;
    }
}
```

That's all! You can easily test it by replacing 5 with 2, and make some requests. You will get a 429 response. You can use this method in conjunction with API keys and users to limit the requests for a certain user.

Limiting access to resources such as DELETE, PUT, and POST for authenticated users

If you are going to expose your API, you need to be sure that only authenticated users can access certain resources. This means that you shouldn't access these resources from a public interface, for example, the frontend. A quick and convenient solution would be to use another header (let's call it TOKEN) that will be used in CRUD operations from the admin interface. Let's perform the following set of steps:

1. Here, we'll first add a new method, `resourceWithToken()`, in `ApiListener.php` as follows, and then update `beforeExecuteRoute()` method:

```
private function resourceWithToken() {
    if (in_array($this->dispatcher->getActionName(),
        ['update','delete','create'])) {
```

```
        if ($this->request->getHeader('TOKEN') !=
          'mySecretToken') {
          $this->response->setStatusCode(405, 'Method Not
            Allowed');
          $this->response->sendHeaders();
          $this->response->send();
          $this->view->disable();

          return false;
        }

        return true;
      }
    }
```

2. Append the following code to the `beforeExecuteRoute()` method:

```
if (false === $this->resourceWithToken()) {
  return false;
}
```

If you try POST, PUT, or DELETE, you will get a 405 error. From now on, you need to append the header named TOKEN with the `mySecretToken` value, as shown in this example:

```
$ curl -i -X PUT    -H "Content-Type:application/json"    -H "APIKEY:6
y85Oei113X3vbz8Ck7Fh7k3xF68Uc0lki41GKs2Z73032T4z8m1I81648JcrY"    -H
"TOKEN:mySecretToken"    -d '{"article_user_id":12,"article_is_publish
ed":1,"translations":{"en":{"article_translation_short_title":"Test API
create","article_translation_long_title":"Test API create","article_
translation_description":"Test API create description","article_
translation_slug":"test-api-create","article_translation_lang":"en"}},"c
ategories":[9,16],"hashtags":[1]}'  'http://learning-phalcon.localhost/
api/v1/articles/6'
```

Remember that this will not secure your API if you call it from a frontend using JavaScript, because the value of the token will be visible to everyone.

There are hundreds of other solutions, and you should carefully study what is needed. Also, securing your API is not enough. Securing the entire application, plus the server (for example, by using firewalls), is important too. But just for the purpose of this chapter, what we did should be enough to protect us from the most common attacks.

Read more, document yourself, and ask for experts' opinions. Most of the time, what seems to be a good solution for someone might not be a good solution for you.

Documenting the API

Documentation is probably one of the most important things you should spend time on. When I discovered Phalcon, the first thing that I did was to develop a simple API. When I needed to create documentation for my API, I found myself in a strange situation; there were just a few solutions out there, and most of them had dependencies. This was back in the summer of 2013 or so.

So, I decided to create my own API documentation generator, without any dependencies—just pure PHP. I am going to use this tool (it is publicly available on GitHub at `https://github.com/calinrada/php-apidoc`) to create and generate the API documentation for our project.

Installation

You should already have it, because I was using the extractor from it to generate comments for the CLI tasks. If you missed it, you can do it in two easy steps:

```
$ php composer.phar require crada/php-apidoc
$ php composer.phar update
```

Usage

We'll perform a couple of steps to properly understand the usage:

1. Let's create a new CLI task named `ApidocTask.php` with the following content:

```php
<?php
use Crada\Apidoc\Builder;
use Crada\Apidoc\Exception;

class ApidocTask extends BaseTask {
  /**
   * @Description("Build API Documentation")
   * @Example("php apps/cli.php apidoc generate")
   */
  public function generateAction($params = null) {
    $classes = [
      'App\Api\Controllers\ArticlesController'
    ];

    try {
      $builder = new Builder($classes, __DIR__.'/../../
        docs/api', 'index.html');
```

```
        $builder->generate();
        exec("ln -s ".__DIR__."/../../docs/api ".__DIR__."/
          ../../public/apidoc");
        $this->consoleLog('ok! : '.__DIR__.'/../../
          docs/api/index.html');

      } catch (Exception $e) {
        $this->consoleLog($e->getMessage(), 'red');
      }
    }
}
```

We are going to use annotation to document each method.

> For additional information on this, check out
> https://github.com/calinrada/php-
> apidoc#usage and https://github.com/
> calinrada/php-apidoc#available-methods.

2. Open `ArticlesController.php` and append the following content to the
    `listAction()` method:

```
/**
 * @ApiDescription(section="Articles",
   description="Retrieve a
   list of articles")
 * @ApiMethod(type="get")
 * @ApiRoute(name="/articles")
 * @ApiParams(name="p", type="integer", nullable=true,
   description="Page number")
 * @ApiReturnHeaders(sample="HTTP 200 OK")
 * @ApiReturn(type="object", sample="{
 *   'items': [{
 *     'id':'int',
 *     'article_user_id':'int',
 *     'article_is_published':'int',
 *     'article_created_at':'string',
 *     'article_updated_at':'string',
 *     'article_translations':[{
 *       'article_translation_short_title':'string',
 *       'article_translation_long_title':'string',
 *       'article_translation_slug':'string',
 *       'article_translation_description':'string',
 *       'article_translation_lang':'string'
 *     }],
```

```
 *      'article_categories':[{
 *        'id':'int',
 *        'category_translations':[{
 *          'category_translation_name':'string',
 *          'category_translation_slug':'string',
 *          'category_translation_lang':'string'
 *        }]
 *      }],
 *      'article_hashtags':[{
 *        'id':'int',
 *        'hashtag_name':'string'
 *      }],
 *      'article_author':{
 *        'user_first_name':'string',
 *        'user_last_name':'string',
 *        'user_email':'string'
 *      }
 *    }],
 *    'before':'int',
 *    'first':'int',
 *    'next':'int',
 *    'last':'int',
 *    'current':'int',
 *    'total_pages':'int',
 *    'total_items':'int',
 *}")
 */
public function listAction() {

}
```

Now switch to the command prompt and execute the following command line:

```
$ php modules/cli.php apidoc generate
```

The task creates a new symlink in your public folder. Now you can access the API documentation at `http://learning-phalcon.localhost/apidoc/`, and you should be able to see exactly the same output as presented in the following screenshot:

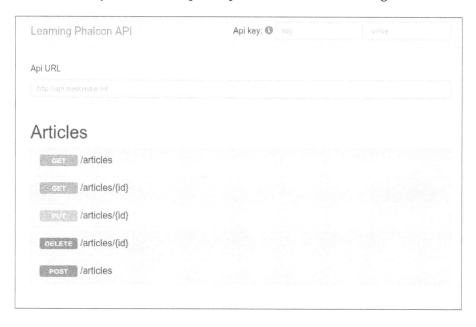

It's time to close this chapter. Please take your time to read as much as possible about developing APIs, especially secure APIs.

Summary

In this chapter, we discovered how easily and quickly we can develop an API. You learned about the recommended practices and a few common ways of securing an API. We covered new topics, such as route grouping and filtering results.

In the next chapters, we will switch layouts and JavaScript integration, but we will continue to adapt, or change, things in the API, database, and models.

6
Assets, Authentication, and ACL

We will make use of our `Backoffice` module for this chapter, since it will be the second module that we will develop.

We will cover the following topics in this chapter:

- Assets management
- Developing an authentication system
- Securing the application using the **Access Control List** (**ACL**) component

Assets management

Before going further, I would like to introduce you to Phalcon's assets manager. This is a very useful component when you need to handle lots of assets (in general, CSS files, images, and JavaScript files). The service should already be available, and you can access it via DI using the following command:

```
$manager = $this->assets;
```

Otherwise, you can use the following command:

```
$manager = $this->getDI()->get('assets');
```

I've heard some people complaining that after its installation, this service does not exist. If you are using Phalcon version 1.3.* (and you should be), then you wouldn't have any problem. If you use an older version, you might need to inject this service into the DI:

```
$di->set('assets', function () {
    return new Phalcon\Assets\Manager();
}, true);
```

Now, let's open the main layout for the back office and do some changes. Open `modules/Backoffice/Views/Default/layout.volt` and remove all the lines containing `stylesheetLink` and `javascriptInclude`.

Now, between `<head>` and `</head>` sections, add the following code:

```
{{ assets.outputCss('headerCss') }}
{% block css %}{% endblock %}
```

And before the `</body>` close tag:

```
{{ assets.outputJs('footerJs') }}
{% block javascripts %} {% endblock %}
```

The `outputJs` and `outputCss` methods contain two parameters (`headerCss` and `footerJs`). These parameters are the names of the assets collections that we are going to build in a few moments. I have added two blocks (`css` and `javascripts`), because we might want to add some special resource for a certain page.

Now, we are going to modify the `BaseController.php` file, and we will add the assets. Open `Backoffice/Controllers/BaseController.php` and append this code:

```php
<?php
namespace App\Backoffice\Controllers;

class BaseController extends \Phalcon\Mvc\Controller
{
    public function afterExecuteRoute()
    {
        $this->buildAssets();
    }

    /**
     * Build the collection of assets
     */
    private function buildAssets()
```

```
    {
        $assets_dir = __DIR__.'/../../../public/assets/';

        $this->assets
            ->collection('headerCss')
            ->addCss($assets_dir.'default/bower_components/
                bootstrap/dist/css/bootstrap.min.css')
            ->addCss($assets_dir.'default/css/lp.backoffice.css')
            ->setTargetPath('assets/default/prod/backoffice.css')
            ->setTargetUri(
                '../assets/default/prod/backoffice.css')
            ->join(true)
            ->addFilter(new \Phalcon\Assets\Filters\Cssmin());

        $this->assets
            ->collection('footerJs')
            ->addJs($assets_dir.'default/bower_components/jquery/dist/
                jquery.min.js')
            ->addJs($assets_dir.'default/bower_components/bootstrap/
                dist/js/bootstrap.min.js')
            ->addJs($assets_dir.'default/js/lp.js')
            ->setTargetPath('assets/default/prod/backoffice.js')
            ->setTargetUri('../assets/default/prod/backoffice.js')
            ->join(true)
            ->addFilter(new \Phalcon\Assets\Filters\Jsmin());
    }
}
```

You can see the new private method `buildAssets()`, where we create the asset groups and use special filters to minify them. After that, we call this method in `afterExecuteRoute()`. You can create your own custom filters, if you want, by extending `Phalcon\Assets\FilterInterface` class. Note that the output goes to a new folder named `prod`. We must create this directory and give it the proper permissions:

```
$ cd public/assets/default
$ mkdir prod && chmod 777 prod
```

If you handle many assets, you might want to save a list in a `config` array or something similar. If you use assets from a CDN, you need to pass some special parameter, for example, something like the following.

```
$js->addJs('cnd.mysite.com/jquery.js', true, false);
// An external resource that does not need filtering.
```

Before checking the result, we need to do two more things. First, remove any content from the `IndexController` class to `indexAction()`. The final `IndexController.php` file should look like this:

```php
<?php
namespace App\Backoffice\Controllers;

class IndexController extends BaseController
{
    public function indexAction()
    {
    }
}
```

Then, open the template for `IndexAction()` that can be found at `Backoffice/Views/Default/index/index.volt`, remove any content from it, and append this code to it:

```
{% extends 'layout.volt' %}
{% block body %}
Welcome, User !
{% endblock %}
```

This is it. You should now be able to access `http://www.learning-phalcon.localhost/backoffice`, and the result should be exactly the same as that shown in the following screenshot:

Fig. 1

This is pretty much everything about assets manager, which is a simple, yet powerful and useful tool.

You can see an example of custom filters in the official documentation at `http://docs.phalconphp.com/en/latest/reference/assets.html#assets-management`.

Developing an authentication system

There are always parts within your application that need to be protected. In this section, we will implement an authentication system that is partially based on the user tables that we created in the previous chapters, and we will use Phalcon's ACL component.

We are not going to reinvent the wheel, so parts of the HTML code are taken from the official Bootstrap website (`http://getbootstrap.com`). In addition, you can find parts of the PHP code in a plugin that I developed a long time ago and which can be found at `https://github.com/calinrada/PhalconUserPlugin`. That being said, let's start developing our authentication system.

The database structure

We will add a few more tables for users, and we will create new ones for the ACL according to the example found at `https://github.com/phalcon/incubator/tree/master/Library/Phalcon/Acl/Adapter` because we will use the database adapter. The incubator page contains a structure for the SQLite database, but we are going to "convert it" for MySQL. The new `user_*` tables are extracted as follows:

```
CREATE TABLE IF NOT EXISTS `user_failed_logins` (
  `id` int(11) NOT NULL AUTO_INCREMENT,
  `user_id` int(11) DEFAULT NULL,
  `ip_address` char(15) CHARACTER SET utf8 COLLATE
    utf8_unicode_ci NOT NULL,
  `attempted` int(11) unsigned NOT NULL,
  PRIMARY KEY (`id`),
  KEY `usersId` (`user_id`)
) ENGINE=InnoDB DEFAULT CHARSET=utf8 AUTO_INCREMENT=1 ;


CREATE TABLE IF NOT EXISTS `user_remember_tokens` (
  `id` int(11) NOT NULL AUTO_INCREMENT,
  `user_id` int(11) NOT NULL,
  `token` char(32) CHARACTER SET utf8 COLLATE utf8_unicode_ci NOT
    NULL,
```

```
  `user_agent` varchar(255) CHARACTER SET utf8 COLLATE
    utf8_unicode_ci DEFAULT NULL,

  `created_at` int(11) NOT NULL,

  PRIMARY KEY (`id`),

  KEY `token` (`token`),

  KEY `user_id` (`user_id`)
) ENGINE=InnoDB DEFAULT CHARSET=utf8 COLLATE=utf8_bin AUTO_INCREMENT=1 ;


CREATE TABLE IF NOT EXISTS `user_success_logins` (

  `id` int(11) NOT NULL AUTO_INCREMENT,

  `user_id` int(11) NOT NULL,

  `ip_address` char(15) CHARACTER SET utf8 COLLATE utf8_unicode_ci
    NOT NULL,

  `user_agent` varchar(255) CHARACTER SET utf8 COLLATE
    utf8_unicode_ci NOT NULL,

  `created_at` datetime NOT NULL,

  PRIMARY KEY (`id`),

  KEY `usersId` (`user_id`)
) ENGINE=InnoDB  DEFAULT CHARSET=utf8 COLLATE=utf8_bin AUTO_INCREMENT=1 ;


ALTER TABLE `user_failed_logins`

   ADD CONSTRAINT `user_failed_logins_ibfk_1`
   FOREIGN KEY (`user_id`) REFERENCES `user` (`id`) ON DELETE
   CASCADE ON UPDATE NO ACTION;


ALTER TABLE `user_remember_tokens`

   ADD CONSTRAINT `user_remember_tokens_ibfk_1`
   FOREIGN KEY (`user_id`) REFERENCES `article_translation` (`id`)
   ON DELETE CASCADE ON UPDATE NO ACTION;


ALTER TABLE `user_success_logins`

   ADD CONSTRAINT `user_success_logins_ibfk_1`
   FOREIGN KEY (`user_id`) REFERENCES `user` (`id`) ON DELETE
   CASCADE ON UPDATE NO ACTION;
```

And the new acl_* tables can look like this:

```
CREATE TABLE IF NOT EXISTS `acl_access_list` (
  `roles_name` varchar(32) COLLATE utf8_unicode_ci NOT NULL,
  `resources_name` varchar(32) COLLATE utf8_unicode_ci NOT NULL,
```

```
  `access_name` varchar(32) COLLATE utf8_unicode_ci NOT NULL,
  `allowed` smallint(3) NOT NULL,
  PRIMARY KEY (`roles_name`,`resources_name`,`access_name`)
) ENGINE=InnoDB DEFAULT CHARSET=utf8 COLLATE=utf8_unicode_ci;

CREATE TABLE IF NOT EXISTS `acl_resources` (
  `name` varchar(32) CHARACTER SET utf8 COLLATE utf8_unicode_ci NOT
NULL,
  `description` varchar(255) CHARACTER SET utf8 COLLATE utf8_unicode_
ci DEFAULT NULL,
  PRIMARY KEY (`name`)
) ENGINE=InnoDB DEFAULT CHARSET=latin1;

CREATE TABLE IF NOT EXISTS `acl_resources_accesses` (
  `resources_name` varchar(32) COLLATE utf8_unicode_ci NOT NULL,
  `access_name` varchar(32) COLLATE utf8_unicode_ci NOT NULL,
  PRIMARY KEY (`resources_name`,`access_name`)
) ENGINE=InnoDB DEFAULT CHARSET=utf8 COLLATE=utf8_unicode_ci;

CREATE TABLE IF NOT EXISTS `acl_roles` (
  `name` varchar(32) CHARACTER SET utf8 COLLATE utf8_unicode_ci NOT
NULL,
  `description` varchar(255) CHARACTER SET utf8 COLLATE utf8_unicode_
ci DEFAULT NULL,
  PRIMARY KEY (`name`)
) ENGINE=InnoDB DEFAULT CHARSET=latin1;

CREATE TABLE IF NOT EXISTS `acl_roles_inherits` (
  `roles_name` varchar(32) CHARACTER SET utf8 COLLATE utf8_unicode_ci
NOT NULL,
  `roles_inherit` varchar(32) CHARACTER SET utf8 COLLATE utf8_unicode_
ci NOT NULL,
  PRIMARY KEY (`roles_name`,`roles_inherit`)
) ENGINE=InnoDB DEFAULT CHARSET=latin1;
```

Models

Now that we have the DB structure, we need to generate the models for the newly created user_* tables. There is really no point in filling pages with complete models because for now, they will contain only getters and setters. The sort version of our models (without getters and setters) is this:

```php
<?php
namespace App\Core\Models;
class UserFailedLogins extends Base
```

```
{
    public function getSource()
    {
        return 'user_failed_logins';
    }
}

<?php
namespace App\Core\Models;
class UserSuccessLogins extends Base
{
    public function getSource()
    {
        return 'user_success_logins';
    }
}

<?php
namespace App\Core\Models;
class UserRememberTokens extends Base
{
    public function getSource()
    {
        return 'user_remember_tokens';
    }
}
```

You can add the getters and setters on your own or check the source code for this chapter.

Next, we will add the relations to the User models so that we can have quick access to the data from these new tables. Open `App\Core\Models\User.php` and append this code to the `initialize()` method:

```
$this->hasMany('id', 'App\Core\Models\UserFailedLogins', 'user_id',
array(
    'alias' => 'failedLogins',
    'foreignKey' => array(
    'action' => \Phalcon\Mvc\Model\Relation::ACTION_CASCADE
    )
));

$this->hasMany('id', 'App\Core\Models\UserSuccessLogins',
    'user_id', array(
    'alias' => 'successLogins',
```

```
    'foreignKey' => array(
    'action' => \Phalcon\Mvc\Model\Relation::ACTION_CASCADE
    )
));

$this->hasMany('id', 'App\Core\Models\UserRememberTokens',
    'user_id', array(
    'alias' => 'rememberTokens',
    'foreignKey' => array(
    'action' => \Phalcon\Mvc\Model\Relation::ACTION_CASCADE
    )
));
```

As for the acl_* tables, for now, we don't need to create any models. The acl database adapter will handle most of the data from them. We can also add data manually or create a task for it. We have database tables and models. Next, we will create an authentication component that will interact with them.

To do this, navigate to modules/Core/ directory and create a new folder named Security:

```
$ cd modules/Core
$ mkdir Security
```

In the security folder, create a new file named Auth.php and add the following content:

```php
<?php
namespace App\Core\Security;

use App\Core\Models\User,
    App\Core\Models\UserRememberTokens,
    App\Core\Models\UserSuccessLogins,
    App\Core\Models\UserFailedLogins;

class Auth extends \Phalcon\Mvc\User\Component
{
    /**
     * Checks the user credentials
     *
     * @param array $credentials
     * @return boolean
     */
    public function check($credentials)
    {
```

```php
    $user = User::findFirstByUserEmail(strtolower(
        $credentials['email']));
    if ($user == false) {
        $this->registerUserThrottling(null);
        throw new \Exception('Wrong email/password
            combination');
    }

    if (!$this->security->checkHash($credentials['password'],
        $user->getUserPassword())) {
            $this->registerUserThrottling($user->getId());
            throw new \Exception('Wrong email/password
                combination');
    }

    $this->checkUserFlags($user);
    $this->saveSuccessLogin($user);

    if (isset($credentials['remember'])) {
        $this->createRememberEnviroment($user);
    }

    $this->setIdentity($user);
}

/**
 * Set identity in session
 *
 * @param object $user
 */
private function setIdentity($user)
{
    $st_identity = [
        'id'    => $user->getId(),
        'email' => $user->getUserEmail(),
        'name'  => $user->getUserFirstName().
            ' '.$user->getUserLastName(),
        'roles' => [
            'Administrator'
        ]
    ];

    $this->session->set('identity', $st_identity);
}
```

```
/**
 * Login user - normal way
 *
 * @param  App\Core\Forms\UserSigninForm $form
 * @return \Phalcon\Http\ResponseInterface
 */
public function signin($form)
{
    if (!$this->request->isPost()) {
        if ($this->hasRememberMe()) {
            return $this->loginWithRememberMe();
        }
    } else {
        if ($form->isValid($this->request->getPost()) ==
            false) {
            foreach ($form->getMessages() as $message) {
                $this->flashSession->error($message->
                    getMessage());
            }
        } else {
            $this->check([
                'email'    => $this->request->getPost(
                    'email'),
                'password' => $this->request->getPost(
                    'password'),
                'remember' => $this->request->getPost(
                    'remember')
            ]);

            $redirect = $this->getDI()->get('config')->
                auth->redirect;

            return $this->response->redirect($redirect->
                success);
        }
    }

    return false;
}

/**
 * Creates the remember me environment settings the related
   cookies and generating tokens
 */
public function saveSuccessLogin($user)
```

```
{
    $successLogin = new UserSuccessLogins();
    $successLogin->setUserId($user->getId());
    $successLogin->setIpAddress($this->request->
        getClientAddress());
    $successLogin->setUserAgent($this->request->
        getUserAgent());

    if (!$successLogin->save()) {
        $messages = $successLogin->getMessages();
        throw new \Exception($messages[0]);
    }
}

/**
 * Implements login throttling
 * Reduces the efectiveness of brute force attacks
 *
 * @param int $user_id
 */
public function registerUserThrottling($user_id)
{
    $failedLogin = new UserFailedLogins();
    $failedLogin->setUserId($user_id == null ?
      new \Phalcon\Db\RawValue('NULL') : $user_id);
    $failedLogin->setIpAddress($this->request->
      getClientAddress());
    $failedLogin->setAttempted(time());
    $failedLogin->save();

    $attempts = UserFailedLogins::count([
        'ip_address = ?0 AND attempted >= ?1',
        'bind' => [
            $this->request->getClientAddress(),
            time() - 3600 * 6
        ]
    ]);

    switch ($attempts) {
        case 1:
        case 2:
            // no delay
            break;
        case 3:
        case 4:
```

```php
            sleep(2);
        break;
        default:
            sleep(4);
        break;
    }
}

/**
 * Check if the user is signed in
 *
 * @return boolean
 */
public function isUserSignedIn()
{
    $identity = $this->getIdentity();

    if (is_array($identity)) {
        if (isset($identity['id'])) {
            return true;
        }
    }

    return false;
}

/**
 * Checks if the user is banned/inactive/suspended
 *
 * @param App\Core\Models\User $user
 */
public function checkUserFlags($user)
{
    if (false === $user->getUserIsActive()) {
        throw new \Exception('The user is inactive');
    }
}

/**
 * Returns the current identity
 *
 * @return array
 */
public function getIdentity()
```

```php
{
    return $this->session->get('identity');
}

/**
 * Removes the user identity information from session
 */
public function remove()
{
    if ($this->cookies->has('RMU')) {
        $this->cookies->get('RMU')->delete();
    }

    if ($this->cookies->has('RMT')) {
        $this->cookies->get('RMT')->delete();
    }

    $this->session->remove('identity');
}

public function getUser()
{
    $identity = $this->session->get('identity');

    if (isset($identity['id'])) {
        $user = User::findFirstById($identity['id']);
        if ($user == false) {
            throw new \Exception('The user does not exist');
        }

        return $user;
    }

    return false;
}

}
```

 Please note that this is not the complete code due to its size. Please check the source code for this chapter. You can see that this file is extending \ Phalcon\Mvc\User\Component. This means that we already have access to the DI, so we don't have to inject any services because they are already available.

Let's analyze a few of the methods from the `Auth` component a little bit:

- `registerUserThrottling($user_id)`: This method logs any failed login attempts with a time stamp, and it checks the number of attempts for a user from a certain IP. If the number of attempts is greater than three, we will delay the response. This is a simple method to reduce the effectiveness of brute force attacks.

- `checkUserFlags($user)`: This method checks whether or not a user is active. Here, you can add other checks, for example, whether a user is banned or temporarily suspended.

- `saveSuccessLogin($user)`: This method saves all the successful logins of a user and contains the user ID, IP, user agent, and the date and time.

- `createRememberEnviroment($user)`: This method (check the source code for `Chapter 6`) creates tokens that we will hold in the database and some cookies. If this operation is successful, next time, we can auto login the user, using this information.

- `setIdentity($user)`: This method simply saves an array containing information about the current authenticated user in the session. We can retrieve this information by using the `getIdentity()` method or directly from the session by calling `$session->get('identity')`.

- `check($credentials)`: This method is the most important one. Here, we first check whether there is any user in our database, registered with the e-mail that we provided. If the user exists, we compare their password with the one that is provided, by making use of the `checkHash()` security component. After that, we check whether the user is active, save a log in successful login table, create a `Remember me` environment, and then save the information of the user in the session, by calling the `setIdentity()` method.

- `signin($form)`: We use this method to log in the user with the help of a form (and we will create this form in a few moments). If the form is valid, we call the `check()` method to validate the credentials. The rest of the methods are quite easy to understand.

We have the `Auth` component, but it is not available just yet. We need to add it to our DI. Open `modules/Backoffice/Config/services.php` and add this code:

```
$di['auth'] = function () use ($di) {
    return new App\Core\Security\Auth();
};
```

Then, open the `config.php` file and append this code to the `$module_config` array:

```php
'auth' => array(
    'redirect' => array(
        'success' => 'index/index',
        'failure' => 'auth/signin',
    ),
),
```

The component is now active, and we can use it. We will create the templates, forms, and controllers for a sign in action. Navigate to `modules/Backoffice/Controllers` and create a new file named `AuthController.php` with the following content:

```php
<?php
namespace App\Backoffice\Controllers;

use App\Core\Forms\UserSigninForm;

class AuthController extends BaseController
{
    public function signinAction()
    {
        $form = new UserSigninForm();

        if ($this->request->isPost()) {
            try {
                $this->auth->signin($form);
            } catch (\Exception $e) {
                $this->flash->error($e->getMessage());
            }
        }

        $this->view->signinForm = $form;
    }

    public function signoutAction()
    {
        $this->auth->remove();

        return $this->response->redirect('auth/signin');
    }
}
```

We don't have the `UserSinginForm`. Navigate to `modules/Core/` directory and create a new folder named `Forms`:

```
$ cd modules/Core
$ mkdir Forms
```

In the `Forms` directory, create a new file named `UserSigninForm.php` with the following content:

```php
<?php
namespace App\Core\Forms;

use Phalcon\Forms\Form;
use Phalcon\Forms\Element\Text;
use Phalcon\Forms\Element\Password;
use Phalcon\Forms\Element\Submit;
use Phalcon\Forms\Element\Check;
use Phalcon\Forms\Element\Hidden;
use Phalcon\Validation\Validator\PresenceOf;
use Phalcon\Validation\Validator\Email;
use Phalcon\Validation\Validator\Identical;

class UserSigninForm extends Form
{
    public function initialize()
    {
        $email = new Text('email', array(
            'placeholder' => 'Email',
        ));

        $email->addValidators(array(
            new PresenceOf(array(
                'message' => 'The e-mail is required',
            )),
            new Email(array(
                'message' => 'The e-mail is not valid',
            )),
        ));

        $this->add($email);

        //Password
        $password = new Password('password', array(
            'placeholder' => 'Password',
        ));
```

```php
        $password->addValidator(
            new PresenceOf(array(
                'message' => 'The password is required',
            ))
        );

        $this->add($password);

        //Remember
        $remember = new Check('remember', array(
            'value' => 'yes',
        ));

        $remember->setLabel('Remember me');

        $this->add($remember);

        //CSRF (Cross-Site Request Forgery)
        $csrf = new Hidden('csrf');

        $csrf->addValidator(
            new Identical(array(
                'value' => $this->security->getSessionToken(),
                'message' => 'CSRF validation failed',
            ))
        );

        $this->add($csrf);

        $this->add(new Submit('signin', array(
            'class' => 'btn btn-lg btn-primary btn-block',
        )));
    }
}
```

You might have noticed that we are using **CSRF** fields in order to prevent **Cross-Site Request Forgery** attacks. If you have no idea what this is, please take a few moments and read about it at `https://www.owasp.org/index.php/Cross-Site_Request_Forgery_(CSRF)_Prevention_Cheat_Sheet`.

Next, we will create the templates. We will use the example template from `http://getbootstrap.com/examples/signin/`, but we will adapt it to our needs. Since our main template, `layout.volt`, contains information that would be available just to authenticated users, we will clone this template and clean it so that we can use it for our sign in action and other actions that requires simple templates. Navigate to `modules/Backoffice/Views/Default/` and duplicate the `layout.volt` file by renaming it to `layout_simple.volt`:

```
$ cd modules/Backoffice/Views/Default/
$ cp layout.volt layout_simple.volt
```

Then, remove the code from `layout_simple.volt` and append the new cleaned code:

```
<!DOCTYPE html>
<html lang="en">
<head>
<meta charset="utf-8">
<meta http-equiv="X-UA-Compatible" content="IE=edge">
<meta name="viewport" content="width=device-width, initial-scale=1">
<title>{% block pageTitle %}Learning Phalcon{% endblock %}</title>

{{ assets.outputCss('headerCss') }}
{% block css %}{% endblock %}

<!--[if lt IE 9]>
    <script src="https://oss.maxcdn.com/html5shiv/3.7.2/html5shiv.
min.js"></script>
    <script src="https://oss.maxcdn.com/respond/1.4.2/respond.min.
js"></script>
<![endif]-->
</head>
<body>
    <div class="container-fluid">
      <div class="row">
        <div class="col-sm-12 main">
          {% block body %}

          {% endblock %}
        </div>
      </div>
    </div>

    {{ assets.outputJs('footerJs') }}
    {% block javascripts %} {% endblock %}
</body>
</html>
```

The final step is to create the template for `signingAction()`. Navigate to `modules/Backoffice/Views/Default` and create a new folder named `auth`. After that, in the `auth` folder, create a file named `signin.volt` with the following content:

```
{% extends 'layout_simple.volt' %}
{% block pageTitle %}Sign in{% endblock %}
{% block css %}
    {{ assets.outputCss('signin') }}
{% endblock %}
{% block body %}

<form class="form-signin" method="post" action="">
    {{ content() ~ flashSession.output() }}
    <h2 class="form-signin-heading">Sign in</h2>
    <label for="inputEmail" class="sr-only">Email address</label>
    {{ signinForm.render('email', {'class':'form-control',
        'required':true, 'autofocus':true, 'type':'email'}) }}
    <label for="inputPassword" class="sr-only">Password</label>
    {{ signinForm.render('password', {'class':'form-control',
        'required':true}) }}
    <div class="checkbox">
        <label>
            {{ signinForm.render('remember') }} Remember me
        </label>
    </div>
    {{ signinForm.render('signin', {'value':'Sign in'}) }}
    {{ signinForm.render('csrf', {'value':security.getToken()}) }}
</form>


{% endblock %}
```

The `signin.volt` template extends the newly created `layout_simple.volt`. Note the new `css` block. We have added a new `css` group named `signin`. We will enable it in a few moments. The `{{ content() ~ flashSession.output() }}` line is a concatenation, because the `flashSession` component is not returned in the `content()` file. So, if we output just the `content()` method, the `flashSession` messages will not be seen.

The template is missing a `css` file. We need to create it and add it to our assets collection. To do this, navigate to `public/assets/default/css/` and create a new file named `lp.backoffice.signin.css` with the following content:

```css
body {
  padding-top: 40px;
  padding-bottom: 40px;
  background-color: #eee;
}

.form-signin {
  max-width: 330px;
  padding: 15px;
  margin: 0 auto;
}

.form-signin .form-signin-heading,
.form-signin .checkbox {
  margin-bottom: 10px;
}

.form-signin .checkbox {
  font-weight: normal;
}

.form-signin .form-control {
  position: relative;
  height: auto;
  -webkit-box-sizing: border-box;
     -moz-box-sizing: border-box;
          box-sizing: border-box;
  padding: 10px;
  font-size: 16px;
}

.form-signin .form-control:focus {
  z-index: 2;
}

.form-signin input[type="email"] {
  margin-bottom: -1px;
  border-bottom-right-radius: 0;
  border-bottom-left-radius: 0;
}
```

```
.form-signin input[type="password"] {
  margin-bottom: 10px;
  border-top-left-radius: 0;
  border-top-right-radius: 0;
}
```

Then, we add this file to our `assets` collection. Open `modules/Backoffice/Controllers/BaseController.php` and append the following code to the `buildAssets()` method:

```
$this->assets
  ->collection('signin')
  ->addCss($assets_dir.'default/css/lp.backoffice.signin.css')
  ->setTargetPath('assets/default/prod/backoffice.signin.css')
  ->setTargetUri('../assets/default/prod/backoffice.signin.css')
  ->addFilter(new \Phalcon\Assets\Filters\Cssmin());
```

This should be all. Our `Backoffice` module is not yet protected, but we can actually do a `signin` action. Using your browser, go to `http://www.learning-phalcon.localhost/backoffice/auth/signin`, and you should be able to see the exact result that is shown in the following screenshot:

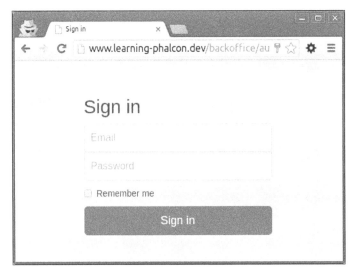

The **Sign in** page

If you already have a user name, you can try to log in. If not, you can create a new user using the task that we created in *Chapter 4, Database Architecture, Models, and CLI Applications*:

```
$ php modules/cli.php user create John Doe john.doe@learning-phalcon.
localhost myPassw0rd 1 Barcelona 1985-03-25
```

This will create a user who has the e-mail address as `john.doe@learning-phalcon.localhost` and the password as `myPassw0rd`. You can use these details to test the form. On success, you will be redirected to index page, on failure; you will see some error messages.

Now that we have a fully functional authentication system, we can secure the entire application. For this, we will make use of Phalcon's `Acl` component.

Securing the application using the ACL component

An ACL is very useful when you have users with different roles. For example, an administrator should have unlimited access, but an editor should have access only to the Articles section. We already have the database structure for the Acl, so we just need to create some relations. First, we will create a new intermediate table named `user_roles` that will hold information about each user's role. A user can have many roles.

```
CREATE TABLE IF NOT EXISTS `user_role` (
  `user_id` int(11) NOT NULL,
  `role` varchar(32) CHARACTER SET utf8 COLLATE utf8_unicode_ci NOT NULL,
  UNIQUE KEY `user_id_2` (`user_id`,`role`),
  KEY `role` (`role`)
) ENGINE=InnoDB DEFAULT CHARSET=latin1;


ALTER TABLE `user_role`
  ADD CONSTRAINT `user_role_ibfk_2` FOREIGN KEY (`role`) REFERENCES `acl_roles` (`name`) ON DELETE CASCADE ON UPDATE CASCADE,
  ADD CONSTRAINT `user_role_ibfk_1` FOREIGN KEY (`user_id`) REFERENCES `user` (`id`) ON DELETE CASCADE ON UPDATE NO ACTION;
```

Another thing that we can do is get rid of the user_group table since we are not going to use it anymore.

1. Delete the `modules/Core/Models/UserGroup.php` file.

2. Remove this code from `User.php`:

```php
$this->hasOne('user_group_id', 'App\Core\Models\UserGroups',
  'id', array(
  'alias' => 'group',
  'reusable' => true,
));
```

3. Remove the column from user table and drop the user_group table:

```sql
ALTER TABLE `user` DROP FOREIGN KEY `user_ibfk_1` ;
ALTER TABLE `user` DROP `user_group_id` ;
DROP TABLE user_group;
```

4. Update the user `create()` method by navigating to `Core/Managers/UserManager.php`, and remove the following lines of code:

```php
$user_group_id = $this->findFirstGroupByName(
  $user_group_name)->getId();
$user->setUserGroupId($user_group_id);
```

5. On the `create()` method, replace the param `$user_group_name = 'User'` with `$user_role = 'Guest'`. (We will implement the functionality in a few moments.)

Now, let's create the models from user_role and acl_roles. Remember that I will not write down the getters and the setters, just the important stuff.

```php
<?php
namespace App\Core\Models;

class UserRole extends Base
{
    public function initialize()
    {
        $this->belongsTo('user_id', 'App\Core\Models\User', 'id',
            array(
            'foreignKey' => true,
            'reusable' => true,
            'alias' => 'user',
        ));
```

```
        $this->belongsTo('user_role', 'App\Core\Models\AclRoles',
            'name', array(
            'foreignKey' => true,
            'reusable' => true,
            'alias' => 'role',
        ));
    }
}


<?php

namespace App\Core\Models;

class AclRoles extends Base
{
// Nothing important here for now, just getters and setters
}
```

We need to make some changes to the `create()` method from `UserManager.php` in order to assign existing roles to a user. The new method should look like this:

```
    public function create($data, $user_role = 'Guest')
    {
        $security = $this->getDI()->get('security');

        $user = new User();
        $user->setUserFirstName($data['user_first_name']);
        $user->setUserLastName($data['user_last_name']);
        $user->setUserEmail($data['user_email']);
        $user->setUserPassword($security->hash(
            $data['user_password']));
        $user->setUserIsActive($data['user_is_active']);


        $o_acl_role  = AclRoles::findFirstByName($user_role);

        if (!$o_acl_role) {
            throw new \Exception("Role $user_role does not
                exists");
        };

        $o_user_role[0] = new UserRole();
        $o_user_role[0]->setUserRole($user_role);
```

```
        $user->roles = $o_user_role;

        $profile = new UserProfile();
        $profile->setUserProfileLocation(
            $data['user_profile_location']);
        $profile->setUserProfileBirthday(
            $data['user_profile_birthday']);

        $user->profile = $profile;

        return $this->save($user);
    }
```

The reason why we define `$o_user_role` as array collection of objects is because the relationship between a user and the roles is one-to-many. We also need to modify the `createAction()` method from the `UserTask.php`. Open the file located at `modules/Tasks/UserTask.php` and append the user's role as follows:

```
$user = $manager->create(array(
    'user_first_name' => $params[0],
    'user_last_name' => $params[1],
    'user_email' => $params[2],
    'user_password' => $params[3],
    'user_is_active' => $params[4],
    'user_profile_location' => $params[5],
    'user_profile_birthday' => $params[6],
), 'Guest');
```

We will use `Guest` by default. Later, we will create a method that will add and remove roles for a user. Now, we are going to implement the security check. Switch to `modules/Core/Security` folder and create a new file with the following content:

```php
<?php
namespace App\Core\Security;

class Acl extends \Phalcon\Mvc\User\Plugin
{
    public function beforeDispatch(\Phalcon\Events\Event $event,
        \Phalcon\Mvc\Dispatcher $dispatcher)
    {
        $controller = $dispatcher->getControllerName();
        $action     = $dispatcher->getActionName();
```

```
$redirect   = $this->getDI()->get('config')->auth->
    redirect;

if ($controller == 'auth' && $action == 'signin') {
    return true;
}

$account = $this->auth->getIdentity();

if (!$account) {
    if ($this->getDI()->get('auth')->hasRememberMe()) {
        return $this->getDI()->get('auth')->
            loginWithRememberMe();
    }
}

if (!is_array($account) || !array_key_exists('roles',
    $account)) {

    $this->view->disable();
    $this->response->setStatusCode(403, 'Forbidden');
    $this->flashSession->error('You are not allowed to
        access this section');
    return $this->response->redirect($redirect->failure);
}

$acl = $this->getDI()->get('acl');

foreach ($account['roles'] as $role) {
    if ($acl->isAllowed($role, $controller, $action) ==
        \Phalcon\Acl::ALLOW) {
        return true;
    }
}

$this->view->disable();
$this->response->setStatusCode(403, 'Forbidden');
return $this->response->redirect($redirect->failure);
    }
}
```

Basically, using the beforeDispatch() method, we check for what the user is requesting, whether it is authenticated, and whether the role that they have allows them to access a certain resource. We need to enable the Acl service and attach the Acl to the events manager. In config/services.php (globally), add the setting for the Acl service:

```
$di['acl'] = function () use ($di) {
    $acl = new \Phalcon\Acl\Adapter\Database([
        'db' => $di['db'],
        'roles' => 'acl_roles',
        'rolesInherits' => 'acl_roles_inherits',
        'resources' => 'acl_resources',
        'resourcesAccesses' => 'acl_resources_accesses',
        'accessList' => 'acl_access_list',
    ]);

    $acl->setDefaultAction(\Phalcon\Acl::DENY);

    return $acl;
};
```

Then, update the dispatcher with the following code:

```
$di['dispatcher'] = function () use ($di) {
    $eventsManager = $di->getShared('eventsManager');

    $eventsManager->attach('dispatch', new
        App\Core\Security\Acl($di));

    $dispatcher = new \Phalcon\Mvc\Dispatcher();
    $dispatcher->setEventsManager($eventsManager);
    $dispatcher->setDefaultNamespace(
        "App\Backoffice\Controllers");

    return $dispatcher;
};
```

We will also need to update the setIdentity() method from Auth.php. Replace it with this code to get the user roles from the database:

```
private function setIdentity($user)
{
    $roles = [];
    foreach ($user->roles as $role) {
      $roles[] = $role->getUserRole();
    }
```

```php
$st_identity = [
  'id'    => $user->getId(),
  'email' => $user->getUserEmail(),
  'name'  => $user->getUserFirstName().' '.$user->
      getUserLastName(),
  'roles' => $roles
];

$this->session->set('identity', $st_identity);
}
```

If you followed the steps closely and did everything by the book, you should be able to access `http://www.learning-phalcon.localhost/backoffice/`; the browser will redirect you to the **Sign in** page (the same page where we saw the **Sign in** page).

We are almost at the end of this chapter. What we will do next is create a task that will handle `Acl`, and we will use this task in the future when we need to modify someone's permissions. Let's see how a simple task for `Acl` can look.

Switch to `modules/Tasks` and create a new file named `AclTask.php`, with the following content:

```php
<?php
class AclTask extends BaseTask
{
    /**
     *
     * @var \Phalcon\Acl\Adapter\Database
     */
    private $acl;

    public function __construct()
    {
        $this->acl = $this->getDI()->get('acl');
    }

    /**
     * @Description("Install the initial(default) acl
         resources")
     */
    public function initAction()
    {
        $roles = array(
            'Administrator' => new
                \Phalcon\Acl\Role('Administrator'),
```

```
            'Guest' => new \Phalcon\Acl\Role('Guest'),
        );

        foreach ($roles as $role) {
            $this->acl->addRole($role);
        }

        $userResources = array(
            'index' => array('index'),
        );

        foreach ($userResources as $resource => $actions) {
            //$this->acl->addResource(new
                \Phalcon\Acl\Resource($resource), $actions);
            foreach ($actions as $action) {
                $this->acl->allow('Administrator', $resource,
                    $action);
            }
        }

        $this->consoleLog('Default resources created');
    }
}
```

We created only one method named `initAction()` that will create the two default acl roles: `Administrator` and `Guest`. An administrator will be allowed to access everything, whereas a `Guest` role will be able to access nothing. Run this task:

$ php modules/cli.php acl init

Now you should be able to see records in your database with the two roles inserted. If you see them, you can navigate to the `user_role` table and insert an `Administrator` role for your user, then try to login, then delete the `Administrator` role and add the `Guest` one. We will add more methods to this task in the next chapters.

Summary

In this chapter, you learned about assets management and Access Control List. We also developed an authentication system for our application. We will continue our journey with the development of the `Backoffice` module, where you will learn more about Forms, Volt, and Models.

7
The Backoffice Module (Part 1)

Unless you are developing a static website, you will need a section/module where an administrator can add and manage content, such as articles, categories, and users. This is where `Backoffice` comes into the picture. In this chapter, we will develop parts of the **CRUD** (**Create**, **Read**, **Update**, and **Delete**) operations needed to administrate our website. We will also use part of the API that we developed in *Chapter 5, The API Module*. We will play more with forms and validations. We will cover this chapter in two parts, namely:

- Hashtag CRUD
- Category CRUD

Editing the main layout

Let's start this chapter with some modifications to the main layout. Edit the main layout located at `modules/Backoffice/Views/Default/layout.volt` and add the following code:

```
<!DOCTYPE html>
<html lang="en">
<head>
<meta charset="utf-8">
<meta http-equiv="X-UA-Compatible" content="IE=edge">
<meta name="viewport" content="width=device-width, initial-scale=1">
<title>{% block pageTitle %}Learning Phalcon{% endblock %}</title>

{{ assets.outputCss('headerCss') }}
{% block css %}{% endblock %}
```

```
<!--[if lt IE 9]>
        <script src="https://oss.maxcdn.com/html5shiv/3.7.2/html5shiv.
min.js"></script>
        <script src="https://oss.maxcdn.com/respond/1.4.2/respond.min.
js"></script>
<![endif]-->
</head>
<body>
    {% include 'common/topbar.volt' %}
        <div class="container-fluid">
          <div class="row">
            <div class="col-sm-3 col-md-2 sidebar">
            {% include 'common/sidebar.volt' %}
            </div>
            <div class="col-sm-9 col-sm-offset-3 col-md-10
              col-md-offset-2 main">
              {% block body %}
              <h1 class="page-header">Dashboard</h1>
              <h2 class="sub-header">Section title</h2>
              <div class="table-responsive">

              </div>
              {% endblock %}
            </div>
          </div>
        </div>

    {{ assets.outputJs('footerJs') }}
  {% block javascripts %} {% endblock %}
</body>
</html>
```

You can see that we are using `include` to include two new files: `topbar.volt` and `sidebar.volt`. In Volt, you can use the `include` method or the `partial()` method. The main difference between `partial` and `include` is that a `partial` method is included in the runtime but an `include` file compiles the content and returns it as part of the view that was included. I prefer `include` because it improves performance. If you need to assign variables to a file that will be included, you need to avoid the file extension. Here is an example:

```
{% include 'common/sidebar' with {'categories': categories} %}
```

You can read more about `include` at `http://docs.phalconphp.com/en/latest/reference/volt.html#include`.

The code for the two new files is the same code that resided in the main layout earlier but with a small modification for the sidebar. Let's create the folder and the files. Go to `modules/Backoffice/Views/Default/` and create a new folder named `common`. In this new folder, create two new files named `sidebar.volt` and `topbar.volt` with the following code.

common/topbar.volt

Here is the code for the navigation bar that can be found at the top of the page. It contains a link to the home page and a link that is used to sign out:

```
<nav class="navbar navbar-inverse navbar-fixed-top"
  role="navigation">
  <div class="container-fluid">
    <div class="navbar-header">
      <button type="button" class="navbar-toggle collapsed"
        data-toggle="collapse" data-target="#navbar"
          aria-expanded="false" aria-controls="navbar">
        <span class="sr-only">Toggle navigation</span>
        <span class="icon-bar"></span>
        <span class="icon-bar"></span>
        <span class="icon-bar"></span>
      </button>
      <a class="navbar-brand" href="{{ url('') }}">Learning
        Phalcon</a>
    </div>
    <div id="navbar" class="navbar-collapse collapse">
      <ul class="nav navbar-nav navbar-right">
        <li><a href="{{ url('auth/signout') }}">Sign out</a></li>
      </ul>
    </div>
  </div>
</nav>
```

common/sidebar.volt

The following is the code for the sidebar (the left menu) and the code that contains the links to different controllers from our application:

```
{% set c_name = dispatcher.getControllerName() %}
<ul class="nav nav-sidebar">
  <li{% if c_name == 'article' %} class="active"{% endif %}>
    <a href="{{ url('article/list') }}">Articles</a></li>
  <li{% if c_name == 'category' %} class="active"{% endif %}>
    <a href="{{ url('category/list') }}">Categories</a></li>
  <li{% if c_name == 'hashtag' %} class="active"{% endif %}>
    <a href="{{ url('hashtag/list') }}">Hashtags</a></li>
  <li{% if c_name == 'user' %} class="active"{% endif %}>
    <a href="{{ url('user/list') }}">Users</a></li>
</ul>
```

There is something new about these two files. We are making use of a method named `url()`, the sidebar has incorporated some logic, and we notice that the dispatcher from DI is available without the need to assign it from a controller.

By default, Volt has access to a number of methods. The `url()` method, which uses the URL service, is one of them. For a list of supported methods, you can check out the official documentation at `http://docs.phalconphp.com/en/latest/reference/volt.html#functions`. Sometimes, you need special functions that are not accessible from Volt. In such a case, you will need to extend the Volt engine and implement your own methods. How do you extend Volt?

In our case, we can do it directly in the `voltService` DI, which can be found in `config/services.php`, for example, we want to add a method named `randomGen()` that generates a number of random strings, and it's located in `modules/Core/Library/Util.php`. The `voltService` DI will look like this:

```php
$di['voltService'] = function ($view, $di) use ($config) {
  $volt = new \Phalcon\Mvc\View\Engine\Volt($view, $di);
  // ... code
  $compiler = $volt->getCompiler();
  $compiler->addFunction('randomGen', function($resolvedArgs,
  $exprArgs) {
    return 'App\Core\Library\Util::randomGen(' . $resolvedArgs . ')';
  });
  //...code

  return $volt;
};
```

We will be able to call this method in Volt by using the following syntax:

```
{{ randomGen(5) }}
```

The preceding method will generate five random strings.

 You can learn more about extending Volt at `http://docs.phalconphp.com/en/latest/reference/volt.html#extending-volt`.

In the sidebar file (`sidebar.volt`), we use `IF` statements to check the name of the current controller. The name is available through the dispatcher, and we assign it to a variable named `c_name`. The equivalent PHP code for our `IF` statements and `set` is as follows:

```php
<?php
$c_name = $this->dispatcher->getControllerName();

if (c_name == 'article') {
    // Link is active
}
```

Of course, there are other ways of generating the code for this menu, but try to use Volt as much as you can, so that you get used to the syntax. Now that we have made a few modifications, let's access `http://www.learning-phalcon.localhost/backoffice/`. If there are no errors, you should see the same things as shown in the following screenshot:

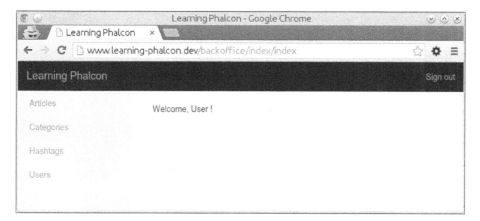

Cleaning the Core module

Let's also clean our `Core` module. We will use this folder as a collection of libraries instead of using it as a module. First, remove the following files:

```
modules/Core/Config/config.php
modules/Core/Config/services.php
modules/Core/Controllers/IndexController.php
modules/Core/Module.php
```

Then remove these lines from `modules/Bootstrap.php`:

```
'core' => array(
    'className' => 'App\Core\Module',
    'path' => __DIR__.'/Core/Module.php',
),
```

Now we have a clean core and our bootstrap will not register it as part of our modules any more. We will make modifications to `modules/Core/Controllers/BaseController.php` and `modules/Backoffice/Controllers/BaseController.php` so that this controller will extend `modules/Core/Controllers/BaseController.php`:

- In the `modules/Api/Controllers/BaseController.php` file:

  ```php
  <?php
  namespace App\Api\Controllers;

  use Phalcon\Http\Response;

  class BaseController extends \App\Core\Controllers\BaseController
  {
    // code
  }
  ```

- In the `modules/Backoffice/Controllers/BaseController.php` file:

  ```php
  <?php
  namespace App\Backoffice\Controllers;

  class BaseController extends \App\Core\Controllers\BaseController
  {
    // code
  }
  ```

These modifications help us reuse some code in all our modules.

Hashtag CRUD

The reason we leave articles at the end is that when we implement it, we will need to assign hashtags, categories, and users to it. Before going further, we will make a slight modification to `layout.volt` and `BaseController`. We will remove this line from `BaseController.php`:

```
->addCss($assets_dir.'default/bower_components/bootstrap/dist/
   css/bootstrap.min.css')
```

Also, we will add this line to `layout.volt`, right before {{ assets. outputCss('headerCss') }}:

```
{{stylesheetLink('../assets/default/bower_components/bootstrap/dist/
   css/bootstrap.min.css') }}
```

We are doing this because the CSS for bootstrap is already minified, and if we do it again, the bootstrap fonts will not be rendered correctly. Remember to apply the same modification to `layout_simple.volt`.

In *Chapter 5*, *The API Module*, when we developed the API module, one of our tasks was to create the rest of the required models and managers. They included the hashtag manager and models. If you didn't do this, don't worry. You have it in the source code. Here, I will show you just the part of the code that we need in order to develop CRUD operations for hashtags. The first thing that you have to do is create the controller in the API module, if you haven't done so already.

The hashtag controller within the API module

All the methods found in this controller follow the same logic:

- We retrieve an instance of the hashtag manager
- We get parameters from the request object
- We call its specific API method and send the response

Let's write the code for this controller. We will start with `listAction()`. All the methods are written between the `try{}-catch(){}` statements:

```php
<?php
namespace App\Api\Controllers;

class HashtagsController extends BaseController{
  public function listAction() {
  try {
```

```
      $manager = $this->getDI()->get('core_hashtag_manager');
      $page    = $this->request->getQuery('p', 'int', 0);

      $st_output = $manager->restGet([], [], $page);

      return $this->render($st_output);
    } catch (\Exception $e) {
      return $this->render([
        'code' => $e->getCode(),
        'message' => $e->getMessage(),
      ], $e->getCode());
    }
  }
}
```

This method calls the hashtag manager and it reads the page number from the request. Next, we output the result of the $manager->restGet() method, which is an array of records with **pagination**:

```
public function getAction($id) {
  try {
    $manager = $this->getDI()->get('core_hashtag_manager');

    $st_output = $manager->restGet([
      'id = :id:',
      'bind' => [
        'id' => $id,
      ],
    ]);

    return $this->render($st_output);
  } catch (\Exception $e) {
    return $this->render([
      'code' => $e->getCode(),
      'message' => $e->getMessage(),
    ], $e->getCode());
  }
}
```

This method is mostly similar to listAction(), the difference being that it will only return one record. Notice that we bind the ID of the requested object to the $manager->restGet() method:

```
public function updateAction($id) {
  try {
    $manager = $this->getDI()->get('core_hashtag_manager');
```

```
        if ($this->request->getHeader('CONTENT_TYPE') ==
          'application/json') {
          $data = $this->request->getJsonRawBody(true);
        } else {
          $data = [$this->request->getPut()];
        }

        if (count($data[0]) == 0) {
          throw new \Exception('Please provide data', 400);
        }

        $result = $manager->restUpdate($id, $data);

        return $this->render($result);
      } catch (\Exception $e) {
        return $this->render([
          'code' => $e->getCode(),
          'message' => $e->getMessage(),
        ], $e->getCode());
      }
    }
```

This method calls the hashtag manager and it reads the page number and content from the request. If the body that we are posting is in the JSON format, we will read it with getJsonRawBody(). The true parameter is used to convert data into arrays. If we don't have data, we throw an exception. Next, we output the result of the $manager->restUpdate() method:

```
  public function deleteAction($id) {
    try {
      $manager = $this->getDI()->get('core_hashtag_manager');

      $st_output = $manager->restDelete($id);

      return $this->render($st_output);
    } catch (\Exception $e) {
      return $this->render([
        'code' => $e->getCode(),
        'message' => $e->getMessage(),
      ], $e->getCode());
    }
  }
```

The `deleteAction()` method simply calls `$manager->restDelete()` with the ID of the object as the argument. If the object is found, it will be deleted:

```php
public function createAction() {
  try {
    $manager   = $this->getDI()->get('core_hashtag_manager');

    if ($this->request->getHeader('CONTENT_TYPE') ==
      'application/json') {
      $data = $this->request->getJsonRawBody(true);
    } else {
      $data = $this->request->getPost();
    }

    if (count($data) == 0) {
      throw new \Exception('Please provide data', 400);
    }

    $st_output = $manager->restCreate($data);

    return $this->render($st_output);
  } catch (\Exception $e) {
    return $this->render([
      'code' => $e->getCode(),
      'message' => $e->getMessage(),
    ], $e->getCode());
    }
  }
}
```

This method is similar to `updateAction()`, but instead of updating an object, it creates it.

The routing is missing, so we are going to add it to `modules/Api/Config.routing.php`. We will create a new routing group for hashtags:

```php
$hashtags = new \Phalcon\Mvc\Router\Group([
    'module' => 'api',
    'controller' => 'hashtags',
]);

$hashtags->setPrefix($versions['v1'].'/hashtags');

$hashtags->addGet('',          ['action' => 'list']);
$hashtags->addGet('/{id}',     ['action' => 'get']);
```

```
$hashtags->addPut('/{id}',    ['action' => 'update']);
$hashtags->addDelete('/{id}', ['action' => 'delete']);
$hashtags->addPost('',        ['action' => 'create']);

$router->mount($hashtags);
```

If everything is okay, you can now insert a few records into the hashtag table and call the API to get the records by using the following command line:

```
$ curl -i -X GET -H "Content-Type:application/json" -H "APIKEY:6y8
250ei113X3vbz78Ck7Fh7k3xF68Uc0lki41GKs2Z73032T4z8mlI81648JcrY"  -H
"TOKEN:mySecretToken" 'http://learning-phalcon.localhost/api/v1/hashtags'
```

The output of the command line should be similar to what is shown in the following screenshot:

This cURL command makes a request to /api/v1/hashtags. The -H option is used to send header information; in our case, we send the token and the API key.

A common method to reduce code duplication

Let's create a method in `modules/Core/Controllers/BaseController.php` that will help us get data from our API. This method will be available within the controllers that extend it:

```php
public function apiGet($uri, $params = []) {
    $config   = $this->getDI()->get('config')->toArray();
    $uri      = $config['apiUrl'].$uri;
    $curl     = new \Phalcon\Http\Client\Provider\Curl();
    $response = $curl->get($uri, $params, ["APIKEY:".$config[
      'apiKeys'][0]]);

    if ($response->header->statusCode != 200) {
    throw new \Exception('API error: '.$response->header->status);
    }

    return json_decode($response->body, true);
}
```

Retrieving the data

To get the data, we just need to provide the URL and extra parameters, if needed. With the help of Phalcon's built-in cURL provider, we make the call. Next, we create a hashtag controller in the `Backoffice` module. It will look like this:

```php
<?php
namespace App\Backoffice\Controllers;

class HashtagController extends BaseController {
  public function indexAction() {
    return $this->dispatcher->forward(['action' => 'list']);
  }

  /**
   * Hashtags list
   */
  public function listAction() {
    $page = $this->request->getQuery('p', 'int', 1);

    try {
      $hashtags = $this->apiGet('hashtags?p='.$page);
```

```
        $this->view->hashtags = $hashtags;
    } catch (\Exception $e) {
        $this->flash->error($e->getMessage());
    }
}
}
```

As you can see, the only thing that we do here is call the API's URL, and it returns an array of paginated items.

The layout structure

Creating the layout for this listing is quite simple. Go to `modules/Backoffice/Views/Default` and create a new folder named `hashtag`. In this new folder, create a new file named `list.volt` with the following content:

```
{% extends 'layout.volt' %}
{% block body %}
<div class="pull-left">
    <h1>Hashtags</h1>
</div>
<div class="pull-right">
  <a class="btn btn-success" href="{{ url('hashtag/add') }}"
    aria-label="Left Align">
    <span class="glyphicon glyphicon-plus" aria-hidden="true">
    </span> New
  </a>
</div>
<div class="clearfix"></div>
<hr>
<div class="panel panel-default">
  <div class="panel-body">
    <table class="table table-striped">
      <thead>
        <tr>
          <th>#</th>
          <th>Hashtag</th>
          <th>Created at</th>
          <th>Options</th>
        </tr>
      </thead>
      <tbody>
        {% for hashtag in hashtags['items'] %}
        <tr>
```

```
        <th scope="row">{{ hashtag['id'] }}</th>
          <td>{{ hashtag['hashtag_name'] }}</td>
          <td>{{ hashtag['hashtag_created_at'] }}</td>
          <td>
            <a class="btn btn-default btn-xs" href="#"
            aria-label="Left Align">
              <span class="glyphicon glyphicon-pencil"
                aria-hidden="true"></span>
            </a>
            <a class="btn btn-danger btn-xs" href="#"
            aria-label="Left Align">
              <span class="glyphicon glyphicon-trash"
                aria-hidden="true"></span>
            </a>
          </td>
        </tr>
        {% else %}
        <tr>
          <td colspan="4">There are no hashtags in your
            database</td>
        </tr>
      {% endfor %}
      </tbody>
    </table>
  </div>
</div>
{% if (hashtags['total_pages'] > 1) %}
{% include 'common/paginator' with {'page_url' : url(
  'hashtag/list'), 'stack' : hashtags} %}
{% endif %}
{% endblock %}
```

Before ending the block of the code for the list template, we include another template named paginator. This is the paginator that will help us navigate through records. Create a file named paginator.volt in modules/Backoffce/Views/Default/ common/ and write this code in it:

```
<nav>
  <ul class="pager">
    <li class="previous {% if (stack['current'] < 2) %}disabled
    {% endif %}"><a href="{{ page_url ~ '?p=' ~ stack['before']
    }}"><span aria-hidden="true">&larr;</span> Previous</a></li>
```

```
    <li class="next {% if (stack['current'] == stack['total_pages'
    ]) %}disabled{% endif %}"><a href="{{ page_url ~ '?p=' ~
    stack['next'] }}">Next <span aria-hidden=
    "true">&rarr;</span></a></li>
  </ul>
</nav>
```

> The preceding code makes use of the paginator variables that are already available (see `http://docs.phalconphp.com/en/latest/reference/pagination.html`).

Now, you can authenticate and access the hashtags listing at `http://www.learning-phalcon.localhost/backoffice/hashtag/list`. You should be able to see something similar to what is shown in the next screenshot:

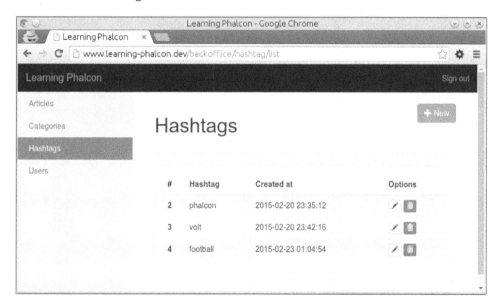

Let's continue with the rest of the actions (create, delete, and update). There are several ways to achieve this, but we will *not* make use of our API for create and update, mainly because of the time needed to cover all the aspects, and also because doing it the "old normal way" is faster. However, you can play with the idea and try to migrate these two actions to be API-driven.

The hashtag form

For create and update, I like to use forms because it's easier to maintain the code and also to validate it. We will start with the create action by writing the code for the create form (the same form will be used for update). Switch to modules/Core/Forms and create a new file named HashtagForm.php with the following code:

```php
<?php
namespace App\Core\Forms;

use Phalcon\Forms\Form;
use Phalcon\Forms\Element\Text;
use Phalcon\Forms\Element\Submit;
use Phalcon\Forms\Element\Hidden;
use Phalcon\Validation\Validator\PresenceOf;
use Phalcon\Validation\Validator\Identical;

class HashtagForm extends Form {
  public function initialize() {
    $hashtag_name = new Text('hashtag_name', array(
      'placeholder' => 'Name',
    ));

    $hashtag_name->addValidators(array(
      new PresenceOf(array(
        'message' => 'Name is required',
      ))
    ));

    $this->add($hashtag_name);

    //CSRF
    $csrf = new Hidden('csrf');

    $csrf->addValidator(
      new Identical(array(
        'value' => $this->security->getSessionToken(),
        'message' => 'CSRF validation failed',
      ))
    );

    $this->add($csrf);
```

```
    $this->add(new Submit('add', array(
      'class' => 'btn btn-lg btn-primary btn-block',
    )));
  }
}
```

Our new form is quite simple. We have three elements: the name of the hashtag, a
csrf field, and a **Submit** button. We validate the name and the csrf field with the
help of two validators: PresenceOf and Identical.

The hashtag controller

We continue by writing the code for the create action and for the template. Open
modules/Backoffice/Controllers/HashtagController.php and add these
two methods:

```
public function addAction() {
  $manager = $this->getDI()->get('core_hashtag_manager');
  $this->view->form = $manager->getForm();
}

public function createAction() {
  if (!$this->request->isPost()) {
    return $this->response->redirect('hashtag/list');
  }

  $manager = $this->getDI()->get('core_hashtag_manager');
  $form    = $manager->getForm();

  if ($form->isValid($this->request->getPost())) {
    try {
      $manager = $this->getDI()->get('core_hashtag_manager');
      $manager->create($this->request->getPost());
      $this->flashSession->success('Object was created
        successfully');

      return $this->response->redirect('hashtag/list');
    } catch (\Exception $e) {
      $this->flash->error($e->getMessage());
      return $this->dispatcher->forward(['action' => 'add']);
    }
  } else {
    foreach ($form->getMessages() as $message) {
```

```
        $this->flash->error($message->getMessage());
      }
      return $this->dispatcher->forward(['action' => 'add',
        'controller' => 'hashtag']);
    }
  }
```

The addAction() method simply renders the form we just created. The processes of creation and validation take place in the createAction() method. This method accepts only POST data, as you can see in the first two lines. When you're working on a big project, you might want to use custom routes, just as we did in the API module.

The hashtag manager

You might notice a new method named getForm() in the hashtag manager. This method returns an instance of HashtagForm and it looks like this:

```
use App\Core\Forms\HashtagForm;
class HashtagManager extends BaseManager{
  ...
  public function getForm($entity = null, $options = null) {
    return new HashtagForm($entity, $options);
  }
  ...
}
```

If you have already created the hashtag manager, you should have a create() method similar to this one:

```
public function create(array $st_inputData)
{
    $st_defaultData = [
        'hashtag_name' => new \Phalcon\Db\RawValue('NULL')
    ];

    $st_data = array_merge($st_defaultData, $st_inputData);

    $hashtag = new Hashtag();
    $hashtag->setHashtagName($st_data['hashtag_name']);

    return $this->save($hashtag, 'create');
}
```

The View template for the add() method

We also need to write the code for the template. Create a new file named `add.volt` in `modules/Backoffice/Views/Default/hashtag` and add the following code:

```
{% extends 'layout.volt' %}
{% block body %}
<h1>Add</h1>
<hr>
<div class="panel panel-default">
  <div class="panel-body">
    <form method="post" action="{{ url('hashtag/create') }}">
      <div class="form-group">
        <label for="hashtag_name">Name</label>
        {{ form.render('hashtag_name',
        {'class':'form-control'}) }}
      </div>
      {{ form.render('add', {'value':'Add'}) }}
      {{ form.render('csrf', {'value':security.getToken()}) }}
    </form>
  </div>
</div>
{% endblock %}
```

Our template extends `layout.volt` and renders the hashtag form elements. At this point, you should be able to add a new hashtag from your `Backoffice` module. Open `http://www.learning-phalcon.localhost/backoffice/hashtag/add`, fill in the name for the hashtag, and click on the **Add** button, like this:

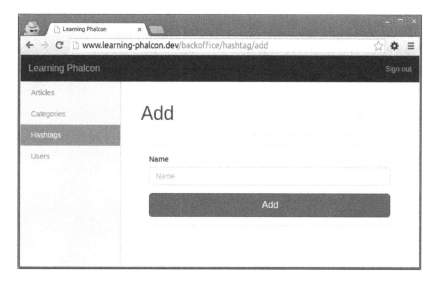

If the hashtag was saved correctly, you will be redirected to a hashtags list page, otherwise an error message will be shown.

Improving the database table structure and adding validation

Now that we can add hashtags, we will face a problem, because we are able to add duplicated hashtags. To fix this, we will make a small change to our hashtags table and implement a new validator in the hashtag model.

The change that we will apply to this table is meant to make the name field unique. Do this by executing the following SQL query against your database:

```
ALTER TABLE hashtag ADD UNIQUE (hashtag_name);
```

If you try to add a new hashtag, you will get an **Integrity constraint violation** error. This is good enough to avoid duplicates in your database, but you will need to implement a more human-friendly error by making use of Phalcon\Mvc\Model\Validator\Uniqueness. Open the hashtag model and append the following code:

```
public function validation(){
  $this->validate(new Uniqueness([
    "field" => "hashtag_name",
    "message" => "This hashtag already exists",
  ]));

  return $this->validationHasFailed() != true;
}
```

This is it! If you try to add the same hashtag, you will get an error message saying **This hashtag already exists**. We can now continue with the edit/update methods for the hashtags.

Editing hashtags

Editing follows the same workflow as creating, except that we need to search for an existing object to edit. Let's first create the update() method in modules/Core/Managers/HashtagManager.php:

```
public function update(array $st_inputData){
  $st_defaultData = [
    'hashtag_name' => new \Phalcon\Db\RawValue('NULL')
  ];
```

```
$st_data = array_merge($st_defaultData, $st_inputData);

$hashtag = Hashtag::findFirstById($st_data['id']);

if (!$hashtag) {
  throw new \Exception('Object not found');
}

$hashtag->setHashtagName($st_data['hashtag_name']);

return $this->save($hashtag, 'update');
}
```

As you can see, there are only two differences between `update()` and `create()`. One is that we searched for a hashtag based on its ID, and the second is that we changed the second parameter from `$this->save()` to `update`. The template is the same as that for the `create()` method. Create a new file named `edit.volt` in `modules/ Backoffice/Views/Default/hashtag` with the following code:

```
{% extends 'layout.volt' %}
{% block body %}
<h1>Edit</h1>
<hr>
<div class="panel panel-default">
  <div class="panel-body">
    <form method="post" action="{{ url('hashtag/update') }}">
      <div class="form-group">
        <label for="hashtag_name">Name</label>
        {{ form.render('hashtag_name', {'class':'form-control'})}}
        </div>
          {{ form.render('save', {'value':'Save'}) }}
          {{ form.render('csrf', {'value':security.getToken()})}}
    </form>
  </div>
</div>
{% endblock %}
```

The only modification that we have done here is that we changed the `<h1>` title from `Add` to `Edit`. We can now switch to `HashtagController` and create two new methods, `editAction()` and `updateAction()`:

```
public function editAction($id){
  $manager = $this->getDI()->get('core_hashtag_manager');
  $hashtag = $manager->findFirstById($id);
```

```
    if (!$hashtag) {
      $this->flashSession->error('Object not found');
      return $this->response->redirect('hashtag/list');
    }


    $this->persistent->set('id', $id);


    $this->view->form = $manager->getForm($hashtag);
  }
```

In this method, we search for an object and output an error message if we can't find it. If it is found, we save the ID in a persistent bag (when using persistent bags, data is temporarily saved in the session and removed the first time you get the variable) and then assign the object to the form to be rendered. The updateAction() method looks like this:

```
public function updateAction(){
  if (!$this->request->isPost()) {
    return $this->response->redirect('hashtag/list');
  }

  $manager     = $this->getDI()->get('core_hashtag_manager');
  $hashtag_id = $this->persistent->get('id');
  $hashtag     = $manager->findFirstById($hashtag_id);
  $form        = $manager->getForm($hashtag);

  if ($form->isValid($this->request->getPost())) {
    try {
      $manager = $this->getDI()->get('core_hashtag_manager');
      $manager->update([
        'hashtag_name' => $this->request->getPost(
          'hashtag_name',['string','trim']),
        'id' => $hashtag_id
      ]);
      $this->flashSession->success('Object was updated
        successfully');

      return $this->response->redirect('hashtag/list');
    } catch (\Exception $e) {
      $this->flash->error($e->getMessage());
      return $this->dispatcher->forward(['action' => 'edit']);
    }
  } else {
    foreach ($form->getMessages() as $message) {
```

```
        $this->flash->error($message->getMessage());
    }
    return $this->dispatcher->forward(['action' => 'edit',
      'controller' => 'hashtag']);
  }
}
```

The main difference between this method and the `createAction()` method is that we get the object ID from the persistent bag and search for it. The final step is to create a link from the listing page to the edit page. Update `list.volt` and replace the current `edit` link with this code:

```
<a class="btn btn-default btn-xs" href="{{ url('hashtag/edit/' ~
hashtag['id']) }}" aria-label="Left Align">
    <span class="glyphicon glyphicon-pencil" aria-hidden="true"></
span>
</a>
```

This is it! You can now access `http://www.learning-phalcon.localhost/ backoffice/hashtag/list`, click on the **Edit** button of an existing record, and try to edit (change the name).

Deleting hashtags

We can move forward and write the code for the last step in this process — deletion. Deletion is very simple and quick. We will use an intermediate page so that a user can confirm when they want to delete an object. Let's start by writing the code for the template. Create a new file named `delete.volt` in the `hashtag` folder and write this code:

```
{% extends 'layout.volt' %}
{% block body %}
<h1>Confirm deletion</h1>
<h3>Are you sure you want to delete the selected element?</3>
<hr>
<div class="panel panel-default">
  <div class="panel-body">
    <form method="post" action="{{ url('hashtag/delete/' ~ id) }}"
      class="form-inline">
    <input type="submit" value="Yes, delete" class="btn btn-sm
      btn-danger btn-block">
    <a href="{{ url('hashtag/list') }}" class="btn btn-lg
      btn-default btn-block">Cancel</a>
    </form>
  </div>
</div>
{% endblock %}
```

This template has a simple form. When a user clicks on the **Yes, delete** button, the actual deletion takes place. Switch to `HashtagController.php` and create a method named `deleteAction()`:

```
public function deleteAction($id){
  if ($this->request->isPost()) {
    try {
      $manager = $this->getDI()->get('core_hashtag_manager');
      $manager->delete($id);
      $this->flashSession->success('Item has been deleted
        successfully');
    } catch (\Exception $e) {
      $this->flash->error($e->getMessage());
    }

    return $this->response->redirect('hashtag/list');
  }
  $this->view->id = $id;
}
```

By default, the `deleteAction($id)` method only renders its template (`delete.volt`). When we confirm the deletion, we make a post and delete the record. If you haven't already written the code for the `delete()` method from manager, here is what it should look like:

```
public function delete($id){
  $object = Hashtag::findFirstById($id);

  if (!$object) {
    throw new \Exception('Hashtag not found');
  }

  if (false === $object->delete()) {
    foreach ($object->getMessages() as $message) {
      $error[] = (string) $message;
    }

    throw new \Exception(json_encode($error));
  }

  return true;
}
```

In the final step, we need to update the `list.volt` template to create a link to the delete page. Open `hashtag/list.volt` and replace the `delete` link with this one:

```
<a class="btn btn-danger btn-xs" href="{{ url('hashtag/delete/' ~
hashtag['id']) }}" aria-label="Left Align">
    <span class="glyphicon glyphicon-trash" aria-hidden="true"></span>
</a>
```

This is pretty much all there is to know about deleting. You can test it by clicking on the **Delete** link from the list. You should see exactly the same output as presented in the next screenshot:

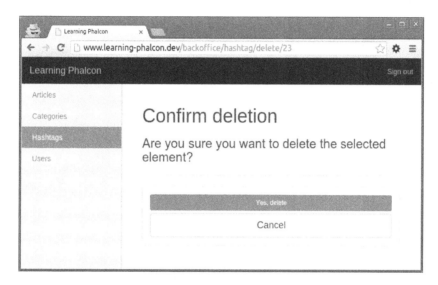

If you click on **Cancel**, you should be redirected to the listing page. If you click on **Yes, delete** and there are no errors, you will be redirected to the listing page and the following success message will be shown: **Item has been deleted successfully**. We will now continue with CRUD development for categories.

Category CRUD

When we created the architecture for category tables, we added a `category_translation` table. We will alter this table and add a unique index to avoid duplicates for the same country code and category ID. Execute the following query:

```
ALTER TABLE `learning_phalcon`.`category_translation` ADD UNIQUE (
`category_translation_category_id` ,
`category_translation_lang`
) COMMENT '';
```

We will add a new array to the `config/config.php` global configuration file that will hold information about i18n:

```
'i18n' => [
  'locales' => [ //ISO 639-1: two-letter codes, one per language
    'en' => 'English'
  ]
]
```

The Category form

We will now create the form for the add/edit categories. Create a new file in `modules/Core/Forms/`, name it `CategoryForm.php`, and write the following code:

```php
<?php
namespace App\Core\Forms;

use Phalcon\Forms\Form;
use Phalcon\Forms\Element\Text;
use Phalcon\Forms\Element\Select;
use Phalcon\Forms\Element\Submit;
use Phalcon\Forms\Element\Hidden;
use Phalcon\Validation\Validator\Identical;

class CategoryForm extends Form{
  private $edit = false;

  public function initialize($entity = null, $options = null) {
    if (isset($options['edit']) && $options['edit'] === true) {
      $this->edit = true;
    }

    $locales = $this->getDI()->get('config')->i18n->locales->
      toArray();

    foreach ($locales as $locale => $name) {

      if (true === $this->edit) {
        $translations = $entity->getTranslations([
          "category_translation_lang = '$locale'"])->toArray();
      }

      $category_name[$locale] = new Text ("translations[
        $locale][category_translation_name]", [
```

```
                    'value' => $this->edit === true ? $translations[0]
                        ['category_translation_name'] : null
                ]);


            $category_slug[$locale] = new Text ("translations[$locale][
                category_translation_slug]", [
                    'value' => $this->edit === true ? $translations[0]
                        ['category_translation_slug'] : null
                ]);


            $category_lang[$locale] = new Hidden ( "translations[
                $locale][category_translation_lang]", [
                    'value' => $locale
                ]);

            $this->add( $category_name[$locale] );
            $this->add( $category_slug[$locale] );
            $this->add( $category_lang[$locale] );
        }

    //CSRF
    $csrf = new Hidden('csrf');

    $csrf->addValidator(
        new Identical(array(
            'value' => $this->security->getSessionToken(),
            'message' => 'CSRF validation failed',
        ))
    );

    $this->add($csrf);

    $this->add(new Submit('save', array(
        'class' => 'btn btn-lg btn-primary btn-block',
    )));
    }
}
```

In this form, we automatically add the required fields based on the available locales.
If we edit a record, we need to retrieve the translations and assign the correct values
to each field. We use the array naming style for easy processing. This means that
the name of the generated field will look like this: translations[en][category_
translation_name].

Next, we need to assign the available locales to the view. Open `BaseController.php` from `modules/Backoffice/Controllers/` and append the following line to the `afterExecuteRoute()` method:

```
$this->view->locales = $this->getDI()->get('config')->i18n
  ->locales->toArray();
```

Creating the Category templates

Let's see how our templates will look. Create a new folder in `modules/Backoffice/Views/Default` and name it `category`. In this new folder, create the `list.volt`, `add.volt`, `edit.volt`, and `delete.volt` template files. The following sections contain the code for each file.

list.volt

Usually, listing is pretty much the same for any section. Here is the `list.volt` template file for `Category`:

```
{% extends 'layout.volt' %}
{% block body %}
<div class="pull-left">
  <h1>Categories</h1>
</div>
<div class="pull-right">
  <a class="btn btn-success" href="{{ url('category/add') }}"
    aria-label="Left Align">
    <span class="glyphicon glyphicon-plus" aria-hidden=
      "true"></span> New
  </a>
</div>
<div class="clearfix"></div>
<hr>
<div class="panel panel-default">
  <div class="panel-body">
    <table class="table table-striped">
      <thead>
        <tr>
          <th>#</th>
          <th>Category</th>
          <th>Slug</th>
          <th>Created at</th>
          <th>Options</th>
        </tr>
```

```
      </thead>
    <tbody>
    {% for record in records['items'] %}
      <tr>
        <th scope="row">{{ record['id'] }}</th>
          <td>{{ record['category_translations'][0]
            ['category_translation_name'] }}</td>
          <td>{{ record['category_translations'][0]
            ['category_translation_slug'] }}</td>
          <td>{{ record['category_created_at'] }}</td>
          <td>
            <a class="btn btn-default btn-xs" href="{{
              url('category/edit/' ~ record['id']) }}"
                aria-label="Left Align">
                <span class="glyphicon glyphicon-pencil"
                  aria-hidden="true"></span>
            </a>
            <a class="btn btn-danger btn-xs" href="{{
              url('category/delete/' ~ record['id']) }}"
                aria-label="Left Align">
                <span class="glyphicon glyphicon-trash"
                  aria-hidden="true"></span>
            </a>
          </td>
      </tr>
        {% else %}
      <tr>
        <td colspan="4">There are no records in your
          database</td>
      </tr>
        {% endfor %}
    </tbody>
  </table>
  </div>
</div>
{% if (records['total_pages'] > 1) %}
{% include 'common/paginator' with {'page_url' : url('category/list'),
'stack' : records} %}
{% endif %}
{% endblock %}
```

add.volt

The only important thing to notice in this template is how we render the elements.
We loop through the `locales` variable that we assigned from `BaseController.php`,
and for each locale, we render the element:

```
{% extends 'layout.volt' %}
{% block body %}
<h1>Add</h1>
<hr>
<div class="panel panel-default">
  <div class="panel-body">
    <form method="post" action="{{ url('category/create') }}">
      {% for locale, name in locales %}
        <h4>Category ({{ name }})</h4>
        <div class="form-group">
          <label for="category_name">Name</label>{{ form.render(
            'translations['~locale~'][category_translation_name]',
              {'class':'form-control'}) }}
        </div>
        <div class="form-group">
          <label for="category_slug">Slug</label>
            {{ form.render('translations['~locale~']
            [category_translation_slug]', {'class':'form-control'
            }) }}
        </div>
        {{ form.render('translations['~locale~']
          [category_translation_lang]') }}
        {% endfor %}
        {{ form.render('save', {'value':'Save'}) }}
        {{ form.render('csrf', {'value':security.getToken()}) }}
    </form>
  </div>
</div>
{% endblock %}
```

edit.volt

The `edit.volt` file is mostly the same as `add.volt`. We just need to change the
form action to {{ `url('category/update')` }}. If you know that you're not going
to develop a complex system, you can use the same file for add/edit. Personally,
I prefer to use two separate files because it happened to me many times that the
complexity of editing was very high compared to adding.

delete.volt

This is the simplest template, but for the same reason as for add/edit, I prefer to keep these files separate:

```
{% extends 'layout.volt' %}
{% block body %}
<h1>Confirm deletion</h1>
<h3>Are you sure you want to delete the selected element?</3>
<hr>
<div class="panel panel-default">
  <div class="panel-body">
    <form method="post" action="{{ url('category/delete/' ~ id)
      }}" class="form-inline">
      <input type="submit" value="Yes, delete" class="btn btn-sm
        btn-danger btn-block">
      <a href="{{ url('category/list') }}" class="btn btn-lg
        btn-default btn-block">Cancel</a>
    </form>
  </div>
</div>
{% endblock %}
```

> If you want, and if you don't have any complex operations, you can create a delete.volt file in the common/ folder and include it from there for all sections. Here is an example of how you can do so:
>
> ```
> {% extends 'layout.volt' %}
> {% block body %}
> {% include 'common/delete' with {'url':url('category/
> delete/' ~ id)} %}
> {% endblock %}
> ```

Creating the Category controller

Now that we have the code for the templates, let's create the controller. Switch to `modules/Backoffice/Controllers/` and create a new file named `CategoryController.php` with the following code:

```
<?php
namespace App\Backoffice\Controllers;

class CategoryController extends BaseController{
  public function indexAction() {
    return $this->dispatcher->forward(['action' => 'list']);
```

```
  }

  public function listAction() {
    $page = $this->request->getQuery('p', 'int', 1);

    try {
      $records = $this->apiGet('categories?p='.$page);

      $this->view->records = $records;
    } catch (\Exception $e) {
      $this->flash->error($e->getMessage());
    }
  }

  public function addAction() {
    $manager = $this->getDI()->get('core_category_manager');
    $this->view->form = $manager->getForm();
  }

  public function editAction($id) {
    $manager = $this->getDI()->get('core_category_manager');
    $object  = $manager->findFirstById($id);

    if (!$object) {
      $this->flashSession->error('Object not found');
      return $this->response->redirect('category/list');
    }

    $this->persistent->set('id', $id);

    $this->view->form = $manager->getForm($object, [
      'edit' => true]);
  }

  public function createAction() {
    if (!$this->request->isPost()) {
      return $this->response->redirect('category/list');
    }

    $manager = $this->getDI()->get('core_category_manager');
    $form    = $manager->getForm();

    if ($form->isValid($this->request->getPost())) {
      try {
```

```php
    $manager   = $this->getDI()->get('core_category_manager');
    $post_data = $this->request->getPost();
    $data      = array_merge($post_data,
      ['category_is_active' => 1]);

    $manager->create($data);
    $this->flashSession->success('Object was created
      successfully');

    return $this->response->redirect('category/list');
  } catch (\Exception $e) {
    $this->flash->error($e->getMessage());
    return $this->dispatcher->forward(['action' => 'add']);
  }
} else {
  foreach ($form->getMessages() as $message) {
    $this->flash->error($message->getMessage());
  }
  return $this->dispatcher->forward(['action' => 'add',
    'controller' => 'category']);
  }
}
}

public function updateAction() {
  if (!$this->request->isPost()) {
    return $this->response->redirect('category/list');
  }

  $manager   = $this->getDI()->get('core_category_manager');
  $object_id = $this->persistent->get('id');
  $object    = $manager->findFirstById($object_id);
  $form      = $manager->getForm($object);

  if ($form->isValid($this->request->getPost())) {
    try {
      $manager = $this->getDI()->get('core_category_manager');
      $manager->update(array_merge($this->request->getPost(),
        ['id' => $object_id]));
      $this->flashSession->success('Object was updated
        successfully');

      return $this->response->redirect('category/list');
    } catch (\Exception $e) {
      $this->flash->error($e->getMessage());
```

```
            return $this->dispatcher->forward(['action' => 'edit']);
        }
    } else {
        foreach ($form->getMessages() as $message) {
            $this->flash->error($message->getMessage());
        }
        return $this->dispatcher->forward(['action' => 'edit',
            'controller' => 'category']);
    }
}
public function deleteAction($id) {
    if ($this->request->isPost()) {
        try {
            $manager = $this->getDI()->get('core_category_manager');
            $manager->delete($id);
            $this->flashSession->success('Object has been deleted
                successfully');
        } catch (\Exception $e) {
            $this->flashSession->error($e->getMessage());
        }

        return $this->response->redirect('category/list');
    }

    $this->view->id = $id;
}
}
```

If you check out the `updateAction()` and `createAction()` methods, you will notice that we use `$post_data` as it is. We can do it this way because the form fields have the array-style name, so we send the data in exactly the same format that the manager expects.

The `editAction()` method renders the form to edit a record. Notice the second parameter from `$manager->getForm()`. It is an array containing the `edit` key and the `true` value, which we use in `CategoryForm.php`.

Creating the Category manager

We are missing the manager. Create a new file named `CategoryManager.php` in `modules/Core/Managers/CategoryManager.php` with the following content:

```php
<?php
namespace App\Core\Managers;
```

```
use App\Core\Models\Category;
use App\Core\Models\CategoryTranslation;
use App\Core\Forms\CategoryForm;

class CategoryManager extends BaseManager{
  public function getForm($entity = null, $options = null) {
    return new CategoryForm($entity, $options);
  }

  public function find($parameters = null) {
    return Category::find($parameters);
  }

  public function findFirst($parameters = null) {
    return Category::findFirst($parameters);
  }

  public function findFirstById($id) {
    return Category::findFirstById($id);
  }

  public function create(array $input_data) {
    $default_data = array('translations' => array(
      'en' => array(
        'category_translation_name' => 'Category name',
        'category_translation_slug' => '',
        'category_translation_lang' => 'en',
      ),
    ),
    'category_is_active' => 0,);

    $data = array_merge($default_data, $input_data);

    $category = new Category();
    $category->setCategoryIsActive($data['category_is_active']);

    $categoryTranslations = array();

    foreach ($data['translations'] as $lang => $translation) {
      $tmp = new CategoryTranslation();
      $tmp->assign($translation);
      array_push($categoryTranslations, $tmp);
    }
```

```php
    $category->translations = $categoryTranslations;

    return $this->save($category, 'create');
  }

  public function update(array $st_inputData) {
    $st_defaultData = array('translations' => array(
      'en' => array(
        'category_translation_name' => 'Category name',
        'category_translation_slug' => '',
        'category_translation_lang' => 'en',
      ),
    ));

    $st_data = array_merge($st_defaultData, $st_inputData);

    $object = Category::findFirstById($st_data['id']);

    if (!$object) {
      throw new \Exception('Object not found');
    }

    foreach ($st_data['translations'] as $locale => $values) {
      $translation = $object->getTranslations([
        "category_translation_lang = '$locale'"]);
      $translation[0]->setCategoryTranslationName($values[
        'category_translation_name']);
      $translation[0]->setCategoryTranslationSlug($values[
        'category_translation_slug']);
      $translation[0]->setCategoryTranslationLang($values[
        'category_translation_lang']);
      $this->save($translation[0], 'update');
    }

    return $this->save($object, 'update');
  }

  public function delete($id) {
    $object = Category::findFirstById($id);

    if (!$object) {
      throw new \Exception('Object not found');
    }
```

```
  if (false === $object->delete()) {
    foreach ($object->getMessages() as $message) {
      $error[] = (string) $message;
    }

    throw new \Exception(json_encode($error));
  }

  return true;
  }
}
```

We need to enable this manager. Add the following code to `config/managers.php`:

```
$di['core_category_manager'] = function () {
    return new \App\Core\Managers\CategoryManager();
};
```

That's all! You can now access `http://www.learning-phalcon.localhost/backoffice/category/list` and you should see something similar to this:

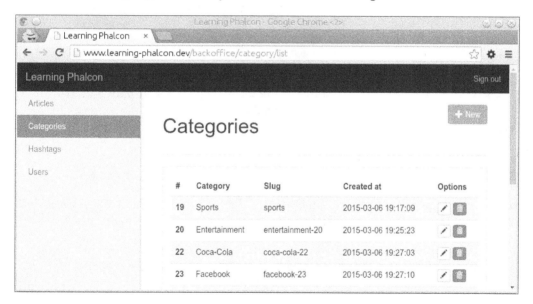

If you don't have any records, click on the **+ New** button to create a new category. This action will render the template for add.volt and you will see the following screenshot:

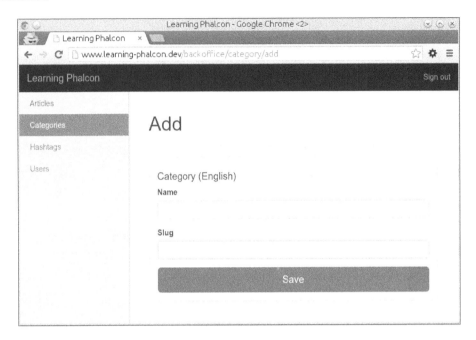

This is it! You can check out the source code for this chapter and play with the API with different categories. Note that the API documentation is always available in docs/api/index.html.

Summary

In this chapter, we developed a functional CRUD for hashtags and categories. You learned how to make API calls and render form elements dynamically.

In the next chapter, we will focus on completing the Backoffice module (developing CRUD for articles and users). We will continue to develop this module by writing code for the user and article CRUD.

8
The Backoffice Module (Part 2)

In this chapter, we will develop the remaining sections of the Backoffice module so that we can get a fully functional administration area. This chapter covers the following topics:

- User CRUD
- Article CRUD

User CRUD

We have already developed part of the code needed for this function, but we will rewrite part of it because, in the meantime, we have made changes to the database that will affect the functionality of our application. What we are going to develop next is similar to the previous CRUD sections. Let's start with the API controller.

Creating the controller (API)

As we did in *Chapter 7, The Backoffice Module (Part 1)*, with hashtag and category, we will need to create a controller for the user. Create a new file in `modules/Api/Controller/` and name it `UsersController.php`. Then, write the following code:

```php
<?php
namespace App\Api\Controllers;

class UsersController extends BaseController{
  public function updateAction($id) {
    try {
```

```
    $manager = $this->getDI()->get('core_user_manager');

    if ($this->request->getHeader('CONTENT_TYPE') ==
      'application/json') {
      $data = $this->request->getJsonRawBody(true);
    } else {
      $data = $this->request->getPut();
    }

    if (count($data) == 0) {
      throw new \Exception('Please provide data', 400);
    }

    $st_data = array_merge($data, ['id' => $id]);
    $result  = $manager->restUpdate($st_data);

    return $this->render($result);
  } catch (\Exception $e) {
    return $this->render([
      'code' => $e->getCode(),
      'message' => $e->getMessage(),
    ], $e->getCode());
  }
}

public function createAction() {
  try {
    $manager   = $this->getDI()->get('core_user_manager');

    if ($this->request->getHeader('CONTENT_TYPE') ==
      'application/json') {
      $data = $this->request->getJsonRawBody(true);
    } else {
      $data = $this->request->getPost();
    }

    if (count($data) == 0) {
      throw new \Exception('Please provide data', 400);
    }

    $st_output = $manager->restCreate($data);

    return $this->render($st_output);
  } catch (\Exception $e) {
```

```
        return $this->render([
          'code' => $e->getCode(),
          'message' => $e->getMessage(),
        ], 500);
      }
    }
  }
```

As you can see, there are not many differences between this controller and the other controllers except for the parameters' binding. We have omitted the list(), get(), and delete() methods, but you can find them in the source code for this chapter.

We will now move on to the creation of the controller in Backoffice.

The user controller from the Backoffice module

Create a new file in modules/Backoffice/Controller/ and name it UserController.php. Then, write the following code in it:

```php
<?php
namespace App\Backoffice\Controllers;

class UserController extends BaseController{
  public function createAction() {
    if (!$this->request->isPost()) {
      return $this->response->redirect('user/list');
    }

    $manager = $this->getDI()->get('core_user_manager');
    $form    = $manager->getForm();

    if ($form->isValid($this->request->getPost())) {
      try {
        $manager   = $this->getDI()->get('core_user_manager');
        $post_data = $this->request->getPost();

        $manager->create($post_data);
        $this->flashSession->success('Object was created
          successfully');

        return $this->response->redirect('user/list');
      } catch (\Exception $e) {
        $this->flash->error($e->getMessage());
```

```
        return $this->dispatcher->forward(['action' => 'add']);
      }
    } else {
      foreach ($form->getMessages() as $message) {
        $this->flash->error($message->getMessage());
      }

      return $this->dispatcher->forward(['action' => 'add',
        'controller' => 'user']);
    }
  }
}

public function updateAction() {
  if (!$this->request->isPost()) {
    return $this->response->redirect('user/list');
  }

  $manager    = $this->getDI()->get('core_user_manager');
  $object_id  = $this->persistent->get('id');
  $object     = $manager->findFirstById($object_id);
  $form       = $manager->getForm($object);

  if ($form->isValid($this->request->getPost())) {
    try {
      $manager = $this->getDI()->get('core_user_manager');
      $manager->update(array_merge($this->request->getPost(),
        ['id' => $object_id]));
      $this->flashSession->success('Object was updated
        successfully');

      return $this->response->redirect('user/list');
    } catch (\Exception $e) {
      $this->flash->error($e->getMessage());

      return $this->dispatcher->forward(['action' => 'edit']);
    }
  } else {
    foreach ($form->getMessages() as $message) {
      $this->flash->error($message->getMessage());
    }

    return $this->dispatcher->forward(['action' => 'edit',
      'controller' => 'user']);
  }
}
}
```

The methods that require more attention are `updateAction()` and `createAction()`, where we validate a user form and assign the data to the right action within the manager.

 The `addAction()`, `deleteAction()`, and `listAction()` methods have been intentionally left out, but you can find them in the source code of this chapter.

The user form

You have already learned how and why we use forms. We will create a form that will help us render and validate the data required for user creation. Create a new file in `modules/Core/Forms/` and name it `UserForm.php`. Then, write the following code in it:

```php
<?php
namespace App\Core\Forms;

use Phalcon\Forms\Form;
use Phalcon\Forms\Element\Text;
use Phalcon\Forms\Element\Password;
use Phalcon\Forms\Element\Submit;
use Phalcon\Forms\Element\Select;
use Phalcon\Forms\Element\Hidden;
use Phalcon\Validation\Validator\PresenceOf;
use Phalcon\Validation\Validator\Email;
use Phalcon\Validation\Validator\StringLength;
use Phalcon\Validation\Validator\Identical;

use App\Core\Models\AclRoles;

class UserForm extends Form {
  private $edit;

  public function initialize($entity = null, $options = null) {
    if (isset($options['edit']) && $options['edit'] === true) {
      $this->edit = true;
    }

    // First name
    $user_first_name = new Text('user_first_name', array(
      'placeholder' => 'First name',
    ));
```

```
$user_first_name->addValidators(array(
  new PresenceOf(array(
    'message' => 'First name is required',
  ))
));

$this->add($user_first_name);

// Last name
$user_last_name = new Text('user_last_name', array(
  'placeholder' => 'Last name',
));

$user_last_name->addValidators(array(
  new PresenceOf(array(
    'message' => 'Last name is required',
  ))
));

$this->add($user_last_name);

// Email
$user_email = new Text('user_email', array(
  'placeholder' => 'Email',
));

$user_email->addValidators(array(
  new PresenceOf(array(
    'message' => 'The e-mail is required',
  )),
  new Email(array(
    'message' => 'The e-mail is not valid',
  )),
));

$this->add($user_email);

//Password
$user_password = new Password('user_password', array(
  'placeholder' => 'Password',
));

$user_password->addValidators(array(
  new PresenceOf(array(
```

```
      'message' => 'Password is required'
    )),
    new StringLength(array(
      'min' => 8,
      'messageMinimum' => 'Password is too short. Minimum 8
        characters'
    ))
  ));

$this->add($user_password);

// User is active
$this->add(new Select('user_is_active', array(
  1 => 'Yes',
  0 => 'No'
)));

// User location
$user_profile_location = new Text('user_profile_location',
  array(
  'placeholder' => 'Location',
));

if (true === $this->edit) {
  $user_profile_location->setDefault($entity->profile->
    getUserProfileLocation());
}

$this->add($user_profile_location);

// User role
$user_acl_role = new Select('user_acl_role', AclRoles::find(),
  array(
  'using' => array('name', 'name')
));

$this->add($user_acl_role);

//CSRF
$csrf = new Hidden('csrf');

$csrf->addValidator(
  new Identical(array(
    'value' => $this->security->getSessionToken(),
    'message' => 'CSRF validation failed',
```

```
        ))
    );

    $this->add($csrf);

    $this->add(new Submit('save', array(
        'class' => 'btn btn-lg btn-primary btn-block',
    )));
    }
}
```

In this form, you may notice a few new things:

- We use `Phalcon\Validation\Validator\StringLength` to validate the length of the password.

- We use a new form element, `Phalcon\Forms\Element\Select`, to generate the `select` form elements.

- We use `Phalcon\Validation\Validator\Email` to validate the e-mail address field.

- We assign the results of `App\Core\Models\AclRoles` as the second parameter of the `select` element, `user_acl_role`. The second parameter for this field is an array that instructs `Phalcon\Forms\Element\Select` to use the field's name when generating the HTML code. Normally, we would use the field's ID and name, or something similar. But in this particular case, the `acl_roles` table does not have an ID.

The user manager

You might already have part of the user manager, or perhaps you have created it in its entirety. Just in case you didn't, create it now. Create a new file in `modules/Core/Managers/` and name it `UserManager.php`. Then, write the following code in it:

```php
<?php
namespace App\Core\Managers;

use App\Core\Models\User;
use App\Core\Models\UserRole;
use App\Core\Models\AclRoles;
use App\Core\Models\UserProfile;

use App\Core\Forms\UserForm;
```

```
class UserManager extends BaseManager{
  public function getForm($entity = null, $options = null) {
    return new UserForm($entity, $options);
  }

  public function create($data, $user_role = 'Guest') {
    $security = $this->getDI()->get('security');

    if (isset($data['user_acl_role'])) {
      $user_role = $data['user_acl_role'];
    }

    $user = new User();
    $user->setUserFirstName($data['user_first_name']);
    $user->setUserLastName($data['user_last_name']);
    $user->setUserEmail($data['user_email']);
    $user->setUserPassword($security->hash($data[
      'user_password']));
    $user->setUserIsActive($data['user_is_active']);

    $o_acl_role  = AclRoles::findFirstByName($user_role);

    if (!$o_acl_role) {
      throw new \Exception("Role $user_role does not exists");
    };

    $o_user_role[0] = new UserRole();
    $o_user_role[0]->setUserRole($user_role);

    $user->roles = $o_user_role;

    $profile = new UserProfile();
    $profile->setUserProfileLocation($data[
      'user_profile_location']);

    $user->profile = $profile;

    return $this->save($user, 'create');
  }
}
```

The `create()` method requires two parameters. The first parameter, `$data`, is an array with the values needed to create our new object. The second parameter is `$user_role`, with a default value. Going further, we check whether the `$data` array has a key named `user_acl_role`. If the key exists, we overwrite the default value of the `$user_role` parameter. Finally, we assign values to each of the `$user` objects and save them:

```
public function update(array $data) {
  $object = User::findFirstById($data['id']);

  if (!$object) {
    throw new \Exception('Object not found');
  }

  $security = $this->getDI()->get('security');

  $object->setUserFirstName($data['user_first_name']);
  $object->setUserLastName($data['user_last_name']);
  $object->setUserEmail($data['user_email']);
  $object->setUserPassword($security->hash($data[
    'user_password']));
  $object->setUserIsActive($data['user_is_active']);

  $o_acl_role  = AclRoles::findFirstByName($data[
    'user_acl_role']);

  if (!$o_acl_role) {
    throw new \Exception("Role $user_role does not exists");
  };

  $o_user_role[0] = new UserRole();
  $o_user_role[0]->setUserRole($data['user_acl_role']);

  $object->roles = $o_user_role;

  $object->profile->setUserProfileLocation($data[
    'user_profile_location']);

  return $this->save($object, 'update');
}
```

The `update()` method is similar to the `create()` method, except that we first check whether the object that we want to update exists. The `delete()` method, shown as follows, will simply search for an object by ID; if the object exists, we delete it:

```
public function delete($id) {
  $object = User::findFirstById($id);

  if (!$object) {
    throw new \Exception('Object not found');
  }

  if (false === $object->delete()) {
    foreach ($object->getMessages() as $message) {
      $error[] = (string) $message;
    }

    throw new \Exception(json_encode($error));
  }
  return true;
}
```

 Again, the `find()`, `findFirstById()`, and `findFirst()` methods have been intentionally left out, but you can find them in the source code of this chapter.

Let's pay attention to the `create()` and `update()` methods and how we store the relations of the profiles and roles. Because the relation between the user and the roles is *1 - N*, to store the values correctly, we use array notation for the `$o_user_role` variable. Otherwise, saving will fail. For the password, we make use of Phalcon's built-in security module, and we encrypt it by using the `$security->hash()` method.

User templates

The final step is to create the templates. Switch to `modules/Backoffice/Views/Default` and create a new directory named `user`. In this new directory, create the four needed files: `add.volt`, `delete.volt`, `edit.volt`, and `list.volt`. There is nothing new to explain about these templates, so we are just going to write the code for them.

The code for `add.volt` is as follows:

```
{% extends 'layout.volt' %}
{% block body %}
<h1>Add</h1>
<hr>
<div class="panel panel-default">
  <div class="panel-body">
    <form method="post" action="{{ url('user/create') }}">
      <h4>User details</h4>
      <hr>
        <div class="form-group">
          <label for="user_first_name">First name</label>
            {{ form.render('user_first_name', {'class':
              'form-control'}) }}
        </div>
        <div class="form-group">
          <label for="user_last_name">Last name</label>
            {{ form.render('user_last_name', {'class':
              'form-control'}) }}
        </div>
        <div class="form-group">
          <label for="user_email">Email</label>
            {{ form.render('user_email', {'class':
              'form-control'}) }}
        </div>
        <div class="form-group">
          <label for="user_password">Password</label>
            {{ form.render('user_password', {'class':
              'form-control'}) }}
        </div>
        <div class="form-group">
          <label for="user_is_active">Is active</label>
            {{ form.render('user_is_active', {'class':
              'form-control'}) }}
        </div>
        <h4>User profile</h4>
        <hr>
        <div class="form-group">
          <label for="user_profile_location">Location</label>
            {{ form.render('user_profile_location',
              {'class':'form-control'}) }}
        </div>
        <h4>User role</h4>
        <hr>
```

```
        <div class="form-group">
          <label for="user_acl_role">Role</label>
            {{ form.render('user_acl_role', {'class':
              'form-control'}) }}
          </div>
        {{ form.render('save', {'value':'Save'}) }}
      {{ form.render('csrf', {'value':security.getToken()}) }}
    </form>
  </div>
</div>
{% endblock %}
```

Here is the code for `delete.volt`:

```
{% extends 'layout.volt' %}
{% block body %}
<h1>Confirm deletion</h1>
<h3>Are you sure you want to delete the selected element?</3>
<hr>
<div class="panel panel-default">
  <div class="panel-body">
    <form method="post" action="{{ url('user/delete/' ~ id) }}"
      class="form-inline">
      <input type="submit" value="Yes, delete" class="btn btn-sm
        btn-danger btn-block">
          <a href="{{ url('user/list') }}" class="btn btn-lg
            btn-default btn-block">Cancel</a>
      </form>
  </div>
</div>
{% endblock %}
```

The `edit.volt` file is nearly the same as `add.volt`. Just replace the `form` action and point it to `user/update`:

```
<form method="post" action="{{ url('user/update') }}">
```

The code for `list.volt` is as follows:

```
{% extends 'layout.volt' %}
{% block body %}
<div class="pull-left">
  <h1>Users</h1>
</div>
<div class="pull-right">
  <a class="btn btn-success" href="{{ url('user/add') }}"
    aria-label="Left Align">
```

```
      <span class="glyphicon glyphicon-plus" aria-hidden=
        "true"></span> New
  </a>
</div>
<div class="clearfix"></div>
<hr>
<div class="panel panel-default">
  <div class="panel-body">
    <table class="table table-striped">
      <thead>
      <tr>
        <th>#</th>
        <th>Name</th>
        <th>Email</th>
        <th>Location</th>
        <th>Created at</th>
        <th>Options</th>
      </tr>
      </thead>
      <tbody>
        {% for record in records['items'] %}
          <tr>
            <th scope="row">{{ record['id'] }}</th>
              <td>{{ record['user_first_name'] }} {{
                record['user_last_name'] }}</td>
              <td>{{ record['user_email'] }}</td>
              <td>{{ record['user_profile'][
                'user_profile_location'] }}</td>
              <td>{{ record['user_created_at'] }}</td>
              <td>
                <a class="btn btn-default btn-xs" href="{{
                url('user/edit/' ~ record['id']) }}"
                aria-label="Left Align">
                <span class="glyphicon glyphicon-pencil"
                  aria-hidden="true">
                </span>
              </a>
              <a class="btn btn-danger btn-xs" href="{{
                url('user/delete/' ~ record['id']) }}"
                  aria-label="Left Align">
                <span class="glyphicon glyphicon-trash"
                  aria-hidden="true">
                </span>
              </a>
            </td>
```

```
        </tr>
          {% else %}
        <tr>
            <td colspan="4">There are no records in your
                database</td>
        </tr>
          {% endfor %}
      </tbody>
    </table>
  </div>
</div>
{% if (records['total_pages'] > 1) %}
{% include 'common/paginator' with {'page_url' : url('user/list'),
'stack' : records} %}
{% endif %}
{% endblock %}
```

And we are done with User CRUD! You should be able to access the `Users` section in Backoffice (`http://www.learning-phalcon.localhost/backoffice/user/list`) and see a list of existing users. Now that we have enabled CRUD for all the sections that are required for adding an article, we will continue with the last part of this chapter — Article CRUD.

Article CRUD

We partially wrote some code for this part. It is probably working for you, but you will be changing mostly everything in it. The API controller has already been developed, so we can move directly on to `ArticleManager` to refactor it.

The Controller (API)

The code for this controller is similar to that of the rest of the controllers. Let's see what it looks like. Open the file located at `modules/Api/Controllers/ArticlesController.php`, clear its content, and write the following code:

```php
<?php
namespace App\Api\Controllers;

class ArticlesController extends BaseController{
  public function updateAction($id) {
    try {
      $manager = $this->getDI()->get('core_article_manager');
```

```
        if ($this->request->getHeader('CONTENT_TYPE') ==
'         application/json') {
          $data = $this->request->getJsonRawBody(true);
        } else {
          $data = $this->request->getPut();
        }

        if (count($data) == 0) {
          throw new \Exception('Please provide data', 400);
        }

        $st_inputData = array(
          'article_user_id' => $data['article_user_id'],
          'article_is_published' => $data['article_is_published'],
          'translations' => [
            $data['article_translation_lang'] => [
              'article_translation_short_title' =>
                  $data['article_translation_short_title'],
              'article_translation_long_title' =>
                  $data['article_translation_long_title'],
              'article_translation_description' =>
                  $data['article_translation_description'],
              'article_translation_slug' => $data[
                  'article_translation_slug'],
              'article_translation_lang' => $data[
                  'article_translation_lang'],
            ],
          ],
          'categories' => $data['categories'],
          'hashtags' => $data['hashtags']
        );

        $result = $manager->restUpdate(array_merge(
          $st_inputData, ['id' => $id]));

        return $this->render($result);
      } catch (\Exception $e) {
        return $this->render([
          'code' => $e->getCode(),
          'message' => $e->getMessage(),
        ], $e->getCode());
      }
    }
```

```php
public function createAction() {
  try {
    $manager    = $this->getDI()->get('core_article_manager');

    if ($this->request->getHeader('CONTENT_TYPE') ==
      'application/json') {
      $data = $this->request->getJsonRawBody(true);
    } else {
      $data = $this->request->getPost();
    }
    if (count($data) == 0) {
      throw new \Exception('Please provide data', 400);
    }

    $st_inputData = array(
      'article_user_id' => $data['article_user_id'],
      'article_is_published' => $data['article_is_published'],
      'translations' => [
        $data['article_translation_lang'] => [
          'article_translation_short_title' =>
            $data['article_translation_short_title'],
          'article_translation_long_title' =>
            $data['article_translation_long_title'],
          'article_translation_description' =>
            $data['article_translation_description'],
          'article_translation_slug' =>
            $data['article_translation_slug'],
          'article_translation_lang' =>
            $data['article_translation_lang'],
        ],
      ],
      'categories' => $data['categories'],
      'hashtags' => $data['hashtags']
    );

    $st_output = $manager->restCreate($st_inputData);

    return $this->render($st_output);
  } catch (\Exception $e) {
    return $this->render([
      'code' => $e->getCode(),
```

```
        'message' => $e->getMessage(),
      ], $e->getCode());
    }
  }
}
```

The only important thing to pay attention to in this controller is the data structure that we expect for `createAction()` and `updateAction()`. Let's continue with the next controller.

 The `addAction()`, `deleteAction()`, and `listAction()` methods have been intentionally left out, but you can find them in the source code of this chapter.

The Article controller from the Backoffice module

Switch to the `modules/Backoffice/Controllers/` folder, create a new file named `ArticleController.php`, and write the following code:

```php
<?php
namespace App\Backoffice\Controllers;

class ArticleController extends BaseController {
  public function createAction() {
    if (!$this - > request - > isPost()) {
      return $this - > response - > redirect('article/list');
    }
    $manager = $this - > getDI() - > get('core_article_manager');
    $form = $manager - > getForm();
    if ($form - > isValid($this - > request - > getPost())) {
      try {
        $manager = $this - > getDI() - > get('core_article_manager');
        $post_data = $this - > request - > getPost();
        $data = array_merge($post_data,
          ['article_user_id ' => $this->auth->getUserId()]);

        $manager - > create($data);
        $this - > flashSession - > success('Object was created
          successfully ');
        return $this - > response - > redirect('article/list');
      } catch (\Exception $e) {
        $this - > flash - > error($e - > getMessage());
```

```
      return $this - > dispatcher - > forward(['action' =>
        'add'
      ]);
    }
  } else {
    foreach($form - > getMessages() as $message) {
      $this - > flash - > error($message - > getMessage());
    }
    return $this - > dispatcher - > forward(['action' => 'add',
      'controller' => 'article'
    ]);
  }
}
public function updateAction() {
  if (!$this - > request - > isPost()) {
    return $this - > response - > redirect('article/list');
  }
  $manager = $this - > getDI() - > get('core_article_manager');
  $object_id = $this - > persistent - > get('id');
  $object = $manager - > findFirstById($object_id);
  $form = $manager - > getForm($object);
  if ($form - > isValid($this - > request - > getPost())) {
    try {
      $manager = $this - > getDI() - > get('core_article_manager ');
      $post_data = $this - > request - > getPost();
      $data = array_merge(
        $post_data, ['article_user_id' => $this - > auth - >
          getUserId(), 'id' => $object_id]);
      $manager - > update($data);
      $this - > flashSession - > success('Object was updated
        successfully ');

      return $this - > response - > redirect('article/list');
    } catch (\Exception $e) {
      $this - > flash - > error($e - > getMessage());
      return $this - > dispatcher - > forward(['action' =>
        'edit'
      ]);
    }
  } else {
    foreach($form - > getMessages() as $message) {
      $this - > flash - > error($message - > getMessage());
    }
```

```
        return $this - > dispatcher - > forward(['action' => 'edit',
          'controller' => 'category'
        ]);
      }
    }
  }
```

Take a look at `createAction()` and `updateAction()`. Here, we use the ID of the authenticated user when we set the value for the `article_user_id` field.

 Again, methods such as `addAction()`, `deleteAction()`, and `listAction()` have been intentionally left out, but you can find them in the source code of this chapter.

The Article form

This form is similar to the one for categories. Let's see what it looks like. Create a new file named `ArticleForm.php` in the `modules/Core/Forms` directory, and write this code in it:

```php
<?php
namespace App\Core\Forms;

use Phalcon\Forms\Form;
use Phalcon\Forms\Element\Text;
use Phalcon\Forms\Element\TextArea;
use Phalcon\Forms\Element\Select;
use Phalcon\Forms\Element\Submit;
use Phalcon\Forms\Element\Hidden;
use Phalcon\Validation\Validator\Identical;

use App\Core\Models\CategoryTranslation;
use App\Core\Models\Hashtag;

class ArticleForm extends Form {
  private $edit = false;
  public function initialize($entity = null, $options = null) {
    if (isset($options['edit']) && $options['edit'] === true) {
      $this->edit = true;
    }
    $locales = $this->getDI()->get('config')->i18n->locales->
        toArray();
    foreach ($locales as $locale => $name) {
```

```php
  if (true === $this->edit) {
    $translations = $entity->getTranslations([
        "article_translation_lang = '$locale'"])->toArray();
  }
  $article_translation_short_title[$locale] = new Text
  ("translations[$locale][article_translation_short_title]", [
    'value' => $this->edit === true ? $translations[0]
    ['article_translation_short_title'] : null
  ]);
  $article_translation_long_title[$locale] = new Text
  ("translations[$locale][article_translation_long_title]", [
    'value' => $this->edit === true ? $translations[0]
    ['article_translation_long_title'] : null
  ]);
  $article_translation_description[$locale] = new TextArea
  ("translations[$locale][article_translation_description]", [
    'value' => $this->edit === true ? $translations[0]
    ['article_translation_description'] : null
  ]);
  $article_translation_slug[$locale] = new Text (
    "translations[$locale][article_translation_slug]", [
    'value' => $this->edit === true ? $translations[0]
    ['article_translation_slug'] : null
  ]);
  $article_translation_lang[$locale] = new Hidden (
    "translations[$locale][article_translation_lang]", [
    'value' => $locale
  ]);
  $this->add( $article_translation_short_title[$locale] );
  $this->add( $article_translation_long_title[$locale] );
  $this->add( $article_translation_description[$locale] );
  $this->add( $article_translation_slug[$locale] );
  $this->add( $article_translation_lang[$locale] );
}
// Categories
$categories = new Select('categories[]',
  CategoryTranslation::find([
      "category_translation_lang = 'en'"]), [
      'using' => [
        'category_translation_category_id',
        'category_translation_name'
      ],
      'multiple' => true
    ]);
```

```
    if ($this->edit === true) {
      $categories_defaults = array();
      foreach ($entity->getCategories(["columns" =>
          ["id"]]) as $category) {
        $categories_defaults[] = $category->id;
      }
      $categories->setDefault($categories_defaults);
    }
    $this->add($categories);
    // Hash tags
    $hashtags = new Select('hashtags[]', Hashtag::find(), [
      'using' => ['id', 'hashtag_name'],
      'multiple' => true
    ]);
    if ($this->edit === true) {
      $hashtags_defaults = array();
      foreach ($entity->getHashtags(["columns" =>
          ["id"]]) as $hashtag) {
        $hashtags_defaults[] = $hashtag->id;
      }
      $hashtags->setDefault($hashtags_defaults);
    }
    $this->add($hashtags);
    // Is published
    $this->add(new Select('article_is_published', array(
        1 => 'Yes',
        0 => 'No'
    )));
    //CSRF
    $csrf = new Hidden('csrf');
    $csrf->addValidator(
      new Identical(array(
        'value' => $this->security->getSessionToken(),
        'message' => 'CSRF validation failed',
      ))
    );
    $this->add($csrf);
    $this->add(new Submit('save', array(
    'class' => 'btn btn-lg btn-primary btn-block',
    )));
  }
}
```

We manage the Article translation in the same way as we did for categories. As for the article hashtags and article categories, when we edit a record, we must somehow retrieve the existing ones and assign them as defaults in the form.

We have created the controllers, managers, and forms. What we need now are the templates. Switch to `modules/Backoffice/Views/Default/article/` and create the three missing files: `add.volt`, `delete.volt`, and `edit.volt`. Here is the code for each of them.

The code for `add.volt` is as follows:

```
{% extends 'layout.volt' %}
{% block body %}
<h1>Add</h1>
<hr>
<div class="panel panel-default">
  <div class="panel-body">
    <form method="post" action="{{ url('article/create') }}">
      {% for locale, name in locales %}
      <h3>Article ({{ name }})</h3>
      <hr>
      <div class="form-group">
        <label for="article_translation_short_title">Title
        </label>
        {{ form.render('translations['~locale~']
        [article_translation_short_title]', {'class':'form-control'})
}}
      </div>
      <div class="form-group">
        <label for="article_translation_long_title">
            Long title</label>
        {{ form.render('translations['~locale~']
          [article_translation_long_title]',
          {'class':'form-control'}) }}
      </div>
      <div class="form-group">
        <label for="article_translation_description">Description
        </label>
        {{ form.render('translations['~locale~']
          [article_translation_description]',
          {'class':'form-control', 'rows': 8}) }}
      </div>
      <div class="form-group">
        <label for="article_translation_slug">Slug
        </label>
```

```
{{ form.render('translations['~locale~']
  [article_translation_slug]',
  {'class':'form-control'}) }}
</div>
{{ form.render('translations['~locale~']
  [article_translation_lang]') }}
{% endfor %}
<div class="form-group">
<label for="article_is_published">Is published
</label>
{{form.render('article_is_published',
{'class':'formcontrol'}) }}
</div>
<h3>Categories</h3>
<hr>
<div class="form-group">
<label for="categories">Select one or more
categories</label>
{{ form.render('categories[]', {'class':'formcontrol'}) }}
</div>
<h3>Hash tags</h3>
<hr>
<div class="form-group">
<label for="hashtags">Select one or more hash tags
</label>
  {{form.render('hashtags[]',
  {'class':'form-control'})}}
</div>
{{form.render('save', {'value':'Save'}) }}
{{form.render('csrf', {'value':security.getToken()}) }}
</form>
</div>
</div>
{% endblock %}
```

After you have created this file, try to access `http://www.learning-phalcon.localhost/backoffice/article/add`. You should see the form.

The code in `edit.volt` is the same as that for `add.volt`. Copy it and change its form action to `article/update` instead of `article/create`.

The `delete.volt` file has the same content as all the `delete.volt` files that we have created so far. Just copy the content from any of them and change the `links` actions to point to `article/delete`.

We have already created the `list.volt` file, but we will need to delete its contents and write the following code in it:

```
{% extends 'layout.volt' %} {% block body %}
<div class="pull-left">
    <h1>Articles</h1>
</div>
<div class="pull-right">
    <a class="btn btn-success" href="{{ url('article/add') }}" aria-
label="Left Align">
        <span class="glyphicon glyphicon-plus" aria-hidden="true"></
span> New
    </a>
</div>
<div class="clearfix"></div>
<hr>
<div class="table-responsive">

  <table class="table table-striped">
    <thead>
      <tr>
        <th>#</th>
        <th>Title</th>
        <th>Is published</th>
        <th>Author</th>
        <th>Created at</th>
        <th>Options</th>
      </tr>
    </thead>
    <tbody>
    {% for record in records['items'] %}
      <tr>
        <td>{{record['id'] }}</td>
        <td>{{record['article_translations'][0]
          ['article_translation_short_title'] }}</td>
        <td>{{record['article_is_published'] }}</td>
        <td>{{record['article_author']['user_first_name']}}
              {{record['article_author']['user_last_name']}}
        </td>
        <td>{{ record['article_created_at'] }}</td>
        <td>
          <a class="btn btn-default btn-xs"
            href="{{url('article/edit/' ~ record['id']) }}"
            aria-label="Left Align">
```

```
            <span class="glyphicon glyphicon-pencil"
              ariahidden="true"></span>
          </a>
          <a class="btn btn-danger btn-xs"
            href="{{url('article/delete/' ~ record['id']) }}"
            aria-label="Left Align">
            <span class="glyphicon glyphicon-trash"
              ariahidden="true"></span>
          </a>
        </td>
      </tr>
      {% else %}
      <tr>
        <td colspan="4">There are no records in your
          database</td>
      </tr>
      {% endfor %}
    </tbody>
  </table>
</div>
{% if (records['total_pages'] > 1) %}
{% include 'common/paginator' with {'page_url' : url('article/list'),
'stack' : records} %}
{% endif %}
{% endblock %}
```

By now, you should have a completely functional administration area. We will close this chapter in a few minutes, but before that, we will prettify the UI (user interface) a little. Let's start this process by adding the name of the authenticated user to the top of the page.

Open the `modules/Backoffice/Controller/BaseControllers.php` file and append the following code to the `afterExecuteRoute()` method:

```
$this->view->identity = $this->getDI()->get('auth')->getIdentity();
```

In this way, we assign the identity of our authenticated user to the views. Next, open the `modules/Backoffice/Views/Default/common/topbar.volt` template file and append the following code before the `"Sign out"` `<li>` tag:

```
<li class="disabled"><a href="#">Welcome, {{ identity['name'] }}</a>
</li>
```

You can now refresh the page, and you should see the name of the authenticated user, as shown here:

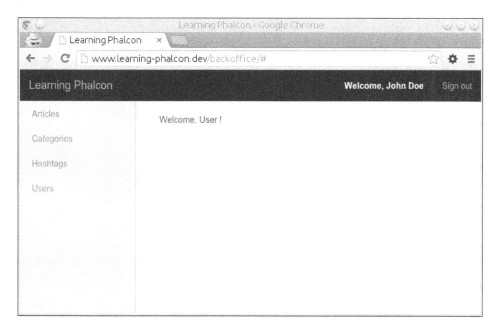

Next, instead of having a default blank page, let's transform it into a simple dashboard. Open `modules/Backoffice/Controller/IndexController.php` and modify the `indexAction()` method with the following code:

```
public function indexAction() {
  $total_articles = $this->getDI()->get(
    'core_article_manager')->find()->count();
  $total_users = $this->getDI()->get('core_user_manager')
    ->find()->count();
  $total_categories = $this->getDI()->get(
    'core_category_manager')->find()->count();
  $total_hashtags = $this->getDI()->get(
    'core_hashtag_manager')->find()->count();
  $this->view->setVar('dashboard', [
    'total_articles' => $total_articles,
    'total_users' => $total_users,
    'total_categories' => $total_categories,
    'total_hashtags' => $total_hashtags,
  ]);
}
```

As you can see, we simply count the total number of articles, users, hashtags, and categories. The template code for `modules/Backoffice/Views/Default/index/index.volt` can look like this:

```
{% extends 'layout.volt' %}
{% block body %}
<div class="row">
  <div class="col-md-6 col-xs-6 text-center">
    <h1>{{ dashboard['total_articles'] }}
      <span class="glyphicon glyphicon-align-justify">
      </span>
    </h1>
    <small>Articles</small>
  </div>
  <div class="col-md-6 col-xs-6 text-center">
    <h1>{{ dashboard['total_categories'] }}
      <span class="glyphicon glyphicon-th">
      </span>
    </h1>
    <small>Categories</small>
  </div>
</div>
<div class="row">
  <div class="col-md-6 col-xs-6 text-center">
    <h1>{{ dashboard['total_hashtags'] }}
    <span class="glyphicon glyphicon-tag">
    </span></h1>
    <small>Tags</small>
  </div>
  <div class="col-md-6 col-xs-6 text-center">
  <h1>{{ dashboard['total_users'] }}
    <span class="glyphicon glyphicon-user">
    </span>
  </h1>
  <small>Users</small>
</div>
</div>
{% endblock %}
```

If you refresh the page, you should be able to see the result of this simple dashboard, as shown here:

The Article manager

Open the file located at `modules/Core/Manager/ArticleManager.php`, clear its contents, and write the following code:

```php
<?php
namespace App\Core\Managers;

use App\Core\Models\Article;
use App\Core\Models\ArticleTranslation;
use App\Core\Models\ArticleCategoryArticle;
use App\Core\Models\ArticleHashtagArticle;
use App\Core\Models\Category;
use App\Core\Models\Hashtag;
use App\Core\Models\User;
```

In these first lines, we insert all the files that we need for the CRUD operations:

```php
class ArticleManager extends BaseManager
{
    private $default_data = array(
        'article_user_id' => 1,
        'article_is_published' => 0,
        'translations' => array(
            'en' => array(
                'article_translation_short_title' => 'Short title',
                'article_translation_long_title' => 'Long title',
                'article_translation_description' => 'Description',
                'article_translation_slug' => '',
```

```
                    'article_translation_lang' => 'en',
                ),
            ),
        'categories' => array(),
        'hashtags' => array()
    );
```

We added $default_data as a private variable to avoid code repetition. We will use it for both the create() and update() methods:

```
    public function getForm($entity = null, $options = null)
    {
        return new ArticleForm($entity, $options);
    }


    public function create($input_data)
    {
        $data = $this->prepareData($input_data);

        $article = new Article();
        $article->setArticleIsPublished($data[
'article_is_published']);

        $articleTranslations = array();

        foreach ($data['translations'] as $lang => $translation) {
            $tmp = new ArticleTranslation();
            $tmp->assign($translation);
            array_push($articleTranslations, $tmp);
        }

        if (count($data['categories']) > 0) {
            $article->categories = Category::find([
                "id IN (".implode(',', $data['categories']).")",
            ])->filter(function ($category) {
                return $category;
            });
        }

        if (count($data['hashtags']) > 0) {
            $article->hashtags = Hashtag::find([
                "id IN (".implode(',', $data['hashtags']).")",
            ])->filter(function ($hashtag) {
                return $hashtag;
```

```
            });
        }

        $user = User::findFirstById((int) $data['article_user_id']);

        if (!$user) {
            throw new \Exception('User not found', 404);
        }

        $article->setArticleUserId($data['article_user_id']);

        $article->translations = $articleTranslations;

        return $this->save($article, 'create');
    }
```

Let's try to understand the create() method. First, we call the prepareData() method. This a helper and we also use it for update(). Next, we initiate a new article object and set the flag for the article_is_published field. An article needs translations and hashtags and we must assign a user to it. We do this by initializing a new object for each translation and hashtag. In the case of a user, we need to check whether the user exists in our database:

```
    public function update($input_data)
    {
        $article = Article::findFirstById($input_data['id']);

        if (!$article) {
            throw new \Exception('Article not found', 404);
        }

        $data = $this->prepareData($input_data);

        $article->setArticleIsPublished($data[
          'article_is_published']);
        $article->setArticleUpdatedAt(
          new \Phalcon\Db\RawValue('NOW()'));


        foreach ($data['translations'] as $lang => $translation) {
            $article->getTranslations()->filter(function($t) use
              ($lang, $translation){

                if ($t->getArticleTranslationLang() == $lang) {
                    $t->assign($translation);
                    $t->update();
```

```
            }
        });
    }

    $results = ArticleCategoryArticle::findByArticleId(
      $input_data['id']);

    if ($results) {
        $results->delete();
    }

    if (count($data['categories']) > 0) {
        $article->categories = Category::find([
          "id IN (".implode(',', $data['categories'])."")",
          ])->filter(function ($category) {
            return $category;
        });
    }

    $results = ArticleHashtagArticle::findByArticleId(
$input_data['id']);

    if ($results) {
        $results->delete();
    }

    if (count($data['hashtags']) > 0) {
        $article->hashtags = Hashtag::find([
            "id IN (".implode(',', $data['hashtags'])."")",
          ])->filter(function ($hashtag) {
            return $hashtag;
        });
    }

    $user = User::findFirstById((int) $data['article_user_id']);

    if (!$user) {
        throw new \Exception('User not found', 404);
    }

    $article->setArticleUserId($data['article_user_id']);

    return $this->save($article, 'update');
}
```

In the preceding code, the `update()` method follows the same logic as the `create()` method. But in the following code, we first need to delete the existing relations of the hashtags and categories, and create new ones. This method also checks whether the article exists in our database:

```php
public function delete($id)
{
    $article = Article::findFirstById($id);

    if (!$article) {
        throw new \Exception('Article not found', 404);
    }

    if (false === $article->delete()) {
        foreach ($article->getMessages() as $message) {
            $error[] = (string) $message;
        }

        throw new \Exception(json_encode($error));
    }

    return true;
}

private function prepareData($input_data)
{
    $data = array_merge($this->default_data, $input_data);

    if (!is_array($data['categories'])) {
        $data['categories'] = $data['categories'] != '' ?
array_map('trim', explode(',', $data['categories'])) : null;

    } else {
        $data['categories'] = implode(',', $data['categories']);
    }

    if (!is_array($data['hashtags'])) {
        $data['hashtags'] = $data['hashtags'] != '' ?
array_map('trim', explode(',', $data['hashtags'])) : null;

    } else {
        $data['hashtags'] = implode(',', $data['hashtags']);
    }
```

```
        return $data;
    }
}
```

The `prepareData()` method is a helper that will help us to avoid code repetition in the `update()` and `create()` methods.

Take a look at the `create()` and `update()` methods. We expect the categories and hashtags to be comma-separated values of IDs. If these fields contain values, we use the `array_map()` method and apply a trim operation to each ID. In the case of `update()`, we always delete the existing hashtags and categories and add them again (or add new ones). I use this approach because Phalcon's ORM doesn't do it automatically.

Important note

In the official documentation, it says you can delete related records in this manner:

```
$robots->getParts()->delete();
```

When using many-to-many relations, as in our case, if you execute the preceding code for categories or hashtags, you will end up deleting the hashtag and the category only. This will not remove the relation from the intermediate model. Also, there is another method for updating related records that is not supported anymore due to some strange functionality, but it can still be found in the official documentation. Don't use it:

```
$robots->getParts()->update($data, function($part) {
    if ($part->type == Part::TYPE_BASIC) {
        return false;
    }
    return true;
});
```

Summary

We're finally done with this module. In general, there are infinite approaches to writing code. In this chapter, I used an approach that I think is easy to understand. Feel free to be different and code the way you like. This book is not intended to teach you coding, but to teach you Phalcon. You might have noticed that for an API, we don't use any validations. You can practice a little and connect your forms to the API.

In the next chapter, we will switch to the `Frontend` module, where we will make some small modifications to the API. We will also try to implement a search engine based on Elasticsearch (`https://www.elastic.co/products/elasticsearch`).

The Frontend Module

Developing the frontend can be a difficult job. You have to take into consideration a variety of aspects, such as **User Experience (UX)**, **Search Engine Optimization (SEO)**, browser compatibility, mobile responsiveness, and so on. We are going to focus on creating a minimal layout and implementing Elasticsearch. We will also use MongoDB to create some logs for articles. Step by step, we are going to cover the following topics in this chapter:

- The frontend layout and basic functionality
- Implementing Elasticsearch
- Implementing MongoDB

The Frontend layout and basic functionality

We are going to use a simple layout for our frontend module. Switch to the `modules/Frontend/Views/Default/common` folder and create the `footer.volt`, `paginator.volt`, and `navbar.volt` files with the following content.

footer.volt

The `footer.volt` file does not contain too much information, but in future, you will want to add more information for sure, such as links, partners, analytics scripts, and so on:

```
<footer class="lp-footer">
    <p>Learning Phalcon</p>
    <p>
        <a href="#">Back to top</a>
    </p>
</footer>
```

paginator.volt

The `paginator.volt` file contains two simple links: **Previous** and **Next**. You can modify these and create a more complex paginator if you wish:

```
<nav>
  <ul class="pager">
    <li><a href="?p={{ records['before'] }}">Previous</a></li>
    <li><a href="?p={{ records['next'] }}">Next</a></li>
  </ul>
</nav>
```

navbar.volt

The `navbar.volt` file contains a link to our home page and all the categories available. We will assign categories to the view later in this chapter.

The code is as follows:

```
<div class="lp-masthead">
  <div class="container">
    <nav class="lp-nav">
      <a class="lp-nav-item active" href="{{ url('') }}">Home</a>
      {% for category in categories['items'] %}
      <a class="lp-nav-item" href="{{ url('categories/' ~
        category['category_translations'][0]
        ['category_translation_slug']) }}">{{ category[
        'category_translations'][0]['category_translation_name']
        }}</a>
      {% endfor %}
    </nav>
  </div>
</div>
```

layout.volt

Let's move on to `layout.volt`. There is already a file located in the `modules/Frontend/Views/Default/` folder. We created it in *Chapter 2, Setting Up the MVC Structure and the Environment for Our Project*. Clear its contents and add the following:

```
<!DOCTYPE html>
<html lang="en">
<head>
<meta charset="utf-8">
<meta http-equiv="X-UA-Compatible" content="IE=edge">
```

```
<meta name="viewport" content="width=device-width, initial-scale=1">
<title>{% block pageTitle %}Learning Phalcon{% endblock %}</title>

{{ stylesheetLink('../assets/default/bower_components/bootstrap/dist/
css/bootstrap.min.css') }}
{{ stylesheetLink('../assets/default/css/lp.css') }}

<!--[if lt IE 9]>
  <script src="https://oss.maxcdn.com/html5shiv/3.7.2/html5shiv.min.
js">
</script>
  <script src="https://oss.maxcdn.com/respond/1.4.2/respond.min.js">
</script>
<![endif]-->
</head>
<body>
  {% block navbar %}
    {% include 'common/navbar.volt' %}
  {% endblock %}

  <div class="container">
    <div class="lp-header">
      <h1 class="lp-title">Learning Phalcon</h1>
      <p class="lead lp-description">The fastest PHP
        Framework</p>
    </div>

    <div class="row">
      <div class="col-sm-12 lp-main">
        {% block body %}

        {% endblock %}
      </div>
    </div>
  </div>

  {% block footer %}
    {% include 'common/footer.volt' %}
  {% endblock %}

  {{ javascriptInclude("../assets/default/bower_components/jquery/
    dist/jquery.min.js") }}
  {{ javascriptInclude("../assets/default/bower_components/
    bootstrap/dist/js/bootstrap.min.js") }}
```

```
    {{ javascriptInclude("../assets/default/js/lp.js") }}
    {% block javascripts %} {% endblock %}
</body>
</html>
```

Notice that here we are using the `javascriptInclude()` and `stylesheetLink()` methods, which are available by default in Volt. If you want, you can use the assets manager as we did for the Backoffice module. We also need a simple CSS file. You should already have a file named `lp.css` in the `public/assets/default/css/` folder. Clear its content and add this:

```
@import url(http://fonts.googleapis.com/
css?family=News+Cycle:400,700);

body { font-family: "News Cycle"; color: #555; }

h1, .h1, h2, .h2, h3, .h3, h4, .h4, h5, .h5, h6, .h6 {
    margin-top: 0; font-family: "News Cycle"; font-weight: normal;
    color: #333;
}

.container {
    width: 720px;
}

.lp-masthead { background-color: #356aa0; -webkit-box-shadow: inset 0
-2px 5px rgba(0, 0, 0, .1); box-shadow: inset 0 -2px 5px rgba(0, 0, 0,
.1); }
.lp-nav-item { position: relative; display: inline-block; padding:
10px; font-weight: 500; color: #cdddeb; }

.lp-nav-item:hover,
.lp-nav-item:focus {
    color: #fff; text-decoration: none;
}

.lp-nav .active        { color: #fff; }
.lp-nav .active:after { position: absolute; bottom: 0; left: 50%;
width: 0; height: 0; margin-left: -5px; vertical-align: middle;
content: " "; border-right: 5px solid transparent; border-bottom: 5px
solid; border-left: 5px solid transparent; }
.lp-header            { padding-top: 20px; padding-bottom: 20px; }

.lp-title       { margin-top: 30px; margin-bottom: 0; font-size: 30px;
font-weight: normal; }
```

```
.lp-description { font-size: 16px; color: #999; }

.lp-main          { font-size: 13px; line-height: 1.5; }

.pager          { margin-bottom: 60px; text-align: left; }
.pager>li>a      { width: 140px; padding: 10px 20px; text-align:
center; border-radius: 30px; }

.lp-post        { margin-bottom: 60px; }
.lp-post-title { margin-bottom: 5px; font-size: 40px; }
.lp-post-meta  { margin-bottom: 20px; color: #999; }

.lp-footer              { padding: 40px 0; color: #999; text-align:
center; background-color: #f9f9f9; border-top: 1px solid #e5e5e5; }
.lp-footer p:last-child { margin-bottom: 0; }
```

Modifying BaseController.php

Now, we should modify `BaseController.php` from the `Frontend` module to extend the core module and to assign categories globally to our views upon each request. Open `modules/Frontend/Controllers/BaseController.php`, clear its contents, and append this code:

```php
<?php
namespace App\Frontend\Controllers;

class BaseController extends \App\Core\Controllers\BaseController
{
    public function afterExecuteRoute()
    {
        $this->view->categories = $this->apiGet('categories');
    }
}
```

We don't actually have a home page (but we can add one anytime we want), so we are going to forward the request to `ArticlesController`. Open `modules/Frontend/Controllers/IndexController.php`, remove `indexAction()`, and append the following code:

```php
public function indexAction()
{
    return $this->dispatcher->forward([
'controller' => 'article',
'action' => 'list'
    ]);
}
```

The last step is to create the `listAction()` method and the view for the articles. First, create a new file named `list.item.volt` in the `modules/Frontend/Views/Default/article/common/` folder with this content:

```
{% for record in records['items'] %}
{% if (record['article_is_published'] == 1) %}
<div class="lp-post">
  <h2 class="lp-post-title">{{ record['article_translations'][0]
  ['article_translation_short_title'] }}</h2>
  <p class="lp-post-meta">
  {{ record['article_created_at']|date("d M Y") }} by
    <a href="#">
  {{ record['article_author']['user_first_name']}}
  {{ record['article_author']['user_last_name']}}
    </a></p>
  <p>
  {{ record['article_translations'][0]
  ['article_translation_long_title'] }}
  <a href="{{ url('article/' ~ record['article_translations'][0]
    ['article_translation_slug']) }}">Read more</a>
  </p>
</div>
{% endif %}
{% endfor %}
```

We also need to modify the layout from `modules/Frontend/Views/Default/article/list.volt`. Open this file, clear its content, and append this code:

```
{% extends 'layout.volt' %}
{% block body %}
    {% include 'article/common/list.item' with {'records':records} %}
    {% if records['total_items'] > 2 %}
    {% include 'common/paginator' with {'records':records} %}
    {% endif %}
{% endblock %}
```

You can see that we show `paginator` only if we have more than two records (you can change this whenever you want). This is related to the `$limit` parameter from the `listAction()` method of `ArticleController`. Open `modules/Frontend/Controllers/ArticleController.php`, and append the following code to it:

```
<?php
namespace App\Frontend\Controllers;

class ArticleController extends BaseController{
```

```
public function listAction() {
  $page = $this->request->getQuery('p', 'int', 1);

  try {
    $records = $this->apiGet('articles',['p' => $page, 'limit'
      => 2]);
    $this->view->records = $records;
  } catch (\Exception $e) {
    $this->flash->error($e->getMessage());
  }
}
```

Basically, we are done with this part. You can now open `http://www.learning-phalcon.localhost/`, and you should see something similar to this screenshot:

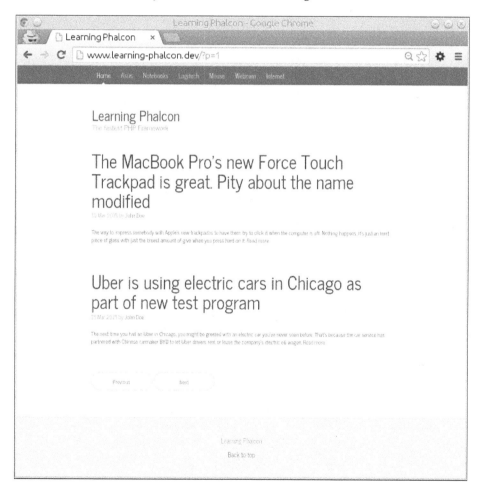

Next, we will make a few changes to the articles controller in order to get an article by its slug. Personally, I like to keep things separated as much as possible, in case I need to implement complex logic in the future. We will create a new method in the API (`ArticlesController`) named `getBySlugAction()`. A slug is a friendly URL used for SEO (**Search Engine Optimization**) purposes. Open `modules/Api/Controllers/ArticlesController.php` and append the following code:

```
public function getBySlugAction($slug) {
  try {
    $manager = $this->getDI()->get('core_article_manager');

    $st_output = $manager->restGet([
      'article_translation_slug = :article_translation_slug:',
      'bind' => [
        'article_translation_slug' => $slug,
      ],
    ]);

    return $this->render($st_output);
  } catch (\Exception $e) {
    return $this->render([
      'code' => $e->getCode(),
      'message' => $e->getMessage(),
    ], $e->getCode());
  }
}
```

This method is similar to `getAction()`. We are searching by slug, therefore we will need to modify the `find()` method from `ArticleManager.php`. Our new `find()` method will look like this:

```
public function find($parameters = null) {
  if (isset($parameters['bind']['article_translation_slug'])) {
    $translation = ArticleTranslation::findFirst($parameters);
    if ($translation->count() !== 1) {
      return [$translation->getArticle()->toArray()];
    } else {
      throw new \Exception('Article not found', 404);
    }
  } elseif (isset($parameters['bind'][
    'category_translation_slug'])) {
      $category_translation = CategoryTranslation::
        findFirst($parameters);
      if ($category_translation->count() !== 1) {
```

```
        return $category_translation->getCategory()->
          getArticles();
      } else {
        throw new \Exception('Article not found', 404);
      }
    } else {
      return Article::find($parameters);
    }
  }
}
```

We check whether the `article_translation_slug` parameter is set. If it is set, instead of calling the `Article::find()` method, we call `ArticleTranslation::findFirst()`. If we get results, we return the object as an array. We apply the same logic when we need to retrieve an article from a certain category. This code will not work unless we also modify the `restGet()` method from `BaseManager.php`. Our current `restGet()` method contains the following line:

```
$result = $objects->filter(function ($object) {
  return $object->toArray();
});
```

Replace this line with the following code:

```
if (is_array($objects)) {
  $result = $objects;
} else {
  $result = $objects->filter(function ($object) {
    return $object->toArray();
  });
}
```

This modified code checks whether the result from `$this->find()` is an array. If it is, we don't need to filter anything. Now, we switch to `modules/Frontend/Controllers/ArticleController.php` and add a new method. It will get an article by its slug:

```
public function readAction($slug) {
  try {
    $records = $this->apiGet("articles/slug/$slug");

    $this->view->records = $records;
  } catch (\Exception $e) {
    $this->flash->error($e->getMessage());
  }
}
```

We are missing the routing information. We need to add routing for both the `Api` and `Frontend` modules. In `modules/Api/Config/routing.php` (the article group), add this line:

```
$articles->addGet('/slug/{slug}', ['action' => 'getBySlug']);
```

Then in `modules/Frontend/Config/routing.php`, replace the last routing line with the following code:

```
$router->add('#^/articles/([a-zA-Z0-9\-]+)[/]{0,1}$#', array(
  'module' => 'frontend',
  'controller' => 'article',
  'action' => 'read',
  'slug' => 1,
));
```

The Article item template

We also need a template for reading an article. Switch to `modules/Frontend/Views/Default/article/common/`, create a new file, name it `item.volt`, and add the following code:

```
{% for record in records['items'] %}
{% if (record['article_is_published'] == 1) %}
<div class="lp-post">
  <h2 class="lp-post-title">{{ record['article_translations'][0]
  ['article_translation_short_title'] }}</h2>
  <p class="lp-post-meta">{{ record['article_created_at']|date(
    "d M Y") }} by <a href="#">
    {{ record['article_author']['user_first_name']}}
    {{ record['article_author']['user_last_name'] }}</a></p>
  <p>
  <strong>{{ record['article_translations'][0]
  ['article_translation_long_title'] }}</strong>
  </p>
  <p>
    {{ record['article_translations'][0]
    ['article_translation_description'] }}
  </p>
</div>
{% endif %}
{% endfor %}
```

The template for `readAction()` (`modules/Frontend/Views/Default/article/`
`read.volt`) should have this code:

```
{% extends 'layout.volt' %}
{% block body %}
{% include 'article/common/item' with {'records':records} %}
{% endblock %}
```

This is it! You can now access `http://www.learning-phalcon.localhost/`.
Click on the **Read more** link and you should see a result similar to this:

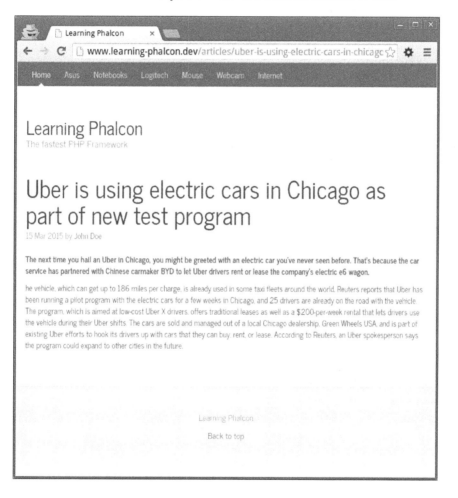

Retrieving articles from a category

We are missing the implementation of retrieving articles from a category (the top bar navigation). We need to do this by following these steps:

1. Add routing information for the `Api` module to `modules/Api/Config/routing.php`:

    ```php
    $articles->addGet('/category/{slug}', ['action' =>
      'getByCategorySlug']);
    ```

2. Create a new method called `getByCategorySlugAction()` in `modules/Api/Controllers/ArticlesController.php`:

    ```php
    public function getByCategorySlugAction($slug) {
      try {
        $manager = $this->getDI()->get('core_article_manager');

        $st_output = $manager->restGet([
          'category_translation_slug =
            :category_translation_slug:',
            'bind' => [
              'category_translation_slug' => $slug,
            ],
        ]);

        return $this->render($st_output);
      } catch (\Exception $e) {
        return $this->render([
          'code' => $e->getCode(),
          'message' => $e->getMessage(),
        ], $e->getCode());
      }
    }
    ```

3. Add routing information for the Frontend module to `modules/Frontend/Config/routing.php`:

    ```php
    $router->add('#^/categories/(([a-zA-Z0-9\-]+)[/]{0,1}$#', array(
        'module' => 'frontend',
        'controller' => 'article',
        'action' => 'categories',
        'slug' => 1,
    ));
    ```

4. Create a new method, `categoriesAction()`, in `modules/Frontend/`
    `Controllers/ArticleController.php`:

```php
public function categoriesAction($slug) {
    $this->view->pick('article/list');

    try {
        $records = $this->apiGet("articles/category/$slug");

        $this->view->records = $records;
    } catch (\Exception $e) {
        $this->flash->error($e->getMessage());
    }
}
```

 Note that we are picking the articles and list view in `categoriesAction()` because there is no point in duplicating the code; it is the same code as that for listing articles.

Now we have a minimal, functional frontend. We can navigate through the articles, get articles from a category, and read an article. We will not go further with this because things can get too complex. In this chapter, we will only add a feature and improve speed by indexing articles in Elasticsearch.

If you want to practice more, you can implement a simple search form to search for articles by title or implement a profile page for authors.

Implementing ElasticSearch

What is **Elasticsearch (ES)**? The short answer is: it's a search server. According to Wikipedia, this is the complete definition:

> *Elasticsearch is a search server based on Lucene. It provides a distributed, multitenant-capable full-text search engine with a RESTful web interface and schema-free JSON documents. Elasticsearch is developed in Java and is released as open source under the terms of the Apache License. Elasticsearch is the second most popular enterprise search engine.*

If you need full-text search, real-time analytics of structured data, or a combination of the two, Elasticsearch is a very powerful tool, fit for you. All the big players use it. We will use ES in front of MySQL to store and search for articles. In this way we will reduce the traffic to MySQL and avoid querying it too often. We are not going to discuss ES in detail, so please spend a few minutes reading about its basic operation at `http://www.elastic.co/guide/`.

Installing ElasticSearch

There is an APT repository available for download. We will perform the following steps:

1. Open a terminal and type the following commands:

    ```
    $ wget -qO - https://packages.elasticsearch.org/GPG-KEY-
    elasticsearch | sudo apt-key add -
    ```

    ```
    $ sudo add-apt-repository "deb http://packages.elasticsearch.org/
    elasticsearch/1.4/debian stable main"
    ```

    ```
    $ sudo apt-get update && sudo apt-get install elasticsearch
    ```

2. After installation, you can configure the repository to start during boot-up by executing this command:

    ```
    $ sudo update-rc.d elasticsearch defaults 95 10
    ```

    The command used to start the service is as follows:

    ```
    $ sudo service elasticsearch start
    ```

    The command used to test whether it is running is the following:

    ```
    $ curl -X GET http://localhost:9200/
    ```

    You should get a JSON response similar to this:

    ```
    {
      "status" : 200,
      "name" : "Lord Pumpkin",
      "cluster_name" : "elasticsearch",
      "version" : {
        "number" : "1.4.4",
        "build_hash" : "c88f77ffc81301dfa9dfd81ca2232f09588bd512",
        "build_timestamp" : "2015-02-19T13:05:36Z",
        "build_snapshot" : false,
        "lucene_version" : "4.10.3"
      },
      "tagline" : "You Know, for Search"
    }
    ```

3. We will need a client library to work with. Fortunately, there is one available. In the terminal, we switch to the root folder of our project and type this command:

    ```
    $ php composer.phar require "elasticsearch/elasticsearch":"1.3.3"
    ```

This will install the PHP client but also a lot of dependencies. It might take a while, so don't worry about it. Next, we will set up this client in our project. If you have no experience with ES, please spend 10 minutes reading the documents for the PHP client at `http://www.elastic.co/guide/en/elasticsearch/client/php-api/current/index.html`.

Enabling a client in DI

Before using the ES client, we need to enable it in DI. Open `config/services.php` and add the following code:

```php
$di['elastic'] = function() {
    return new \Elasticsearch\Client();
};
```

Indexing (storing) documents

If we want to index documents, we will need to add some methods to our manager. Also, we will have to make some modifications for data types. First, we will create a common method to paginate array results. Open `modules/Core/Managers/ArticleManager.php` and append the following code:

```php
protected function paginate($data, $limit, $page)
{
    $paginator = new \Phalcon\Paginator\Adapter\NativeArray(
      array(
          "data" => $data,
          "limit"=> $show,
          "page" => $page
      )
    );

    $items = $paginator->getPaginate();

    if ($items->total_items > 0) {
      return $items;
    }

    return false;
}
```

We create a method that should normalize the data before we send it to the ES index:

```
protected function esNormalize($article) {
    $body = json_decode(json_encode($article->toArray(),
        JSON_NUMERIC_CHECK), true);
    $body['article_created_at'] = str_replace(' ', 'T',
        $body['article_created_at']);
    if ($body['article_updated_at'] != '') {
        $body['article_updated_at'] = str_replace(' ', 'T',
            $body['article_updated_at']);
    } else {
        $body['article_updated_at'] = $body['article_created_at'];
    }
    return $body;
}
```

The json_encode and json_decode methods are used to force the conversion of string values that contain only numbers to numeric/integer values. We also replace the empty space between the date and time from MySQL with T. This ISO format is auto-recognized by ES as a date and it will then set the field type accordingly. We also force the article_updated_at field to get a valid date value. If we don't do this, we will not be able to search for an article between certain intervals of time. Next, we will create a method in the same manager that will index the article in ES. Append this code in the manager:

```
public function esIndex($article) {
    $elastic_manager = $this->getDI()->get('elastic');

    $params             = array();
    $params['index']    = 'learningphalcon';
    $params['type']     = 'article';
    $params['id']       = 'article-' . $article->getId();
    $params['body']     = $this->esNormalize($article);

    $elastic_manager->index($params);

    return true;
}
```

Whenever we index data, ES expects a certain format. This format is represented in the `esIndex()` method. To compare the parameters with a MySQL structure, you can think about something like this:

- `index`: The database name
- `type`: The table name
- `id`: The ID (primary key)
- `body`: A field named body from a table that contains a JSON-encoded database

The `esIndex()` method always returns true, but we must be careful and always use `try {}`, `catch() {}` because `esindex()` can throw exceptions. If an article already exists in the ES index, it will be updated. Let's create a simple task that will retrieve all the articles from MySQL and index them into ES. Open `modules/Task/ArticlesTask.php` and append this code:

```php
public function esindexAction() {
    $article_manager = $this->getDI()->get('core_article_manager');

    foreach ($article_manager->find() as $article) {
        try {
            $article_manager->esindex($article);
            $this->consoleLog("Article {$article->getId()} has been
                indexed");
        } catch (\Exception $e) {
            $this->consoleLog("Article {$article->getId()} has not been
                indexed. Reason: {$e->getMessage()}", "red");
        }
    }
}
```

Make sure that you have some articles in the database. If not, navigate to Backoffice and add some. Then open a terminal, switch to the root folder of your project, and execute the following command:

```
$ php modules/cli.php article esindex
```

You should see an output similar to this:

```
vagrant@thex:/projects/learning-phalcon.dev-(git/ master )$ php modules/cli.php article esindex
Article 30 has been indexed
Article 31 has been indexed
Article 32 has been indexed
```

At this point, we have articles indexed in ES. Each time we update, add, or delete an article from MySQL, we have to reflect this action in ES. We are already doing this when we add an article. Let's implement it for updates and deletions.

We don't need to create a special method to update articles in ES. It is enough to submit the index of the same article. ES will find it by ID and update it automatically. All we need to do is implement the functionality as we did for createAction().

Let's follow these steps:

1. Open modules/Backoffice/Controllers/ArticleController.php.

2. Go to the updateAction() method:

    ```
    $this->persistent->set('es_add_to_index_id', $object_id);
    ```

3. Append the preceding code right after the following line:

    ```
    $this->flashSession->success('Object was updated successfully');
    ```

4. We need to modify the editAction() method. Remove the current method and replace it with this one:

    ```
    public function editAction($id) {
      $manager = $this->getDI()->
        get('core_article_manager');
      $object = $manager->findFirstById($id);
      if (!$object) {
        $this->flashSession->error('Object not found');
        return $this->response->redirect('article/list');
      }
      if ($es_add_to_index_id = $this->persistent->
        get('es_add_to_index_id')) {
        $article = $manager->findFirstByid(
          $es_add_to_index_id);
          try {
            $manager->esindex($article);
          } catch (\Exception $e) {
            $this->flash->error("Article was not added to ES
              index");
          }
        }
      }

      $this->persistent->set('id', $id);
      $this->view->form = $manager->getForm(
        $object, ['edit' => true]);
    }
    ```

This is all we need to do when updating an article. From now on, whenever you make changes, those changes will be reflected in ES. When we delete an article from MySQL, we will have to delete it from ES too. Let's create a simple delete method in `ArticleManager.php`:

```php
public function esdelete($article_id)
{
    $elastic_manager = $this->getDI()->get('elastic');

    $params['index'] = 'learningphalcon';
    $params['type']  = 'article';
    $params['id']    = 'article-'.(int)$article_id;

    try {
        $elastic_manager->delete($params);
    } catch (\Exception $e) {

    }
}
```

As you can see, all that we need to do is provide three keys: `index`, `type`, and `id`. Then we call the `delete()` method, and if it is found, the article is removed. The last step is to call `esdelete()` when we delete an article. Open `modules/Backoffice/Controllers/ArticleController.php` again, go to `deleteAction()`, and append the `$manager->esdelete($id);` line right after `$manager->delete($id);`. Now, when we remove articles from MySQL, they will be removed from ES too.

We will not go further into ES. You should spend some time and implement a search form to retrieve articles from ES. As a tip, here is a simple way to search ES articles by category slug:

```php
public function elasticSearchByCategorySlug($categorySlug, $show,
$page, $limit)
{
    $elastic_manager = $this->getDI()->get('elastic');
    $params['index'] = 'learningphalcon';
    $params['type']  = 'article';

    $params['body']['from'] = 0;
    $params['body']['size'] = $limit;
```

```
$params['body']['query']['bool']['must'] = array(
    array('match' => array('category_translation_slug' =>
        $categorySlug))
);

$params['body']['sort'] = [
    'post_id' => ['order' => 'desc']
];

$queryResponse = $elastic_manager->search($params);

foreach ($queryResponse['hits']['hits'] as $hit) {
    $tmp['items'][] = $hit['_source'];
}

return $this->paginate($tmp['items'], $show, $page);
}
```

Implementing MongoDB

In this section, we will implement a simple log for articles. Of course, you can have your entire website running on Mongo. It is incredibly fast, but personally, I don't like to use it for big projects because Mongo can be very greedy with space. In order to get an overall idea, in the past, I had to index prices for nearly 5,000 properties (apartments, villas, and houses) for 4 years and the size requirement was approximately 50 GB. At my current workplace, we have migrated SMS logs to Mongo and we have nearly 3 million SMS logs for about 20 GB of space. For a relatively small website, MongoDB is perfect, or if you know that space won't be an issue, just go for it.

We will not cover Mongo in this section, but there will an example that shows how to implement it using Phalcon. If you have no idea about Mongo, spare some time and read the basics at http://docs.mongodb.org/manual/.

That being said, let's start implementing the logs. What are we going to log? Article IDs, user IP addresses, user agents, and timestamps. From this, you will be able to show the number of times an article was read and also generate simple reports.

Mongo models

Switch to `modules/Core/Models` and create a new folder named Mongo. In this new folder, create two new files with the following code.

modules/Core/Models/Mongo/BaseCollection.php

The `modules/Core/Models/Mongo/BaseCollection.php` file is a simple base class that extends `\Phalcon\Mvc\Collection`. You can use it in the future to add common logic as follows:

```php
<?php
namespace App\Core\Models\Mongo;

class BaseCollection extends \Phalcon\Mvc\Collection
{
}
```

modules/Core/Models/Mongo/ArticleLog.php

This class is the model for our `article_log` collection and has two important methods: `log()` and `countVisits()`. We are going to use them to log article visits and count them:

```php
<?php
namespace App\Core\Models\Mongo;

class ArticleLog extends BaseCollection
{
    public $article_id;

    public $client_ip;

    public $user_agent;

    public $timestamp;

    public function getSource()
    {
        return 'article_log';
    }

    public function log($article_id, \Phalcon\Http\Request $request)
    {
        $log = new self();
```

```php
        $log->article_id = (int) $article_id;
        $log->client_ip  = $request->getClientAddress();
        $log->user_agent = $request->getUserAgent();
        $log->timestamp  = time();

        $log->save();
    }

    public function countVisits($article_id, $unique = false)
    {
        if (false === $unique) {
            return $this->count(array(
                array(
                    "article_id" => $article_id
                )
            ));
        } else {
            $result = $this->getConnection()->command(
                array(
                    'distinct' => 'article_log',
                    'key' => 'client_ip',
                    'query' => ['article_id' => $article_id],
                )
            );

            return count($result['values']);
        }
    }

    public function columnMap()
    {
        return [
            'article_id' => 'article_id',
            'client_ip'  => 'client_ip',
            'user_agent' => 'user_agent',
            'timestamp'  => 'timestamp',
        ];
    }
}
```

The `log()` method is pretty much straightforward. We assign values to variables and save the information in the `article_log` collection. The `countVisits()` method expects two parameters: `$article_id` and `$unique`. If we don't want to show the number of unique visits, this parameter must be set to `false` (the default value), and we can simply query the collection using the built-in `count()` method. If we need to show only the unique visits (unique by IP address), then we execute the `command()` action, which is available in MongoClient (Phalcon does not have this method implemented).

Let's switch to `ArticleManager.php` from the Core module and add these two methods so that we can call them from DI:

```
public function mongoLog($article_id, \Phalcon\Http\Request
  $request)
{
    $log = new ArticleLog();
    $log->log($article_id, $request);
}

public function countVisits($article_id, $unique = false)
{
    $alog = new ArticleLog();
    return $alog->countVisits($article_id, $unique);
}
```

Now, we will modify the `readAction()` method from `ArticleController.php` (Frontend module). Remove the current one and append this code:

```
public function readAction($slug){
  try {
    $records = $this->apiGet("articles/slug/$slug");
    $manager = $this->getDI()->get(
      'core_article_manager');
    $total_views = $manager->countVisits(
      $records['items'][0]['id']);
    $manager->mongoLog($records['items'][0]['id'],
      $this->request);
    $this->view->records = $records;
    $this->view->total_views = $total_views;
  } catch (\Exception $e) {
    $this->flash->error($e->getMessage());
  }
}
```

Notice the line that contains `$total_views = $manager->countVisits($records['items'][0]['id']);` — we are not providing the `$unique` parameter. This means that by default, we will not show unique visits. If you want to show them, append `true` like this:

```
$total_views = $manager->countVisits($records['items'][0]['id'], true);
```

The final step consists of making small modifications to our templates. Open `modules/Frontend/Views/Default/article/read.volt` and append the `total_views` parameter to `include`:

```
{% extends 'layout.volt' %}
{% block body %}
    {% include 'article/common/item' with {'records':records, 'total_
views' : total_views} %}
{% endblock %}
```

Then, open `modules/Frontend/Views/Default/article/common/item.volt`, clear its contents, and append this code:

```
{% for record in records['items'] %}
{% if (record['article_is_published'] == 1) %}
<div class="lp-post">
  <h2 class="lp-post-title">
    {{ record['article_translations'][0]
      ['article_translation_short_title'] }}</h2>
  <p class="lp-post-meta">
    {{ record['article_created_at']|date("d M Y") }}
    by <a href="#">
    {{record['article_author']['user_first_name'] }}
    {{ record['article_author']['user_last_name'] }}</a>
    {% if dispatcher.getActionName() == 'read') %}
    <span class="pull-right glyphicon glyphicon-eye-open">
    {{ total_views }}
    </span>
    {% endif %}
  </p>
  <p>
    <strong>{{ record['article_translations'][0]
    ['article_translation_long_title'] }}</strong>
  </p>
  <p>
    {{ record['article_translations'][0]
      ['article_translation_description'] }}
  </p>
</div>
{% endif %}
{% endfor %}
```

The difference between the old `item.volt` file and new one is the code under `{% if dispatcher.getActionName() == 'read') %}`. We show the number of visits only in `readAction()`.

That's all about MongoDB and Phalcon. The functionality of Phalcon's ODM is similar to the ORM functionality, but it is not so advanced. You might find yourself in situations where you will be forced to use MongoClient from PHP. You can read more about the ODM at `http://docs.phalconphp.com/en/latest/reference/odm.html`.

Summary

In this chapter, you learned a few new things about ElasticSearch and MongoDB. We created a simple Frontend module, and we now have a simple, fully functional website.

In the next and final chapter, we will discuss things that we didn't cover in previous chapters, such as uploading images and the annotation router.

10
Going Further

In this chapter, we will try to cover a few things that we didn't use in this book. In April 2015, Phalcon released version 2.0. You don't have to worry about it because it is perfectly compatible with what you have learned so far.

The big difference is that version 2.0 was completely rewritten in the Zephir language (http://www.zephir-lang.com/). You can upgrade to version 2.0.* if you want.

We will cover the following topics in this chapter:

- Uploading files with Phalcon
- Using the Annotation router

Uploading files with Phalcon

Uploading files with Phalcon is a piece of cake. We just need to check whether the request object has files and move them to our upload directory. Let's create the following controller in the Backoffice module:

```php
<?php
namespace App\Backoffice\Controllers;

use App\Core\Forms\MediaForm;

class MediaController extends BaseController {
  public function addAction() {
    $this->view->form = new MediaForm();
  }

  public function uploadAction() {
    if (true == $this->request->hasFiles() &&
      $this->request->isPost()) {
```

```
$upload_dir = __DIR__ . '/../../../public/uploads/';

if (!is_dir($upload_dir)) {
  mkdir($upload_dir, 0755);
}
foreach ($this->request->getUploadedFiles() as $file) {
  $file->moveTo($upload_dir . $file->getName());
  $this->flashSession->success($file->getName().' has been
    successfully uploaded.');
}

$this->response->redirect('media/add');
    }
  }
}
```

The uploadAction() method first checks whether the request object has a file and the request method is POST. We assign the path to the upload directory to the $upload_dir variable. Then we check whether this directory exists in public, otherwise we create it. Next, we move each uploaded file to public/uploads/. You can find the forms and the views for this example in the source code for this chapter. The file object has some built-in methods that are very helpful:

- $file->getSize();

- $file->getRealType();

- $file->getName()

Using these methods, we can implement a simple validator for an image. Let's assume that we only accept JPEG files that are no larger than 1 MB. This is what an improved version of the uploadAction() method can look like:

```
<?php

class MediaController extends BaseController {
  private $valid_mime = [
    'image/jpeg'
  ];

  private $max_size = 125000;

  public function uploadAction() {
    if (true == $this->request->hasFiles() && $this->request->
      isPost()) {
      $upload_dir = __DIR__ . '/../../../public/uploads/';
```

```
        if (!is_dir($upload_dir)) {
          mkdir($upload_dir, 0755);
        }

        foreach ($this->request->getUploadedFiles() as $file) {

          if (!in_array($file->getRealType(), $this->valid_mime)) {
            $this->flashSession->error($file->getName().' is
              invalid');
            continue;
          }

          if ($file->getSize() > $this->max_size) {
            $this->flashSession->error($file->getName().' is too
              big');
            continue;
          }

          $file->moveTo($upload_dir . $file->getName());
          $this->flashSession->success($file->getName().' has been
            successfully uploaded.');
        }

        $this->response->redirect('media/add');
      }
    }
  }
```

Phalcon also supports image manipulation. Unfortunately, this is not documented, but you can take a look at the official repository at https://github.com/phalcon/cphalcon/tree/master/ext/phalcon/image to find out the available methods, or the source code for the IDE stubs at https://github.com/phalcon/phalcon-devtools/tree/master/ide/1.3.4/Phalcon/Image.

A simple example of image manipulation can be as follows:

```
$image = new Phalcon\Image\Adapter\GD($file);
$image->resize(200, 200)
if ($image->save()) {
  $this->flashSession->success('Image has been successfully
    resized');
}
```

We can also use an external library, such as https://github.com/avalanche123/Imagine, which you will find very well documented at http://imagine.readthedocs.org/en/latest/usage/introduction.html.

Using the Annotation router

In this book, we used a configuration file for the router. If you come from Symfony, for example, you might want to use annotations. For this, you need to change the router information in the DI:

```php
<?php

use Phalcon\Mvc\Router\Annotations;

$di['router'] = function() {
    $router = new Annotations(false);
    $router->addResource('Articles', '/api/v1/articles');

    return $router;
};
```

Then you must modify `ArticlesController` to look like this:

```php
<?php
namespace App\Api\Controllers;

/**
 * @RoutePrefix("/api/v1/articles")
 */
class ArticlesController extends BaseController {
  /**
   * @Get("/")
   */
  public function listAction() {

  }
}
```

You can read more about the Annotation router at `http://docs.phalconphp.com/en/latest/reference/routing.html#annotations-router`. If you need/want, you can also develop your own router, implementing `Phalcon\Mvc\RouterInterface`.

Summary

In this chapter, we saw how we can upload files with Phalcon. Also, we saw how to use the Annotation router.

Phalcon is a completely decoupled framework. There are no real "best practices", so you, as a developer, can build your own conduit. I also recommend that you take a look at Vegas CMF for Phalcon at `https://github.com/vegas-cmf`, especially if you are going to work with a big team.

Thank you for reading this book, and I really hope that it was helpful. You can now start developing your own application.

Index

A

ACL component
used, for securing application 187-194
Annotation router
URL 296
using 296
Apache
configuration files 5, 6
API
about 129
documenting 160
recommended practices 129, 130
reference link, for examples 130, 131
API documentation
installation 160
reference link 160
usage 160-163
API module
hashtag controller, creating within 201-205
API, securing
about 155
access to resources, limiting to
    authenticated users 158, 159
API key, adding for extra
    protection 155-157
number of requests per second, limiting
    from same IP 157, 158
SSL used 155
application
securing, ACL component used 187-194
Article-Category-Article model 122-128
Article CRUD
about 247
Article controller, from Backoffice
    module 250-252

Article form 252-260
Article manager 261-266
Controller (API) 247-250
Article model 121
Articles
CRUD operations, creating for 140-154
Article translation model 120
assets management 165-168
Auth component
methods 179
authentication system
database structure 169, 170
developing 169
models 171-187

B

Backoffice module
reference link, for adding new hashtag 213
BaseController.php
Article item template 276
articles, retrieving from category 278, 279
modifying 271-275
base layout
creating 52-55
blameable behavior
reference link, for article 115
Bootstrap
URL 169
Bower
URL 52

C

cache component 27-29
categories 116

[299]

request component 10, 11
response component 12-14
root folder 5
router
  preparing 41-43
router component
  about 18, 19
  using, in module 44-51

S

session component 26
Smarty 23
software
  requisites 2
SQL database
  versus NoSQL database 57, 58
SQL-to-MongoDB mapping chart
  URL 58
SSL
  enabling, on local machine 131-133
structure
  creating, for project 36, 37

T

TLD (Top Level Domain) 6
Twig 23

U

user CRUD
  about 233
  controller (API), creating 233-235
  user controller, from Backoffice
      module 235-237
  user form, using 237-240
  user manager 240-243
UserGroup model 98
UserGroup table 95
User model 97
UserProfile model 99
UserProfile table 95
User table 94
user templates 243-247

V

view component
  about 22-25
  reference link 26
Volt engine
  references 198, 199

Z

Zephir
  about 1
  URL 1

Thank you for buying
Learning Phalcon PHP

About Packt Publishing

Packt, pronounced 'packed', published its first book, *Mastering phpMyAdmin for Effective MySQL Management*, in April 2004, and subsequently continued to specialize in publishing highly focused books on specific technologies and solutions.

Our books and publications share the experiences of your fellow IT professionals in adapting and customizing today's systems, applications, and frameworks. Our solution-based books give you the knowledge and power to customize the software and technologies you're using to get the job done. Packt books are more specific and less general than the IT books you have seen in the past. Our unique business model allows us to bring you more focused information, giving you more of what you need to know, and less of what you don't.

Packt is a modern yet unique publishing company that focuses on producing quality, cutting-edge books for communities of developers, administrators, and newbies alike. For more information, please visit our website at www.packtpub.com.

About Packt Open Source

In 2010, Packt launched two new brands, Packt Open Source and Packt Enterprise, in order to continue its focus on specialization. This book is part of the Packt Open Source brand, home to books published on software built around open source licenses, and offering information to anybody from advanced developers to budding web designers. The Open Source brand also runs Packt's Open Source Royalty Scheme, by which Packt gives a royalty to each open source project about whose software a book is sold.

Writing for Packt

We welcome all inquiries from people who are interested in authoring. Book proposals should be sent to author@packtpub.com. If your book idea is still at an early stage and you would like to discuss it first before writing a formal book proposal, then please contact us; one of our commissioning editors will get in touch with you.

We're not just looking for published authors; if you have strong technical skills but no writing experience, our experienced editors can help you develop a writing career, or simply get some additional reward for your expertise.

Getting Started with Phalcon

ISBN: 978-1-78328-767-3   Paperback: 138 pages

Design, implement, and deliver superior web applications using the most popular PHP framework available

1. Build impressive web applications with the pace of C, the ease of PHP, and the structure of the MVC framework.

2. Use Phalcon Developer Tools to build a scaffolding for your project in minutes.

3. Detailed instructions and examples help you build an impressive blog application using Phalcon PHP quickly and easily.

Persistence in PHP with Doctrine ORM

ISBN: 978-1-78216-410-4   Paperback: 114 pages

Build a model layer of your PHP applications successfully, using Doctrine ORM

1. Develop a fully functional Doctrine-backed web application.

2. Demonstrate aspects of Doctrine using code samples.

3. Generate a database schema from your PHP classes.

Please check **www.PacktPub.com** for information on our titles